CARDUS
UNCOVERED

Second edition

CARDUS UNCOVERED

Neville Cardus: The Truth, the Untruth and the Higher Truth

Second edition

———⚜———

Christopher O'Brien

Whitethorn Range Publishing

Copyright First edition © Christopher O'Brien 2018
Second edition © Christopher O'Brien 2020

First edition: ISBN: 978-1-9999105-0-1
Second edition ISBN: 978-1-9999105-3-2
Kindle edition: ISBN: 978-1-9999105-1-8

First edition published in 2018 in the UK
Second edition published in 2020 in the UK by
Whitethorn Range Publishing,
64 Hillside Road, Beeston,
Nottingham NG9 3AY
whitethorn.range@gmail.com

Design and layout by Amanda Helm
amandahelm@uwclub.net

Printed and bound in Great Britain
by Short Run Press, Exeter, EX2 7LW
www.shortrunpress.co.uk

Cover images: Neville Cardus,
courtesy of Guardian News and Media

CONTENTS

LIST OF TABLES

FOREWORD

It was when I saw his *Autobiography* in a sale of second-hand books at Trent Bridge cricket ground that I realised I ought to know more about Neville Cardus than I then did. After all, I was born and brought up in Manchester and spent much of my youth watching Lancashire cricket at Old Trafford. My interest in classical music developed afterwards, and in my late teens and twenties I was often at the Free Trade Hall in Manchester to hear concerts of the Hallé orchestra. So, I felt I really should be more familiar with the life of Neville Cardus, whose work on both cricket, especially Lancashire cricket, and classical music had led to his reputation as a writer, sufficient to lead to his being knighted.

Having bought and read the book, the problem was that *Autobiography* didn't provide all the answers I wanted. Some help was at hand as the sale at Trent Bridge also included Christopher Brookes' biography, *His Own Man*. But I still didn't know who Neville's father was. Or when Neville was born. The description of his early family life contained much that was vague. Given modern genealogical techniques and sources, surely it was possible to do better?

It didn't make sense to stop at Neville's childhood. There were other enigmas. When and why did he change his name from Fred to Neville? And what about his wife, about whom Neville wrote little? He wrote about his wedding day, but this was, according to *His Own Man*, a delightful story and not true. What else of his life was not true? There was also a mistress, the so-called Milady, about whom Neville Cardus did write following his wife's death: was this the truth or was there embellishment?

I also wished to know more about Neville Cardus's work as cricket writer and music critic. The challenge here is that much of his cricket writing was focussed on the characters of the game, and we know that it wasn't all literal truth. Cardus used the justification that he employed the "higher truth". Can we separate what was the truth and what was the higher truth? And some of what was written was neither, but still could be an intriguing story that helped make Neville Cardus the writer that he was. The story of Neville Cardus's life is similarly an intriguing challenge.

January 2018

I have taken advantage of the reprint to make a number of changes, taking into account new research. In particular, I have extended chapter 12, have inserted a new chapter (no. 13) on the writing style of Neville Cardus; and added an analysis of his cricket reports for the *Manchester Guardian* in 1919–39 as the new Appendix 4. Other sections that have been expanded include the material on Cardus's time at Shrewsbury School (in Chapter 5) and the relationship with his mistress (Chapter 9).

December 2019

NOTE ON SOURCES

Information on cricketers and cricket matches is taken from Cricket Archive: wwwcricketarchive.com

Family history information is documented in Appendix 5, indicating the sources used.

"GRO Index" is the General Register Office Index of births and deaths.

"Register" is the Register of the British population taken on 29 September 1939.

"Slater" indicates Slater's (later Kelly's) annual directory of Manchester.

Passenger journeys: information on passenger lists is at www.ancestry.com and www.findmypast.co.uk, supplemented by newspaper reports for dates of departure and arrival if not otherwise recorded.

Books by and relating to Cardus are referred to in notes by short titles for convenience.

Chapter 1

IT'S A MATTER OF STYLE

In the opening match of the 1927 cricket season, Lancashire hosted Warwickshire at Old Trafford on a chilly day, and a journalist from the *Manchester Guardian* described Lancastrian Richard Tyldesley coming on to bowl:

> "A northerly wind blew over Old Trafford on Saturday, chilling the bone's marrow. When the Lancashire side took the field it seemed to me that Richard Tyldesley was wearing about half a dozen sweaters. But indeed he wasn't. Later, he went on to bowl and revealed to us that he had only one sweater to remove – the rest of him was just Richard Tyldesley. And, come to think of it, Richard Tyldesley is too hardy a man to require more than one sweater. 'One's enough,' we can imagine him saying, 'Don't be nesh.' (If any reader should not understand what 'nesh' means he is no true Lancashire man and ought to resign immediately from the county membership.)"[1]

That journalist, a Lancastrian himself, was Neville Cardus. He became Sir Neville Cardus in 1967 in recognition of his contributions on cricket and music. He had delighted countless readers with his style of writing about not only events on the field and in the concert hall but also the characters he had observed.

Cardus was arguably one of the greatest sports writers

the world has seen. Despite that, much of his life remains an enigma. For example, Neville Cardus was previously called John Frederick Newsham, although he may not have known this and he certainly didn't mention it. There are plentiful omissions and contradictions in his writing. Now, using new sources of information for the first time, we are in a better position to separate the myth from the reality and work out what is the truth.

Cricket was where Cardus had the greatest impact. We can still learn about the man from his writing, from which his emotions become apparent. He was keen to share his sense of excitement of cricket, and when the 1921 Australians were narrowly defeated by a scratch England XI team put together by Archie MacLaren, readers could enjoy:

> "All cricketers know well the infinite changefulness of the great game, but to overthrow the might of Australia from no better base than a first innings total of 43 – why, the miraculous is here, black magic, the very imps of mischief. There were the most thrilling fluctuations in the day's play: now the game was safe in [Australian] Armstrong's keeping, now it slipped from his grasp, now, by a desperate motion of the will, Armstrong clutches it again, and then, as, indeed it looked his for good, out it slipped and MacLaren and his men stuck greedily to it… MacLaren was rather overcome with emotion, and through a deputy announced that this was his farewell to cricket." [2]

It was also necessary to convey what was happening in a cricket match even when there wasn't much action, in which case Cardus could add in some action, as when he recalled writing about slow-scoring batsman Trevor Bailey:

"Before he had gathered together 20 runs, a newly-married couple could have left Heathrow and arrived in Lisbon, there to enjoy a honeymoon. By the time Bailey had congealed 50, this happily-wedded pair could easily have settled down in a semi-detached house in Surbiton; and by the time his innings had gone to its close they conceivably might have been divorced."[3]

There was something special about someone who could make his name in two fields for a major newspaper. Cardus had been chief cricket writer for the *Manchester Guardian* from 1919. However, he had trained himself in musical criticism, and in 1927 he became the paper's senior music critic. He had the gift of being able to convey his enthusiasm for music and musicians. A particular favourite of his was singer Kathleen Ferrier, in whose obituary he paid her this tribute:

"… the most beautiful of all English singers of her time, beautiful of voice and musical expression, and beautiful to look at. Her contralto avoided the booming impersonal stateliness of her kind; it was warm of tone. Her warm nature went into it. The range of her voice touched altitudes belonging to the mezzo-soprano: and it would lose nothing of her own heart and throb as it arched the intent and far-flung phrases of the 'Abschied' of Mahler's *Das Lied von der Erde*."[4]

On the other hand, he did not mince his words if need be, and pianist Vladimir Horowitz was the subject of a critical notice when Cardus, based in London post-war, wrote:

"Horowitz surely commands a technique which by now is free to relax and hint of the reserve power that is the proof of mastery. This performance did, indeed, protest too much; at times it suggested a sort of musical speedway and the tumult of the shouting heard at the end was in much the same vocal key, and meant much the same, as the acclamation emitted any evening at the White City [a stadium for greyhound racing and previously speedway]."[5]

Both in music and cricket Cardus used allusions to help tell readers what he meant.

Cardus did write about his own life, initially in *Autobiography*, published in 1947, followed by *Second Innings* in 1950. A further book, *Full Score*, issued in 1970, contains many reminiscences, and these three autobiographical volumes naturally contain valuable information, as does the record of his discussions with Robin Daniels: *Conversations with Cardus*. His life was, when we read the introduction to *Autobiography*, a rags-to-riches story. He lived in a slum, was the son of a prostitute and did not know his father. Cardus apparently only had four years at school and learned little; he later worked hard to educate himself.

He looked back on his life and in 1945 recalled the first time he went to the cricket ground at Old Trafford. Lancashire were playing a Gloucestershire team that included Gilbert Jessop, a fierce hitter of the ball:

"I can remember the first time I ever went to Old Trafford, on a June morning in 1899: Lancashire were playing Gloucestershire... I saw a refreshment-room. As I was thirsty, as only a boy of nine can be on a hot summer day, I stood on tiptoe reaching up at the counter asking for a glass of lemonade. There was a sudden explosion of mirrors and bottles and other hardware… As I shrank from flying splinters a cheerful Lancashire voice reassured me. 'It's all reight, sonny,' said a man in a cloth cap. 'Don't worrit thiself, it's only Jessop just coom in.' Jessop did not score many runs at Old Trafford that day… Tom Lancaster was one of the Lancashire eleven and I think [Lancastrian] Jack Sharp scored sixty, and at the day's end, H.F.B. Champain and Wrathall began Gloucestershire's innings. I can here say quite honestly that I am writing far away from my books."[6]

That suggests a good memory for events that took place some 46 years previously, although the lemonade had become ginger beer when he wrote about the same match two years later in *Autobiography*. And when he referred to it in 1951, the month had changed to July, the weather had deteriorated to be a dull day, and Jessop left no indelible impression on him.[7] Indeed, he was puzzled why he went to watch cricket at all as his passion at the time was football. The month had switched back to June when Cardus mentioned the match in 1952,[8] but was again July in 1957, when Cardus admitted that he had been hungry rather than thirsty: his visit to the refreshment room was for a halfpenny bun when the glass splintered from Jessop's hit.[9] Elsewhere, he added the further detail that Jessop drove perfect off-breaks for six.[10]

What do we make of this mixed-up information? The lesson is that we cannot read too much into Cardus's writing. His memory was fallible, and he was inclined to embellish his stories. We can now work out that the match actually began on Monday 24 July, when there was bright sunshine and a cool breeze.[11] Lancashire did not have off-break bowlers in their side. Readers don't really know whether Cardus was hungry or thirsty or indeed whether he visited the refreshment room at all. We conclude that we cannot believe all that Cardus wrote. There are truths and untruths, and it is not always possible to tell them apart. And to confuse us further, Cardus introduced the concept of "higher truth" as a justification for what may not be the (literal) truth.

The autobiographical volumes also have some significant gaps. They do not say when Cardus was born or who his father was (Cardus said he did not know). He does not admit that he changed his name to Neville. There is little about his mother, Ada. His wife, Edith, is mentioned less than "Milady", his mistress in the 1930s. After his first visit to Australia on the 1936/37 MCC cricket tour, he does not reveal that he went to Australia for health reasons the following winter.

There are also plentiful mistakes in what Cardus wrote. He lived for some years with his maternal grandparents. He recorded their deaths, although claimed that his grandmother died first, which is incorrect.[12] Grandfather Robert, according to Neville, "fell down the cellar steps with fatal results shortly before the relief of Ladysmith",[13] which would date this in 1899. Robert actually died from apoplexy in October 1900. Grandmother Ann is said to have died of bronchitis at the age of 73.[14] The facts are that she died from a heart condition at the age of 68 in 1907, over seven years after her husband.

However, the essence of Cardus's legacy is not its factual content. It is the quality of his writing, the sweep of history that he encompasses, with a literary construction of the Golden Age of cricket in late Victorian and Edwardian times,[15] and his portrayal of the characters on the field. Benny Green encouraged readers to savour what Cardus had written, even if not the literal truth.[16]

Cardus's writing, in his autobiographical volumes and elsewhere, contains gaps and conflicting information. The objective of this book is, as far as possible, to fill in what is missing and to resolve the contradictions; and to establish a firmer factual basis for Cardus's life and his family background.

This search for the truth about Cardus uses sources not previously employed in published work. Genealogical information enables me to piece together the family history in a way not done before. There are, naturally, some pitfalls. Both Neville's birth certificate and baptism record included (different) deliberate mistakes. Nevertheless, his father can at last be revealed. And we can find out more about people in the family from records of cases that went to court, police records and lists of passengers who went abroad.

Some of the problems of the missing and inconsistent information about Cardus's adult life can also be addressed. Not only British but also Australian newspapers help work out the events that took place. Archive sources are also valuable, including the new collection of Neville Cardus papers in the Guardian News and Media Archive. Light is shone on his introduction to writing on cricket for the *Manchester Guardian* and his first review of serious music for the newspaper. There are other issues around, for example, his music responsibilities being extended to cover London in the 1930s, his stay in Australia in the 1940s, and his reporting on Test matches in 1953. By piecing together the evidence we finally start to understand what is the truth, the untruth and what is the "higher truth".

Chapter 2

FAMILY BACKGROUND:
BEFORE NEVILLE CARDUS WAS BORN

-------- ❦ --------

Neville Cardus's grandfather: Robert – his origins

Neville Cardus spent several of his early years with his maternal grandparents, so we begin with them: Robert and Ann. There is rather more to say about Robert, who Neville said, "originally was a policeman, or to use his own fastidious language, a constable. He was wholly Victorian."[1]

While Neville was well-known as a Lancastrian, his grandfather Robert was born in Yorkshire: probably in 1829, at Switchers Farm in the village of Hellifield, about 7 miles (11km) south-east of Settle. He was baptised later in 1829 at nearby Long Preston.

Oddly, Robert didn't start off life as a Cardus: he was born Robert Carradice. His father (Neville's great grandfather) was John Carradice, who was baptised in 1787 in Long Mitton, Yorkshire, and married Rebecca Preston in Long Preston in 1824. He was an agricultural labourer. The family changed surname: it was recorded in the 1841 census as Carradice and in the 1851 census as Cardus; the two names are both forms of Carruthers.[2] The new name was in place by 1848 as it was then that John died, his death certificate showing "Cardus". Although Robert's mother, Rebecca, was shown as a Cardus in the 1851 and later censuses, the certificate of her death in 1882 shows her surname as Carradice.

The 1841 census shows Robert, then aged 11, living in Long Preston with his parents, four sisters (Betty, Anne, Mary and Bridget) and two brothers (John and Michael); his elder brother William is absent from the household. By 1851 the family was in Airton, a village about 4 miles (7km) east of Long Preston.[3] In addition to the family being depleted by the death of father John, two of Robert's sisters had left home: his eldest sister Betty had married in 1849 and was living nearby in Settle; while Mary had gone to be a servant for her aunt in Skipton, about 7 miles (11km) south-east of Airton. However, brother William was back at home.

So, in 1851, Robert was living in Airton with his widowed mother, three brothers and two sisters. Robert, like his elder brother William, was recorded in the census as a common carrier; he may have been helping transport goods locally using a horse-drawn carriage. The 1850s was, however, to be a time when the family split up.

Robert and his seven siblings had all left home by 1861. Three were nearby in Airton, Settle or Skipton: Betty and Mary as before, and also William. Two of the siblings had moved to Lancashire: John to Burnley, Bridget to Lancaster. One travelled much further: Anne had become a housemaid in London. The last had passed away: Michael died, aged 12, in 1852. Robert's mother, Rebecca, remained in Airton, now accompanied by her son Henry Preston, whom she had borne before marrying John.

What happened to Robert as the family dispersed? First, he moved to Skipton, and worked as a labourer at Skipton Castle. Then, in 1854, he made the move to Lancashire: he went to live in Much Woolton (now known as Woolton). This was a village then outside the boundaries of Liverpool, it being incorporated in the city in 1913. It may well be a journey that he undertook on his own. Apart from his sister Anne who had relocated to London, Robert travelled further from his home village than any of the others in the family.

Robert Cardus's career as a police constable

Robert Cardus's work in Lancashire was with the county police force, to which he was appointed in June 1854. He was attached to the division at Prescot, just outside Liverpool and not far from Much Woolton. We are fortunate that his police record is available, so we know that Robert was 5ft 8in (173cm) tall, had grey eyes, dark brown hair and a fresh complexion.

Robert Cardus was in the news in April 1859, when he identified a theft by John Banks and William Nelson of 64lb (29kg) weight of crushed oats and a sack from the premises of Ambrose Lace of Little Woolton.[4] However, there was an unwelcome event later in the year.[5] On 28 October he was drunk in a railway carriage at St Helens, and assaulted Isaac Hatton, an earthenware dealer, whom he falsely accused of having stolen a purse containing two sovereigns. The Prescot magistrates fined Robert £1. Present during the investigation was Captain William Elgee, chief constable, who dismissed Robert from the police force. He then earned his living as a self-employed greengrocer.

He rejoined Lancashire police less than a year later, on 3 October 1860, this time attached to the Manchester division.[6] His hair was then brown rather than dark brown; and the temptation cannot be resisted to suggest that his complexion, then described as ruddy, may have owed something to his drinking habits.

It was July 1867 when a dramatic incident took place.[7] Robert Cardus, in plain clothes, saw a man, John (also known under an alias, William) Langford, entering gardens in Moss Lane, Manchester, and leaving with a bundle containing two rabbits and some onions, which

Robert found had been stolen from a garden. Robert told the man that he was a police officer and that it was his duty to take him into custody. Langford responded by picking up two bricks and throwing them at Robert, who was injured and unable to pursue him. A few days later, Robert saw Langford going along Oxford Street, Manchester with a hand cart and, with the assistance of a colleague, Isaac Wild, attempted to capture him. Langford said he would go quietly if allowed to take his hand cart and tools, which was accepted. Then,

"After walking about thirty yards he let go the cart, from which he took a crowbar, and struck Cardus with two blows, one with both hands, which cut through the officer's helmet, and the other inflicted a serious blow upon his head. He also hit Cardus with a blow on the shoulder, and struck Wild on the head with the crowbar. The blow on Cardus's head incapacitated the officer from duty for a week, and placed him under surgical treatment for about the same time."[8]

Langford was 6ft 0½in (184cm) tall, rather more than Robert Cardus's 5ft 8in. With a heavy iron crowbar, Langford was able to inflict serious harm on both constables. It was also reported, "There was not much room for doubt that the helmet which Cardus was wearing and which was broken by the first blow, saved his life."[9] Langford was sentenced to prison for seven years.

Neville's account in *Autobiography* is:

"My grandfather retired from the constabulary on a small pension, after receiving several blows on the head, administered in person by Mr Charles Peace with a crowbar. My grandfather was proud of these bumps on the head, lasting evidence of an intimate association with a famous and, in his day, much respected criminal."[10]

Charles Peace was indeed famous: he was guilty of burglaries and of two murders, one victim being a police officer in Manchester, and he spent several years of his life in prison.[11] However, there is no evidence that he was ever involved in an incident with Robert Cardus, and the crowbar in question did belong to John Langford. The reference in *Autobiography* to Charles Peace may make the story more impressive, and responsibility for this may, of course, lie with Robert himself, but it is not true.

In May 1870 Robert Cardus was transferred to the police division at Leyland, near Preston. Later that year, on 6 September, he resigned from the force to look for other employment, as his family did not wish to make the move north.[12] Indeed, it may also be the case that Robert did not want to move; such transfers were typically at the request of the police force. Research into Lancashire police pension records in Preston has been unable to find any trace of a pension for Robert, who left the force at the age of about 40, or for his widow.

After leaving the police, Robert Cardus had a variety of jobs. Records indicate that he was a greengrocer, gardener and farmer, although these may not have been distinct occupations; perhaps equivalent to what we would now call market gardening. He is also shown as a labourer and porter, in addition to helping in the family laundry business. Nevertheless, Robert Cardus's death certificate showed his occupation as "formerly a police constable": although this was his job for only about 16 years it was what he was to be remembered as.

Enter Ann Cardus, Neville's grandmother

Robert Cardus was married in July 1859 to Ann Rawlinson. Ann had been born in 1840 in Allerton, then a village near (and now a suburb of) Liverpool; her father John was a gardener, with earlier records showing him as a labourer. The wedding took place in the parish church of Childwall, near to Allerton.

Ann was described by Neville as, like Robert, God-fearing and hard-working.[13] She ran the family laundry, which was not a female preserve but also involved Robert and, at times, Neville. Ann had a pride in home-made things, devoting a day a week to baking, and would not stoop to buying bread in a shop.[14] By the 1901 census, when a widow, Ann was described as a retired laundress.

The Cardus family grows and moves to Summer Place

Robert and Ann's first child was born in January 1860: a boy named George. The family were then living at Allerton Road, Much Woolton. Finding a house in Manchester after rejoining the force in October 1860 looks to have been difficult. In the 1861 census Robert, Ann and son George are shown as living at the police station in Prestwich, near Manchester. A second child was born in October 1861: Alice, whose birth certificate shows the family address as Woolton St, Much Woolton, implying that the family were still searching for a new home.

The first definite information of a house in the Manchester area is from the birth on 1 February 1865 of their third child, Samuel, at Union Street, Rusholme.[15] Rusholme was a village just to the south of Manchester, of which it became a part in 1885. Two further children were born there: Annie and Arthur, in 1866 and 1868 respectively.

Robert and Ann now had five children, and their house in Union Street may not have been large enough for their needs: the houses in the street each had four rooms.[16] The family moved to 4 Summer Place, Rusholme, about a five-minute walk away. The rateable value of the house in Union Street had been only £9.00, whereas in Summer Place, with six rooms, it was £15.25.[17] The new house appears to have been built in the late 1830s.[18] The Manchester rate books suggest that the Cardus family was the occupier on 6 June 1869, although this may not be the date they moved in. This was to be the family home for over 25 years.

Summer Place is where the sixth child, Ada, Neville's mother, was born in October 1870. Neville said very little about her in *Autobiography*; he doesn't even mention her by name. Shortly afterwards, Arthur died of scarlet fever, aged 2. However, four further children were born at the house: Helena, Robert, Jessie and Beatrice, in 1873, 1874, 1876 and 1879 respectively. Altogether, this meant that Robert and Ann had ten children: four sons and six daughters, all but one (Arthur) surviving to adulthood. Neville was not to be short of aunts and uncles.

Ann and Robert ran a home-laundry. From *Autobiography* we learn that this also occupied "her three daughters".[19] Since there were six daughters, this isn't specific. Census records indicate that Alice, Ada and Helena were involved. It is fair to think that Annie, Jessie and Beatrice helped as well.

By the time Neville was born, his eldest uncle, George, had left the family home. On Christmas Eve 1882 he had married Sarah Ann Gaul in Liverpool, although they returned to Manchester to make their family home. But 4 Summer Place remained a busy house in which Neville was brought up, although there would be some secrets in his family life.

Chapter 3

A SECRETIVE EARLY LIFE

———— ❧✦❧ ————

When was Neville Cardus born?

In *Autobiography*, Neville Cardus did not say when he was born. A strange omission perhaps. But it shows that the problem of establishing the truth about Cardus starts from the outset. His book, written in 1947, does have some indirect references such as "In 1911 I arrived at the age of 21… the spring of 1919, when I was twenty-nine", mostly implying that he was born in 1890.[1] Hence, when Rupert Hart-Davis wrote the introduction to *The Essential Neville Cardus* in 1949 he indicated that Neville was born in 1890.[2]

That is only the beginning of the problem. Alternatively, look at *Who's Who*, in which Cardus was first included in 1936: it shows he was born on 2 April 1889. This is consistent with the information on birthdays in the list in *The Times* when he was included from 1964 (age 75) onwards. It is also true for the dates in the *Manchester Guardian* (later, the *Guardian*) for his 70th, 75th and 80th birthdays. It appeared on his passport[3] and on his death certificate. Hence, 2 April 1889 became accepted as Cardus's birthdate and was used by Brookes in *His Own Man*.[4]

However, this was not the end of the matter, as a search of the register of births in 1889 produced no sign of the boy in question.[5] The solution is to go back to 1888. The birth certificate of the boy who we have come to know as Neville shows that he was born to Ada Cardus, laundress of 4 Summer Place, Rusholme, Manchester, on 3 April 1888: this is therefore the third birthdate we have.[6] No father is shown, so we deduce that Neville was illegitimate. The name Neville is absent: the boy's Christian names were John Frederick. This third date, 3 April 1888, has been taken as correct in the *Oxford Dictionary of National Biography*.

A further look at the birth certificate is instructive. The birth was registered on 15 May 1888, which was 42 days after the birthdate of 3 April. That was the maximum time allowed by law for registration, and a genealogical perspective is that, in such a case, if there is evidence from a baptism record that the child was born on an earlier date, "I would strongly suspect that the parent registering the birth falsified the date in order to avoid a fine for late registration."[7]

We need to find Neville's baptism record. We can, and it indicates that a son, although named John Henry rather than John Frederick, was born to parents John Henry and Ada Newsham, who were living in Rusholme, the father being a smith.[8] The baptism was on 3 June 1888, and the birthdate is indeed earlier than that on the birth certificate: it is 2 April 1888.

Now we know that, on 14 July 1888, Ada Cardus married John Frederick Newsham, a smith. Therefore, the baptism record must surely refer to the boy whose birth was registered on 15 May. On the face of it, the baptism record disguised some of the facts. At the time of the baptism, the parents were not yet married: this could be why the names of both the father and the son were changed from John Frederick to John Henry. Later census records confirm they were actually John Frederick. However, the key point is the birthdate of 2 April 1888. This makes good sense. There was no reason to lie about the birthdate on the baptism record, which avoided the deadline that birth registration had. Therefore, we finish with a fourth birthdate, 2 April 1888, for the boy who was later to adopt the name Neville.

Hence, I am confident that 2 April 1888, as shown on the baptism record, is the true birthdate of Neville Cardus. This is consistent with the date of 2 April when he celebrated his birthday, but he was wrong about his year of birth, so he missed out on a year's pension. We see that both the birth certificate and baptism record contain (different) deliberate mistakes; the problem of establishing the truth about Neville Cardus is to continue throughout his lifetime.

Why did Neville Cardus wrongly claim that he was born later than 1888?

Why should Neville claim to have been born later than the truth of 1888? It could have been a deliberate mistake, for example, to cover up his illegitimacy: if born in 1889, this would have been after his parents' marriage.[9] However, while it is fair to accept Brookes' comment[10] that illegitimacy must have caused embarrassment at times, he goes on to say that it provided enormous conversational capital. So, it is not clear that illegitimacy was a problem for the adult Cardus.[11] Of course, another possibility is that he wished to be regarded as younger than the truth: he asserted that, in 1929, he looked younger than he was.[12]

On the other hand, it is possible that the mistake was not Neville's: he may have been misinformed by others, possibly by uncle Robert, with whom he lived when a young adult. He had a difficult family environment and may have never known, or may have forgotten, the truth.

There is an inconsistency that should be noted. When asked for his date of birth Neville's usual answer was 2 April 1889: for example, in his *Who's Who* entry from 1936 onwards and in the 1939 Register, a form of census taken in September 1939.[13]

But there is then a problem with the answers he gave when asked his age. After the censuses of 1891 and 1901, when Neville's age was correctly based on 1888, things went wrong in 1911. The census date of 2 April was his 23rd birthday, so 23 should have been recorded. Instead, he was said to have been 21, implying he was born in 1890.

Neville continued to err, implying birth in 1890 when disclosing his age on his marriage certificate in 1921, and when travelling to Australia in September 1936 and in December 1937.[14] He also implied 1890 in *Ten Composers* (1943),[15] *Autobiography* (1947) and *Second Innings* (1950).[16] And inconsistencies abound in post-war passenger lists for his journeys to and from Australia: you can deduce from the age he declared that he was born in either 1888, 1889 or 1890. He even claimed to be age 60 when leaving Australia in 1948, but only 59 when returning later that year.

There is likely a simple explanation for implying 1890: Cardus was a literary person rather than a mathematician,[17] and made mistakes in recalling years, so on being asked to say how old he was when completing forms, he just didn't do the arithmetic properly. He used 1890 rather than the bothersome sum of subtracting 1889 (or 1888) from the current year. Later on, Cardus appears to have begun calculating his age as based on being born in 1889, writing in *Full Score* (1970) that he was then in his 82nd year and had been 50 in 1939.[18] But struggles with arithmetic would continue over his lifetime.

Neville Cardus's birthplace: 4 Summer Place

Neville's birth certificate specifies that he was born at 4 Summer Place, which was, of course, the Cardus family home. This was where he spent the early years of his childhood, with his maternal grandparents, some of his aunts and uncles and, for a short period, his mother. One enigma is that *Autobiography* referred to him being born at 2 Summer Place[19] and that the house where he lived "stood at the end of a small row",[20] i.e. no.2. Of course, this may be just a mistake. It may also be a mistake when we read elsewhere that Ada lived with her husband at 2 Summer Place.[21]

However, it is just possible that 2 Summer Place was relevant in some way. This is because it was a much less crowded household. The censuses of 1881 and 1891 show that there were 11 and 9 people, respectively, living at no.4. But at no.2 in 1881 there were only Thomas Lilliman and his wife, and a lodger; in 1891 Thomas Lilliman was there alone. So, while this is admittedly speculation, perhaps Ada lived with her husband and Neville for a few days at 2 Summer Place, where the extra space would provide more privacy. Nevertheless, for Neville's birthplace, the contemporaneous evidence of the birth certificate does support 4 Summer Place as the answer.

The 1891 census is the first that includes Ada's son, as Frederick Newsham. However, Table 1 (*see overleaf*) confirms that the house was beginning to thin out as Robert and Ann's children moved away.

A point of debate is whether 4 Summer Place was a slum. Neville Cardus thought so, writing in *Autobiography*: "Manchester was my place of birth, in a slum."[22] However, some authors have argued that Summer Place was not a slum.[23] The photograph in *Autobiography* shows us that it was a semi-detached house with bay windows and a small strip of earth that was the garden. Cardus himself modified his view on this point. In *Second Innings* and *Full Score*, he described it as a semi-slum,[24] a term he also used in conversation with Geoffrey Mather.[25] With Daniels he referred to it both as a slum and as a semi-slum.[26]

Table 1. Census records for 4 Summer Place 1871–1891

	1871		1881		1891	
	occupation	age*	occupation	age*	occupation	age*
Robert	labourer	37	greengrocer	49	porter	55
Ann		31	laundress	41		51
George	scholar	11	tin man	21		
Alice	scholar	9	laundress	19	dress maker	29
Samuel	scholar	6	blacksmith's apprentice	16		
Annie	scholar	4	scholar	15		
Ada		0	scholar	10	laundress[a]	20
Helena			scholar	8	laundress	17
Robert			scholar	6	estate agent's clerk	16
Jessie			scholar	4	scholar	14
Beatrice				2	scholar	11
Frederick Newsham[b]						3

[a] surname Newsham [b] i.e. Neville Cardus. *Some reported ages are incorrect.

Some indication of the nature of Summer Place at the time is available from the 1891 census records. The Cardus home had 9 people and 6 rooms; below are data on the other houses. Included are the occupations of the heads of household; while not conclusive, they suggest that semi-slum was more appropriate than slum.[27]

- Joiner, 1 person, 6 rooms
- General labourer, 8 people, 7 rooms
- Coach driver, 9 people, 7 rooms
- Infants' schoolteacher, 1 person, 4 rooms
- Commercial clerk, 6 people, 5 rooms.

Ada Cardus is married

Ada was married on 14 July 1888 at St Clement's parish church, Longsight, Manchester. Her husband was John Frederick Newsham (the "sh" was pronounced "s" as in newspaper). The bride and groom were aged 17 and 21 respectively. The marriage certificate indicated that the couple were both living at 21 Victoria Street before the marriage: there is no other reference to this address, and it is not clear whether it is true (errors in the addresses of spouses are not uncommon).

The couple's fathers are shown as John Newsham, master smith; and Robert Cardus, gentleman. Both witnesses represented the bride's family: Annie, one of Ada's elder sisters, and Arthur Albert Rushworth Smith, who was to marry Annie in 1889.

Parental consent was necessary for Ada to marry, but not for her husband, who had reached age 21 in November 1887. If parental consent had been a problem for him, this would not have prevented a wedding taking place before Neville's birth on 2 April 1888.

Who was Neville Cardus's father?

We know who Neville's mother married, but this does not necessarily tell us who Neville's father was. In none of *Autobiography*, *Second Innings* and *Final Score* does Neville tell us much about his parents, and one of the Cardus mysteries is that Neville did not know who his father was; he suggested that he could derive his temperament from an unknown father.[28] In *Autobiography* he wrote about having been told in infancy that his father had gone to the coast of west Africa on business and had died there. But he realised that this could hide a family secret. He continued:

"I can account for my mother's reticence. But why didn't my Aunt Beatrice tell me? … The most she ever told me of my father is that he was tall, saturnine of countenance, and one of the first violins in an orchestra.... My father and his violin never entered Summer Place."[29]

As Neville's birth was swiftly followed by his mother marrying John Frederick Newsham, who will be referred to as JFN senior (to distinguish him from the boy who was to become Neville but whose birth was registered as John Frederick), it is clearly on the cards that this was Neville's father. A further positive sign is that the son's names were also John Frederick: it was common for a son to take the name of the father. On the other hand, those names may have been given to conceal the fact that JFN senior was not the father.[30]

Recall that son John Henry on the baptism record was really John Frederick (he would be called Frederick Newsham in the 1891 census).[31] So, was the father on the baptism record, John Henry Newsham, really John Frederick Newsham, the man that Ada was to marry?

Neville did, on his marriage certificate, indicate that his father was Frederick Cardus, deceased, a clerk in the civil service. This is an untruth, although Frederick was part of the truth, of which Neville perhaps had some inkling. Later, Cardus's 1936 *Who's Who* entry referred to his parents as Robert Stanislaw Cardus and Ada Newsome. Stanislaw appears to be a made-up name, but using 'Newsome', as Newsham was pronounced, suggests that Cardus had heard his father's name, though maybe not seen it in print, and had some idea of what went on, perhaps misunderstood, misremembered or deliberately disguised.[32]

What happened was that JFN senior left for America just four days after the wedding, when Neville was only 3½ months old. It is therefore not surprising that Neville had no recollection of him. Then, having returned to England, JFN senior divorced Ada in 1899. The divorce papers[33] indicate that there were no children of the marriage; of course, Neville was born before the marriage. However, the divorce was reported in *The Times*, which recorded that JFN senior's lawyer stated, in court:

> "The parties were married on July 14, 1888, at St Clement's Church, Longsight, near Manchester, both being at the time quite young, the respondent [Ada] having in the previous April given birth to a child of which the petitioner [JFN senior] was the father."[34]

Another press report indicated that, "He [JFN senior] had had a child by her [Ada] before marriage, and it was in consequence of this that he married her."[35]

There is therefore a specific statement, on behalf of JFN senior, that he was the father of Neville. Added to the plentiful indirect evidence, this is sufficient to convince me that Neville's father was indeed John Frederick Newsham, who married Neville's mother shortly after his birth.

One minor point: there is no evidence that JFN senior was a violinist. This looks to be a red herring, and Neville's supposition that he inherited his feeling for music from his father[36] reflects his ignorance of what happened.

Neville Cardus's father: his upbringing

JFN senior was born in Chorlton-on-Medlock, Manchester in 1866. His father was John Newsham, who was a blacksmith, born in Manchester in 1841; he was later described as a master blacksmith. In 1864 John married Emma Plant, who was born in Blackley, near Manchester, in 1840. Emma's occupation was given as cotton weaver in 1861 and crinoline maker on her marriage certificate.

At the time of the 1871 census, JFN senior was living in Chorlton-on-Medlock with his parents and two younger brothers and a servant. JFN senior attended a Presbyterian school and then Ducie Avenue school in Manchester.[37]

Ten years later the family were in Rusholme, this time without a servant; JFN senior was an apprentice to a smith, presumably working for his father.

By 1891 JFN senior had, of course, left, and the family then had a servant again. Both parents died at the age of 52: Emma in 1893 and John in 1894. John's death certificate referred to chronic alcoholism as a cause of death.

Did Neville Cardus's father desert his family?

A reader of *Autobiography* may well conclude that Neville's father was guilty of deserting Neville and his mother. However, all is not what it seems.

Neville's parents were divorced in 1899. The case came before the courts on 24 June 1898.[38] The essence of the case was that JFN senior (the petitioner in the divorce) alleged that Ada (the respondent) had committed adultery with Eliahoo Joseph (the co-respondent). In the papers prepared for the court Ada denied the adultery and claimed that JFN senior was guilty of desertion from July 1888. However, by the time the court met, Ada and Joseph had changed their minds, and dropped their allegation of JFN senior's desertion. The judge said that the case was practically undefended.

JFN senior and Ada did not live together for long. On 18 July 1888, four days after the wedding, JFN senior was in Liverpool on the *Britannic*, which then began its journey to America. Ada saw him off on the ship, which arrived in New York on 28 July. The plan, agreed between the couple, was for JFN senior to seek employment, and a home at which his wife (and presumably son) would join him. JFN senior's evidence was robust:

> "It had been arranged before the marriage that the petitioner should join his uncle in America and get a home together there, and that the respondent should

subsequently join him; and accordingly in July, 1888, he and the respondent's brother sailed for America."[39]

The brother who also went to America appears to be Samuel, who died in New York in March 1896.[40] Another of Ada's brothers followed. This was Robert, the youngest of the boys, and he travelled from Liverpool to New York on the *Teutonic* on 22 February 1893. As he had 12 pieces of luggage, this was presumably not a short holiday.

JFN senior therefore argued that he did not desert Ada, his travel to and staying in America being with her consent to provide a home for them there. He wrote from time to time to Ada, and the correspondence between the couple was on affectionate terms, but this was not to last. JFN senior asked Ada to come out to America with him but she always refused to do so, supported by her mother Ann. Indeed, Ada said she would not come to America even if her husband stayed there 20 years. JFN senior provided money to Ada but she wrote that this was no longer required as she was earning her own living at her mother's laundry.

Ada does not come out well in the evidence. JFN senior suffered ill health in America. Ada had, in one letter to him, wished that he was dead. She also told him that his mother would not go to heaven when she was dead.

Ada was taking advantage of her husband's absence to enjoy other male company. Suspicions about Ada's conduct reached JFN senior, who wrote to her on that subject in 1892. Her reply asked him to get a divorce, and said that she did not intend to join him in America. The new man in her life was a merchant, Eliahoo Joseph. JFN senior was to allege in the divorce case that, in July 1893, Joseph frequently visited Ada at 4 Summer Place, and committed adultery with her on a number of occasions.

JFN senior decided to come to England, travelling on the *Umbria* from New York to Liverpool, arriving on 29 December 1894. He called at the home of Ann Cardus, who told him that Ada was with "her chap", i.e. the co-respondent, and JFN senior found that his suspicions were correct. When he was satisfied that his wife was living with Eliahoo Joseph, he returned to America, where he planned to increase his earnings so that he would be able to take divorce proceedings. Ada's relationship with Eliahoo Joseph continued. JFN senior alleged that, from about May 1896 onwards, the pair had lived together at 3 Clyde Road, Withington, Manchester, as husband and wife, and habitually committed adultery together.

JFN senior's further return to England was on the *Campania* from New York, arriving in Liverpool on 22 October 1897. This is described in *The Times*:

> "In October, 1897, he again came to England, and finding that his wife was living maritalement with the co-respondent, he, with the help of his friends, filed his petition. The respondent had in her answer pleaded that the petitioner had deserted her, but that plea was not now persisted in."[41]

JFN senior discovered his wife living with Eliahoo Joseph at the latter's house at 3 Clyde Road, calling herself Mrs Joseph. His visit to the house was eventful:

> "He remembered on the 19th March going with a witness to a house in Clyde Road, Withington. He saw his wife with the co-respondent, and touched the latter on the shoulder, remarking, 'Do you know you are with my wife?' The co-respondent screamed and ran into the house. The respondent denied she was petitioner's wife, and said she did not know him at all. He followed them to the door, and put his foot against it. She said, 'Come in, come in, don't make a disturbance there.'"[42]

A nurseryman, Mellor, who was in charge of Joseph's vinery at Clyde Road, said that he had seen Ada and Joseph courting in Lapwing Lane, and had seen them together when Ada was not properly dressed. Ada told Mellor that her husband had died of tuberculosis in America. Joseph, however, looks to have bribed Mellor with drink, asking him not to say anything about his, i.e. Joseph's, women.[43]

The jury found that Ada and Eliahoo Joseph had committed adultery and that JFN senior was not guilty of desertion. Since JFN senior did not have evidence that Joseph knew that Ada was already married to him, he could not claim costs and damages from him; he also had to pay Ada's costs.

What did Neville say about his mother in *Autobiography*? One answer would be "not much". He does not name her. However, he does say that his mother and aunts went "dancing down the primrose path" and brought shame into Summer Place.[44] Neville claimed to have inherited his baser self from his mother, "the buxom wench who conceived me in sin."[45] And he told readers that his mother went to live with a "stout gentleman in a fez and gold spectacles", a Sultan who fascinated Neville with his flapping heelless slippers.[46] Now since Ada specifically asked Neville not to include anything about her in the book,[47] an alternative answer is that there was too much about his mother. Of course, it would have been a challenge to Neville to write an autobiography without mentioning either his mother (because she had asked him not to) and his father (because he did not know him). It is, though, also possible that Neville did have information about his father which he did not reveal because of his mother's wishes. In *Full Score* Neville did provide his mother's name, Ada – this being some years after her death – and confirms that she, and his aunts Jessie and Beatrice were prostitutes ("adorned the oldest profession").[48]

Ada's night-time work did enrich the rags-to-riches story. It is worth reflecting that if Ada had not been a prostitute, she would presumably have gone to America with her son. And America would not have led to Neville gaining fame as a writer on cricket.

Eliahoo Joseph's background: "a scoundrel"

Eliahoo Joseph, the man who was the lover of Neville's mother, had a colourful life. He was a Turkish citizen, born in Baghdad, around 1856–61.[49] In 1886 he became a merchant in Manchester, running a company, E. Joseph & Co.[50] He was married, and had a son and two daughters, although was separated from his wife, who was still in Baghdad.

Joseph came to the notice of the British public in 1892 when he was found guilty in an "extraordinary breach of promise case".[51] Both parties in the case were Jews and gave their evidence in Arabic. The plaintiff was teenager Sophia Hettena, daughter of a merchant in Port Said, Egypt. Sophia had become engaged to Joseph on 24 April 1892 in a ceremony in Port Said known as a kiddushin, carried out in accordance with Jewish law. This meant that the couple were married, in the sense that a Jewish divorce was needed if they were to break up, but they were not allowed to live together as man and wife until a further stage, the nisu'in, was completed. Amazing as it seems to modern eyes, Joseph was not present at the ceremony, "but he executed a power of attorney in favour of the rabbi at Port Said, instructing him to carry out the ceremony as if he had been there himself." At this stage the engaged couple had corresponded by mail but had not met each other!

In June 1892 Joseph asked Sophia Hettena to meet him at the Grand Hotel in Paris. However, Joseph's plan to share a bedroom with his fiancée was thwarted by the latter's mother, who was also at the hotel and insisted that the couple first had to be married in a way acceptable to French law, not merely engaged. Joseph said he could not do that as he was already married. He argued that the bride belonged to him and that it was the custom in Turkey and France for engaged couples to live together without being married. The fiancée's mother said she would go to the Consul the following morning to check this, and Joseph agreed to be there – but he didn't turn up.

Thereafter, "The new terror of the suggestion of bigamy seemed to have such a disheartening effect on the intending bridegroom that he fled straight away back to Manchester. Thither the jilted bride and her energetic mother followed, inexorable as fate."[52] The parties met in Joseph's office, where Joseph "renewed his efforts to consort with the plaintiff. This was resisted by both the mother and her daughter."[53] The Hettena family then sought legal advice with a view to claiming breach of promise.

In December 1892 the jury found in favour of Sophia Hettena, and awarded her £1350. Joseph appealed, but lost, the Master of the Rolls saying that Joseph was a scoundrel and had behaved disgracefully.[54] Joseph and Sophia Hettena were subsequently divorced in accordance with Jewish law.[55]

Ada Cardus's relationship with Eliahoo Joseph

Ada Cardus and Eliahoo Joseph were in a relationship from July 1893, as recorded in the divorce papers, and possibly earlier. Joseph was around 10 years older than Ada, perhaps more. As a foreign merchant, he was not the boyfriend we would ordinarily expect for someone in her early twenties living in Summer Place. It is therefore reasonable to think that Joseph was linked to Ada's prostitution. The earlier reference to asking Mellor not to say anything about Joseph's women (plural) also suggests it was not a simple relationship.

Autobiography tells us that Ada and Joseph met through Ada's sister, Beatrice. Joseph is not named but we read that he was a friend of the Turkish consul in Manchester.[56] Unfortunately, Cardus's interpretation of events is not correct. Ada's relationship with Joseph began earlier, and Joseph introduced the Turkish Consul to Beatrice,[57] which may back up the suggestion that Joseph was a pimp.[58]

It was reported that Ada was aware of Joseph's wife and children in Baghdad.[59] Joseph knew that he could not marry Ada in accordance with English law; however, in a synagogue in Southport, he married her "on the Bible"[60] or "by word of God."[61] The 1901 census records the couple living together as married at Park Lane, Timperley.

School and education

Meanwhile, Neville Cardus needed education. He described his school years in *Autobiography*, beginning:

> "I attended what was known as a Board school, a place of darkness and inhumanity. I learned scarcely anything there, except to read and write. For four years only did I attend school, delicate years and miserable. At the age of thirteen my formal education came to an end."[62]

Elsewhere he wrote that he went to school for not four years but three[63] or five (from age 8 to 13),[64] and indicated 14 as the school leaving age.[65] His schooling was interrupted by illness which kept him in bed for nearly a year.[66] In *Full Score* he described his school as "a place of mental and aesthetic darkness".[67] Cardus obviously had a poor opinion of his education and, in particular, little music was taught.[68] The lack of learning may reflect his admission that he was not interested at school.[69] Cardus also referred to having been taught scripture at Sunday school.[70]

There is a puzzle as the Education Act 1870 prescribed a school starting age of 5, and the usual school leaving age was 13. So, Cardus's memory may be at fault, although there could be an explanation of which we are unaware.

Cardus did refer to "the Board school round the corner."[71] Just round the corner from Summer Place was the Holy Trinity National School, which was opened in 1861.[72] It is reasonable to suppose that this is where Cardus attended; when his uncle George moved to 4 Summer Place in the late 1890s his children went there. The buildings still stand, as Trinity House Community Centre; the original separate entrances for girls and infants on the one hand, and boys on the other, are still visible. Unfortunately, the school admission registers are only available from 1895, and unsurprisingly there is no record of Cardus, who would have been 5 years old in 1893.

Another puzzle is that this was not a board school, which was one under the auspices of the local council school board following the Education Act 1870, either because the board built the school or it took over responsibility for an existing school. However, Holy Trinity was a "National" rather than a board school and remained the responsibility of the church.

Cardus's writing implied that he went to just one school. However, he had moved away from Summer Place before he was aged 13, although perhaps always near enough to make a change of school unnecessary. However, we do not know whether he joined his grandparents and aunt Beatrice at Rose Cottage, Northenden, which was around 4 miles (6km) from Rusholme. It is possible that Cardus also attended some other school which was a board school.

The family home was, according to Cardus in *Autobiography*, illiterate and there was no music.[73] On the other hand, there were some positive signs: in *Second*

Innings the home is described as semi-literate and it is clear that there were some books.[74] Cardus's mother and aunts frequented the variety theatres of Manchester and sang music hall songs at home.[75] Aunt Beatrice used to sing him to sleep with melodies from *Norma*,[76] and encouraged him to read reasonably good books.[77]

Cardus regarded himself as, in effect, self-educated. After his school years he devised a schedule of the hours to devote to studying a range of subjects, involving metaphysics, sociology, economics, comparative religion and literature.[78] *Who's Who in Australia* indicated that his education began seriously in the Manchester libraries, theatres, concerts and cafés. He made use of libraries: the Municipal Lending Library, the Free Library in Rusholme and Manchester reference library.[79] With a great appetite for reading, he recalled that, "I discovered Charles Dickens and went crazy."[80] There were also free lectures at the University of Manchester, Manchester Art Gallery and elsewhere.[81] Meetings of the Ancoats Settlement were enjoyable, including a talk by George Bernard Shaw on the Ten Commandments; this was on 21 October 1906.[82] Hence, Cardus's educational achievements reflected his own efforts more than the results of the Manchester school system.

Chapter 4

MORE DIFFICULTIES WITH FAMILY AND FRIENDS

———— ◦◦◦•◦◦◦ ————

The breaking up of 4 Summer Place

Robert and Ann's large family meant that 4 Summer Place was a crowded home, but as the children grew up, the family began to disperse. George, a tinplate worker, was the first child to marry, in 1882, and moved away to live with his wife, Sarah Ann. Samuel, a farrier, was married in 1888 and emigrated to New York: like JFN senior, without his wife. Annie married a commercial traveller in the following year, moving away from Summer Place.

George's children included a girl named Esther. Brookes mentioned that those who knew the family in Summer Place recalled that Esther later owned a dress shop in Great Western Street and that she was the daughter of Ada.[1] However, this is incorrect: she was a cousin and not a sister of Neville.

Ada also left 4 Summer Place. Cardus wrote, "My mother withdraws to the wings as the more effulgent personality of my Aunt Beatrice commands the stage."[2] The divorce papers indicate that Ada was living at the home of Eliahoo Joseph by 1896 at the latest. It is therefore no surprise that we read of Neville being put to bed by his grandmother and by his aunt Beatrice.[3]

Robert and Ann's need for space was diminishing and, in 1896 or 1897, they departed for Rose Cottage,

Northenden. Beatrice confirmed that she was living there with her mother when she first met Mustafa Karsa, which was in April 1899.[4] However, by 1900, the family had relocated again: to 12 Claremont Street, Chorlton-on-Medlock, Manchester. Beatrice indicated that, before this move, she lived in Raby Street, Moss Side, Manchester, although it is unclear when this happened and whether other family members accompanied her.[5]

The family may have had further addresses. In *Second Innings* Cardus wrote as follows, although it is not clear what period it relates to:

"my own family seldom stayed at one address long enough to become enrolled on the official list of rent and ratepayers. According to the vicissitudes of fortune they moved from house to house; it was called, in the vivid poetic imagery of the lower orders of the period, 'flitting'... My grandmother spent the better part of the last few years of her life in, as she called it, 'getting straight'."[6]

As for 4 Summer Place, this remained a Cardus home, being occupied from 1896/97 by Robert and Ann's son George and his wife and family. They had six children by 1896 and presumably needed the space. However, by the time of the 1901 census, they had left for 9 Syndall Street, Chorlton-on-Medlock. The association of 4 Summer Place with Carduses, which lasted around 30 years, thereby came to an end.

Neville's grandfather Robert died in 1900 so, at the time of the 1901 census, Ann was the head of the household in Claremont Street, with Neville, his uncle Robert, and aunts Jessie and Beatrice (Table 2). Jessie's husband Harry was also present. This address is where Ann died in 1907.

Table 2. 12 Claremont Street in the 1901 census

	occupation	age
Ann Cardus	retired laundress	61
Robert Cardus	stone mason	26
Jessie Davies	usher, Comedy Theatre	24
Harry Davies	store keeper	23
John Frederick Cardus	school	12
Beatrice Cardus	working at home	21

Neville's uncertain whereabouts

Although Neville was at Claremont Street in 1901, what happened thereafter is uncertain. While not living permanently with his mother, Neville did stay with her at Eliahoo Joseph's house in Timperley from time to time, for several weeks in 1901, and in 1902.[7] He mostly lived in the kitchen with the cook.[8] Beatrice also spent time there: indeed, there is an unusual occurrence in that she is shown twice in the 1901 census, both with her mother and others at Claremont Street and also with Ada and Joseph at Timperley.

What Neville does say is that he went to live with his aunt Beatrice:

> "A year or two after the breach of promise action [1902, see below], both my grandfather and grandmother were dead. The family broke up. Beatrice was compelled to live in a long mean street that was not even a Place; and I went with her. A house with a backyard, sordid beyond description."[9]

It is not clear when this happened as grandmother Ann did not die until 1907, five years after the breach of promise case. Another complication is that Beatrice gave birth to an illegitimate son in 1903; we do not know how this fits in with Neville going to live with her.

The following paragraph of *Autobiography* is especially difficult to understand:

> "After the breaking-up of Summer Place and the passing of Beatrice I lived precariously for a while… I dwelt in a single back room in a Manchester lodging, so cold in the winter for want of a blanket that I collected newspapers and periodicals to pile on my bed over my feet."[10]

This appears before the section on his work for the Fleming brothers (which began in December 1904) so one might assume it refers to about 1902–04. The passing of Beatrice is a mistake, as she did not die until 1918.

It is worth setting out some facts that we do know, starting with a letter that Neville wrote to the editor of the *Manchester Courier* on 5 April 1909.[11] Neville complained that Edward German's song *Glorious Devon* was an honest, pure song rather than "music-hally", the word used by the newspaper's music critic in a review of a concert at the Manchester Free Trade Hall. Neville's contribution brought forth a letter from another correspondent in agreement. The significant point here, though, is that Neville's address is given as 129 Rosebery Street, Moss Side, Manchester.

Turning to the 1911 census, Neville was still at 129 Rosebery Street. His name is shown as Frederick Cardus, as he was then known, and his occupation was insurance clerk. The head of the household was his uncle Robert, who was living there with his wife Eliza. The house had five rooms. In Slater's directory, Robert is listed there in 1910; the 1909 directory entry for the address is blank, but it is reasonable to think, given the letter to the *Manchester Courier*, that Robert, and Neville, were there in 1909.[12] When Robert married in July 1908 he was living in Kippax

Street, Moss Side, but we do not know if Neville was there (Robert's wife died in 1920).

Let us review Neville's whereabouts between 1901 (with grandmother Ann at Claremont Street) and 1909 (with uncle Robert at Rosebery Street). He may have continued to live for a time with his grandmother, although she was in poor health for some time before her death.[13] He spent some weeks with his mother and Joseph. There was a period with his aunt Beatrice, but when and where is unknown. A possibility is living by himself: Neville has admitted being a solitary individual. Further, while he appears to have been with his uncle Robert in April 1909, this arrangement may have started before then. The truth is proving elusive.

Living with uncle Robert

Following Robert being listed at 129 Rosebery Street in the 1911 census, he remained there in the 1912 directory, is absent from the 1913 edition but, in 1914, is shown to be living at a terraced house, 154 Moseley Road, Fallowfield, Manchester. Although there may have been an intermediate address, it looks as if Robert moved from Rosebery Street to Moseley Road in around 1912–14. Moseley Road was also from where Neville wrote his letter to the *Manchester Guardian* in January 1917.

The Moseley Road address reappears in 1921. It was where Robert was living when he remarried in February 1921, with Neville and his future wife Edith as the witnesses. The same address was given for Neville when he married in June and Robert when he died in September. This therefore suggests that Neville was living with his uncle Robert at Rosebery Street from about 1909 and Moseley Road from about 1912–14 until 1921 (although Neville was to be at Shrewsbury in the summers of 1912–16: see chapter 5).

Neville commented about his living arrangements in early 1921 in *Second Innings*: "My bedroom was in a back attic, and my landlady and her husband slept on the floor below".[14] What is strange is that there is no mention of uncle Robert in Neville's writing. He bemoans his aunt Beatrice not telling him more about his father,[15] but we might expect Neville to have heard about this from his uncle Robert, who, like JFN senior, went to New York (in 1893; we do not know when he came back to England). It may well be that Neville had information about his father that he did not disclose in his writing.

Ada Cardus and Eliahoo Joseph: the litigious years

Ada and Joseph continued their relationship in the new century, although it was to be an eventful period, with Joseph making frequent appearances in court.

Joseph's business – Eliahoo Joseph & Co., shipper of cotton and woollen goods to Baghdad and the Persian Gulf – was deteriorating in 1902 and he was unable to obtain credit.[16] His solution was to change the name of his company to Elias Brothers, thinking that this would attract custom intended for a stronger competitor, Abdullah Elias and Co, owned by Abdullah Elias, a wealthy Manchester merchant. The move failed: Elias took Joseph to court and obtained an injunction to restrain Joseph from using Elias Brothers or a similar name. Joseph's business remained unsuccessful and, in May 1903, a court order was made to appoint a receiver to manage Joseph's bankrupt business.

Joseph nursed a grievance against Elias. In court on 13 May 1903 he made an allegation against Elias, which was followed on 15 May when he went to the police and provided a statement that Elias and Charles Battat, a young man employed by Elias, had committed homosexual acts, then illegal, in March and April 1901.[17] Elias and Battat were arrested but, after investigation, acquitted. Elias and

Battat then brought a case of conspiracy against Joseph, together with four others who held a grievance towards Elias. There followed several anonymous letters, written by one of the accused, John Reekie, said to be "demanding money with menaces, and without reasonable probable cause".[18] The accused were arrested; all were bailed, except Joseph, who was kept in prison.

The prosecution case was that Joseph acted at first out of spite and malice, and that the case grew into a conspiracy, in which others joined to try to get money out of Elias. The trial took place at the Manchester Assizes in November 1903. Joseph and one of the others accused, Sion Levy, were found guilty and sentenced to two years' hard labour. Following his release from prison, Joseph was receiving money from his brother in Baghdad; it was not thought that he was employed in business.

Ada appeared to stand by Joseph despite these upheavals. In 1903 Joseph signed a requisition that some property he had when arrested should be passed to her. And there is evidence that Joseph and Ada were living together for six months towards the end of 1906, in a boarding house in Cecil Street, Manchester.[19] The house in Timperley with its vinery was no longer an option in straitened circumstances.

In order to carry on business, Joseph decided to apply, in October 1907, for naturalisation as a British citizen. The issue came to court because declarations by three men in support of Joseph were regarded by the prosecution as false.[20] Additionally, Joseph's statement was, according to the prosecution, almost entirely false: he was a disreputable person, and not the fit and proper person needed for naturalisation. In any event Joseph went abroad immediately after his naturalisation application; it was thought that he went to Marseilles and thereon to Baghdad.[21] He had left Manchester and Ada behind. Manchester was doubtless happy at Joseph's departure, and perhaps the same was true of Ada if she had by then learned that he was, in fact, a scoundrel.

Aunt Beatrice and the lustful Turk

Joseph wasn't the only foreign visitor to the Cardus household. We find Mustafa Karsa making the newspaper headlines in another court case, when Justice Wills described him as the "Lustful Turk" in the case for breach of promise that Neville's aunt Beatrice brought in April 1902. Beatrice was Cardus's favourite aunt, always charming to him and calling him "darling".[22] Neville remembered her vividly: "Beatrice frankly joined the oldest of professions and became an adornment to it... I well remember her face, her blue eyes, her lovely weak mouth without lipstick; red as a rose. She was tall and walked like one of the well-born of the earth."[23] Neville described in some detail her relationship with Mustafa Karsa, the Turkish Consul in Manchester, her "greatest conquest, amongst many".[24]

In court, the jury heard that, in April 1899, Beatrice met Karsa at the house of Eliahoo Joseph.[25] The couple became intimate, and shared a bedroom when visiting Liverpool. Beatrice said that, in 1900, he promised to marry her, this being supported by several of her family members. Later, Karsa said that he couldn't be bothered and was too old to marry her, and the court case followed.

Karsa's home situation was of particular interest to the jury. Beatrice had visited Karsa's home in Sale, and had been introduced to a lady who Beatrice was told was a housekeeper although referred to as Mrs Karsa. There were eight children present; Beatrice claimed it was stated that their mother was dead. Karsa, on the other hand, stated that he had never referred to the lady as a housekeeper: she was his wife, whom he had married in a Muslim ceremony in that house some 16 years ago, with a registration ceremony in Beirut about 7 years ago to legitimise the children. Karsa's evidence was that Beatrice had heard the children calling Mrs Karsa "mother". Asked if he had told Mrs Karsa of his intimate relations with Beatrice, he replied, "No, I would get the poker if I did." Of course, not everything is what it seems.

Mustafa Karsa was a Muslim merchant, born in Damascus. He appears to have arrived in Britain in or around 1881, when the firm of M. Karsa & Co. was advertising for a youth aged 15–20 who spoke English and French (no anti-ageism laws then).[26] He appeared in the 1881 census: he was shown as a 31-year-old married merchant, lodging with a German family in Chorlton-on-Medlock, without his wife present. In 1898 he was appointed Vice-Consul of Turkey in Manchester.[27]

Although the court case focussed on Karsa's family with eight children, he had an earlier family: with Hassibi Karsa (née Leham). They had three children born in England: in Manchester (1883) and Altrincham (1884 and 1886).[28] There is no trace of a marriage in England nor any further record of the mother or these children, who may have gone abroad.

Mustafa Karsa's second family appeared in the 1891 and 1901 censuses. Karsa was shown as married to Helen, who was born in 1870, about 20 years younger than her "husband", but 10 years older than Beatrice. Helen appeared to have borne eight children, or possibly nine,[29] in the twelve years from 1888 to 1900. The couple had a further child in 1906.

A week before the court case in 1902, Karsa married Helen, whose maiden name was Saunders, in accordance with English law. The certificate shows Karsa to be a widower, perhaps a reference to Hassibi having died. He had also been stripped of his consular title; in August 1902 he was reinstated as Imperial Ottoman Consul for Manchester.[30]

The case was heard on 21 April, and the jury found in favour of Beatrice. She may have been lucky. There were no affectionate letters or photographs in the case. It was said that there were no wounded affections. And, of course, we know from Neville Cardus that Beatrice was engaged in prostitution.[31] The award to Beatrice of £200 was much less than the £3000 she had been offered in settlement, and half of what she received was said, perhaps wrongly, to have been dissipated in an unsuccessful bet on a horse.[32]

Beatrice's luck may also reflect insufficient emphasis on one point, namely that the writ was brought after there had been a disagreement on money matters between Karsa and Eliahoo Joseph. Surely it was possible that Joseph had suggested that Beatrice bring the case in order to embarrass Karsa, both personally and financially? Joseph and Ada were away in Blackpool at the time of the court hearing and could not be contacted: perhaps rather convenient for the prosecution.

Karsa died in Southport in 1907.[33] There was a sad incident in 1909, when his widow Helen was accused of theft: she "appeared in the dock in a pitiable state of collapse".[34] She was acquitted provided that her son, as promised, made restitution.

What happened to Aunt Beatrice?

Neville Cardus related a sad end for Beatrice:

> "Her life came to an end soon after in circumstances which may appear a little abject. She became inexplicably compassionate about an elderly man who for years had been the gardener at a house when she picked up a temporary job as a laundress, deep down in the cellar, two days a week. She married him, kept him, and bore him a daughter and died at the age of twenty-eight."[35]

As usual, the truth is not quite so straightforward. In 1903 Beatrice was living in Chorlton-on-Medlock, when she gave birth to a son, Cecil, who was born in Sale, at 65 Roebuck Lane. The birth was illegitimate, and the surname was spelt Cardross. Some disguising of the facts was taking place, presumably as Beatrice did not want publicity about such an event so soon after her winning the breach of promise case. Slater's Directory for 1904 shows the head of household at 65 Roebuck Lane to be George Wilkinson, labourer (earlier directories show no entry for this house). Although not certain, this appears to be Beatrice's brother-in-law, husband of Helena, helping at a difficult time by letting her give birth at his home.

In 1911 Beatrice and Cecil were living with Ada in Withington, Manchester. The householder is described as "Mrs Beatrice Cardus" in Slater's Directory. It was in August of the following year that Beatrice married her gardener: he was Edward Mann, a 61-year-old widower. Beatrice's marriage to a man 27 years older was doubtless related to her being pregnant, and about five weeks later she gave birth to their daughter, Irene. The couple had a son, Edward James Mann, in 1916. Beatrice died in 1918 in Baguley sanatorium, Wythenshawe.

So, Neville Cardus was on the right lines, although his favourite aunt lived to be 39 not 28.

Friends of Neville Cardus: the "Gang"

If Neville Cardus had a difficult family, what do we know about his friends? The young Cardus was part of what he called a Gang and in *Second Innings* he mentioned his fellow members, Johnny Howard, Billy Clegg, Harry Pinkerton and Herbert Ramsbottom.[36] There is insufficient detail to identify them from genealogical records; while it is possible to trace some young men with these names in the Manchester district, it is not clear which, if any, are the individuals in question. Cardus also referred to Sammy Ogden and the Moffitt brothers as friends;[37] again, it has not been possible to trace them.

The information that Cardus provides about Billy Clegg[38] does, however, raise some questions.[39] It is said he was small and bow-legged, played football for Manchester City, being a good dribbler and chewing a toothpick while playing. Cardus added that he thought Billy scored a goal to win the FA Cup Final. However, no-one of that name played for Manchester City. The description instead fits Welsh international Billy Meredith, who played for Manchester City from 1894. Indeed, Cardus wrote about "the bow-legs and ball jugglery of that wiry Welsh dribbler Meredith, whose toothpick was to become as profound an object of veneration as WG's black beard" and who scored a goal in the FA Cup Final of 1904.[40] Meredith was born in 1874, and lived in Wales until he joined Manchester City. Rather than a member of the Gang – he was some 14 years older than Cardus – Meredith was his boyhood hero when football was his favourite sport,[41] and he claimed to have seen him play.[42]

There may have been other members of the "Gang"; indeed, Cardus wrote, "the 'Gang' was the nursery of no fewer than two county players and a professional cricket coach."[43] He later added that the urchins produced two professional cricketers (one an England player), a music critic of international renown and a political writer for the *Manchester Guardian*.[44] We know Cardus himself was a professional cricketer (at Shrewsbury School) and music critic, but the information about Clegg leads us to be sceptical about the rest of Cardus's remarks.

A further friend – not a member of the Gang but more an "hon. member" – was Eric Brindley, whose family story was discussed at length.[45] After the family's financial problems Eric reappeared in the Far East and was married there; further, Cardus indicated that Eric scored a century in a first-class cricket match against an English tour team. The Brindley household was described as superior, giving Cardus his first glimpse of the English middle classes, although when we learn that they lived in a semi-detached house with bay windows, it is worth recalling that those features also applied to 4 Summer Place.

It has not been possible to identify the family in genealogical records. Neither is there an E. Brindley on the Cricket Archive website.[46] There is a **William** Thomas Brindley who played first-class cricket in both England and Ceylon. Cardus may have come across the name as W.T. Brindley opened the batting for Ceylon against MCC on 3 October 1936 at Colombo, where the MCC team, with Cardus, stopped en route to Australia. Cardus did not report on the match; *Autobiography* records that he was bored by Colombo and, with no reference to a cricket match being played, explained that he went back to the ship.[47] This Brindley was born in Buckinghamshire in 1896; his highest score in first-class matches was 59 not out.[48] Perhaps the episode of Cardus's interaction with a "superior" family is correct but the household's financial difficulties necessitated some name changes. On the face of it, the story, or some elements of it, was made up.

Cardus doubtless did have some friends with whom he played informal cricket in Rusholme. In *Autobiography* he mentioned Smith and Thompson. As these happen to be the two names he also used in a story about his cricket when at Shrewsbury School,[49] perhaps they were plucked out of thin air.

There therefore remains considerable doubt about Cardus's friends. Indeed, was there any such gang? It is not mentioned in *Autobiography*. Cardus admitted he was a shy, delicate, self-conscious, introverted and solitary boy.[50]

He confessed that much of his early youth was spent alone and that he walked round Manchester by himself,[51] while he later admitted that he spent hours in solitude.[52] This is consistent with when he wrote, "When his [Neville's] home crashed and the family dispersed, he was still a boy more or less without companions".[53] While there might be some truth in what is recorded about the Gang, Cardus may have wished to give the impression that he was a more sociable individual than he really was.

Further friends

When Cardus was working as an insurance clerk (1904–12, see chapter 6), he became involved with another group of friends, meeting outside the gates of Alexandra Park, Moss Side, in summer evenings and in a Lyons café in Albert Square in the city centre.[54] The group comprised W. (called Tom, "a sort of partner in a small chemical agency", about 30 years old), his younger brother Edgar and Bobbie Burns (with a game leg and an interest in Karl Marx). There is again insufficient information to trace the group members in other sources.

A somewhat older friend was George Popper. We know that he was real as Cardus wrote several letters to him from Shrewsbury in 1916.[55] He appears to be the Georg Popper, living in Withington, who married Maria Elisabeth Spengler on 22 April 1909; he was aged 24 and a salesman.[56] The 1911 census reveals that he was born in Vienna in 1885/86 and had Hungarian nationality. His occupation was yarn salesman; his wife had been born in Russia and was a German national. Popper died in Manchester on 6 September 1926.[57]

Neville Cardus's father after the divorce

Neville Cardus didn't know his father, but what happened to him? JFN senior didn't waste time: within three days of the divorce absolute on 30 January 1899, he married Jane Hope at the register office in Fallowfield, Manchester. Jane was about 2½ years older than Ada, and had been a patent lint maker; her father Charles was a mechanic.[58] The marriage certificate confirms that JFN senior was a smith.

What the divorce papers don't reveal is that JFN senior was, at the time, in a relationship with Jane Hope, and that Jane was pregnant. Their daughter was born on 7 October 1898, and was therefore illegitimate. According to the birth certificate her name was Harriet Newsham Hope; it was common practice in illegitimate births to include the father's surname as the child's middle name. There was logic in delaying the baptism until a fortnight after the wedding; the child's name was then Harriet Newsham.

Harriet had a sister: Nellie was born in 1901. These girls were half-sisters that Neville never knew he had.

The census returns for 1901 indicated that Jane was living with her parents and Harriet in the parents' home at Prestwich, but her husband was not there. This may reflect his occupation as a journeyman blacksmith travelling to where the work was. By 1911 JFN senior, then described as an engineer's smith, was back with his wife Jane, who was living in the same house as in 1901, with her father, then retired, but without her mother, who had died.

Neville Cardus's half-sisters

What happened to the half-sisters?

First, Harriet. In 1917 she married Alfred A. Scowen, a 20-year-old musician on *HMS Lion*. It is intriguing to note that their first child, born in 1919, was named Alfred Neville Scowen. It is unlikely that JFN senior or daughter

Harriet was aware that Neville was the name adopted by JFN senior's son. Alfred Neville was a steward on *SS Fort Missanable* and was killed at sea in 1944. After her husband died in 1938, Harriet remarried in 1945, her new husband being Alfred G. Grist, a 45-year-old engineer. The couple emigrated to South Africa in the 1950s. Harriet (also known as Hettie) died in Durban in 1972. What was Harriet's occupation? The passenger lists tell us. Neville, master of the English language, had a half-sister who was an English teacher.

The second half-sister, Nellie, first married Harry Hides, a 25-year-old band corporal from the Royal Navy School of Music in Portsmouth in 1919. So, there was a similarity in the occupations of the husbands of the sisters. Nellie and Harry subsequently divorced and, in 1931, Nellie married Rudolph Edward Meyers. He was a 29-year-old Dutch national, living in South Africa and over in England as an export merchant, based at the Midland Hotel, Manchester. Nellie, also known as Eileen, died in Johannesburg in 1995.[59]

Chapter 5

YOUNG NEVILLE TAKES TO CRICKET

—— ∞•∾ ——

Watching cricket: Neville Cardus's first
Test matches

Cricket was to be a large part of Cardus's life, and it was 1902 when he saw his first Test match, at Old Trafford on 24–26 July.[1] He could not have wished for a better first Test: it turned out to be one of the most memorable of all time. England needed 124 in the fourth innings to defeat Australia, but after being 68–1 they collapsed. Wilfred Rhodes was joined by last man Fred Tate with eight needed for victory. Tate, in his only Test, was bowled when four were still required, compounding his misery of having dropped a catch from Australia's captain Joe Darling in their second innings.

There was another remarkable incident on the first day of the Test: the century before lunch by Australian Victor Trumper, which, according to *Autobiography*, Cardus saw.[2] This is consistent with an article in the *Manchester Guardian* ("MG") in 1934, when he said he played truant from school, and saw Trumper and Duff in their opening partnership.[3] He wrote in 1937 that he saw the century[4] and, writing in Australia in 1940, confirmed that this was the first Test match he watched; he described Trumper's century on the first day and the implication is that he was then there.[5] Later, in 1953, he referred to the match, with the century (on the first day) and the Australian victory (on the third day), and added, "watching it *all* [italics added], with the rapt attention of a schoolboy, was Manchester's own Neville Cardus".[6]

However, deciphering what went on is not easy. The truancy is questionable: Cardus was aged 14 and may well have left school. It is not clear when Neville was at Old Trafford. Was this the first day, when Trumper scored his century? Or the second day, when Darling played an innings that Cardus said he would never forget?[7] Or the third day, when Australia won, which would be would be consistent with his memory of the scenes on the third day that he recalled in 1930.[8] Further, in describing "The greatest test match at Old Trafford" in the MG, he referred to play on the second day and the climax on the third day but without any mention of Trumper's century on the opening day.[9] Hence readers are left confused by what Cardus actually saw, which may well not have included Trumper's first-day century.

The next Test at Old Trafford was in 1905: Cardus wrote that he saw (at least the start of) the match; Australia were comprehensively defeated.[10]

The third Old Trafford Test of the 20th century, in 1909, is more of a problem. In *Conversations* Cardus recalled seeing Trumper score 48 (the figure is correct) in Australia's second innings.[11] Unfortunately, this is contradicted by the possibly more reliable earlier confession in *Second Innings* that music was now his obsession, and that he did not see the 1909 Test even though Trumper was in the Australian team.[12]

Hence, we see that Cardus had problems in recalling events from his childhood. This would be no different from most people finding that their memory lets them down about events that took place 40–50 years before.

When was Cardus's first visit to Old Trafford?

Cardus's first visit to Old Trafford preceded that first Test, but exactly when is not easy to determine. His writing on the subject reveals a confusing combination of truths and untruths, reflecting both inevitable memory problems and a wish to fill in the gaps with an interesting story. Indeed, the answer could well be the game between Lancashire and Gloucestershire in 1899, referred to in chapter 1 with the varied accounts of Cardus's visit, and hunger or thirst. On several occasions he confirmed that this was the first match he saw.[13]

Perhaps Cardus had forgotten this in 1975, when he claimed he first watched Lancashire at Old Trafford in June 1900, Kent being the visitors. The information provided about the match was largely though not completely right.[14] In an article in 1964 he confirmed that he was then present, the details of the match and weather being mostly but not wholly correct.[15] And he went on to say that he was also there on the following day (5 June 1900), when Briggs scored 50, while he recalled being present at the next fixture at Old Trafford, when Essex were the visitors.[16] He appears to have had sufficient pocket money to indulge his passion for watching Lancashire cricket.

However, his 1964 article refers to his having previously seen one of the greatest feats in Lancashire cricket of all time, when Johnny Briggs took all ten wickets of Worcestershire's first innings. This was on 24 May 1900. So, was "Briggs's match" the first time Cardus visited Old Trafford?[17] He claimed in 1951 to have been present then, though also admitted that he had seen Lancashire in the year before, against Gloucestershire, with Jessop. I suspect he didn't see Briggs's feat as the autobiographical volumes don't refer to it, and when he saw Freeman take 10 wickets in 1931 he mentions Briggs in 1900 but fails to say he saw him.

There is, however, one further candidate for the first match. According to an article written in 1931, it is June 1899, with Lancastrian Archie MacLaren driving a ball from Paish of Gloucestershire to the boundary. Then rain ended play for the day, although it was 3pm or 4pm before spectators were sent home.[18] Unfortunately, this is incorrect, as MacLaren did not play in the 1899 match against Gloucestershire, which actually began on 24 July (see chapter 1).

Autobiography has something similar.[19] Cardus saw MacLaren open the batting and drive the ball to the boundary; the bowler's name had been forgotten and the visiting team not mentioned. Then rain fell in torrents and play was abandoned after lunch. *Conversations* has further detail on the match.[20] It was between Lancashire and Gloucestershire, played after W.G. Grace had retired, with Jessop and Roberts among those in the away team. MacLaren, it was said, batted for only 10 minutes on a gloomy morning, though hooked (not drove) Roberts (not Paish) for four. Following rain, play was abandoned.

Unfortunately, the match descriptions do not match reality. The best we can do is mention the 1901 match between Lancashire and Gloucestershire, due to begin on 25 July.[21] A club match at Old Trafford on the previous day was abandoned because of rain, but the weather forecast for the 25th was "fine, generally". As it turned out, rain fell heavily throughout the day and no play took place: the abandonment was early in the afternoon. 1.975ins (5cm) of rain fell in Manchester in the 24 hours to 9pm. The match therefore began on the second day, with the players Cardus mentions being included in the teams. Gloucestershire were bowled out and Lancashire reached 108–1 but MacLaren had not batted by close of play. On the third and last day MacLaren scored 11 and the game was drawn.

We can't tell what the truth is. It is plausible that Cardus first went to Old Trafford in 1899 and saw Jessop and Gloucestershire. If that is so, promoting the Kent game to the first match looks like an error from Cardus's memory bank of so much cricket. Briggs's match had perhaps appeared from the list of cricket he wished he had seen rather than had seen. As for the Gloucestershire match where rain led to abandonment, it looks as if it is a story, possibly with some basis in fact, but with elaboration and not convincing as the truth. We can't be entirely sure about a conclusion as we know that the 1899 match with Jessop itself has different versions: in the understandable absence of a firm foundation from memory, Cardus would entice the reader with embellishment.

One complication is that Cardus referred to walking to Old Trafford from Summer Place, giving the distance as 6 to 7 miles (it is actually 3 to 3.5 miles).[22] This would imply that his first visit to Old Trafford was no later than 1897, which is unlikely. For a possible solution we turn to *Wisden*, 1951, when Cardus recalled walking home to Rusholme, down Shrewsbury Street and past Brooks's Bar. While these are indeed on the route from Old Trafford to Summer Place, they are also on the way to Claremont Street, where he was living in 1901 and probably earlier. The vivid memory of Summer Place may have been planted in his mind when it was not in fact the home from where he walked to Old Trafford.

Roses matches

Matches between Lancashire and Yorkshire were to be an important part of Cardus's cricket-watching. Between the world wars it was often the case that the scoring was slow but the crowds large. Cardus wrote, "the Lancashire and Yorkshire match in the 1920s and 1930s was the greatest, severest and most humorous cricket match in the living universe."[23] There were to be plenty of characters, on both sides, to help fill the columns of the MG.

Cardus recalled, in 1971, seeing his first Lancashire v Yorkshire match on 21 July 1901.[24] He mentioned 12 players taking part; the hero was Wainwright, whose obstinate innings enabled Yorkshire to narrowly escape defeat. However, the 1901 match was won comfortably by Yorkshire and two of the 12 players named did not in fact participate. This instead looks to be the Roses match of 19 July 1900 when, batting at number 8, an innings of 50 by Wainwright enabled Yorkshire to avoid losing. That match did have all the players mentioned in the 1971 article.

Some caution is warranted, however. Cardus did claim that he had seen Wainwright play for Yorkshire against Lancashire at Old Trafford;[25] he took part in the matches in 1888–1897 and 1899–1901. The pair were to work together at Shrewsbury, and it is reasonable to think that Wainwright would have told Cardus about his playing record at Old Trafford; some of that may have become fixed in Cardus's mind as if he had been present even if that were not the case.

The memory of Wainwright being unsurprisingly vague, Cardus later wrote that his earliest recollection of a Roses match that was vivid was when George Hirst was out leg before wicket to Walter Brearley around 1903, an appeal that he argued should not have been made.[26] However, the dismissal was vivid in Cardus's imagination rather than in reality, as such a dismissal did not happen either in 1903 or indeed any other year.

We see another problem when Cardus reported watching Spooner scoring a century for Lancashire against Yorkshire at Old Trafford; he missed school one day in August, reporting that his absence was due to suffering from scarlatina (scarlet fever) and his face was as red as a beetroot.[27] It was in 1904 when Spooner first scored a century (dismissed for 126) in a Roses match at Old Trafford. Accuracy of memory is again a problem: the match was in May, the weather was poor,[28] and the 16-year-old Cardus would no longer have been at school.

Other early cricket memories

Cricket at Old Trafford was a source of delight for the young Cardus; we can read in *Autobiography*, "During the whole of the summer of 1902 I seem to have lived free as the wind watching and playing cricket".[29] He admitted that he became an addict for Lancashire cricket.[30] However, it becomes clear that we cannot compile his life story from his writing about cricket matches he states that he saw.

Cardus did claim to have once seen W.G. Grace, who, he indicated, had spoken to him when he was a boy.[31] Grace played at Old Trafford in 1898, 1896 and earlier years. However, Cardus made no mention of seeing Grace in his autobiographical volumes or in the pieces quoted about early matches he attended, and it is therefore deduced that this reference to Grace is incorrect. It looks like an example of Cardus writing what he wished had happened rather than reality. Indeed, the revelation in *Close of Play* was that, when Cardus first saw Gloucestershire, Grace had moved on to play for London County.[32]

One of the early matches that Cardus described in some detail was when Lancashire met Surrey in 1902. It is a mixture of the true and the not true. When writing in 1921 he indicated that he went on 26 June, a public holiday, sat on the popular side of the ground under the scoreboard and, in hot weather, saw J.T. Tyldesley flog the Surrey bowlers to all corners of the field.[33] From Cardus's later writing,[34] we find that Tyldesley had been 36 not out at the end of the first day (was actually 105) and was bowled by Richardson for 165 (the correct score though he was caught). This was followed by Barnes dismissing Surrey batsmen Abel (right), Hayward and Brockwell (wrong, although Barnes did take four wickets). Then Surrey recovered through dashing batting by Crawford and a stubborn innings by Bush (they were not out at close of play). In addition, Cardus appears to have been present on not the first day but the second, 27 June. Both days were public holidays; Edward VII was due to be crowned on the earlier day, although the ceremony was postponed because of his appendicitis.

Some other memories are clearly inaccurate. Nottinghamshire feature in several of Cardus's reminiscences and he wrote in 1931 that, the first time he saw them, William Gunn scored a century.[35] That implies the timing was 1899 (27–29 July). However, he added that Arthur Shrewsbury played a long innings that afternoon when, in fact, he was out for a duck.

Cardus had a number of favourites, one of whom was Lancashire batsman Reg Spooner. Cardus wrote that he read in the newspaper that George Wilson, playing for Worcestershire, dismissed Spooner for a pair of spectacles.[36] Spooner did indeed bag a pair against Worcestershire, in June 1904, but the bowler for the second of Spooner's ducks was Arnold.

Another favourite was Yorkshireman Emmott Robinson. Cardus wrote that he saw him play against Middlesex at Bradford and bowling Hearne (for at least 57), the visitors having been 128–2.[37] Robinson's Yorkshire career was from 1919 to 1931, and he played against Middlesex at Bradford in 1920, 1923, 1926 and 1929. However, in these four matches, Middlesex were never 128–2, and while Hearne was one of Robinson's three wickets, he was caught for 15 not bowled for at least 57. Further, in none of Yorkshire's other matches against Middlesex, home or away, did Robinson bowl Hearne.

The need to be cautious about believing Cardus's writing is further illustrated by the assertion that playing truant enabled him to see Garnett score a century for Lancashire against Middlesex.[38] Checking the records shows that Garnett played against Middlesex at Old Trafford only four times, in 1904, 1905, 1911 and 1914, all after Cardus had left school, and with a highest score of just 31.

Cardus playing cricket: early days

Cardus was not just passionate about watching cricket; it led to employment to provide economic independence so that he could educate himself.[39] In 1912 he was appointed assistant cricket coach at Shrewsbury School. But what cricket did Cardus play before this? It is another puzzle where it is difficult to establish the truth.

As a youngster, Cardus did play informal cricket with his friends on rough ground (brickcrofts) near his home. He has described how there would be one bat for the whole side, and the ball dwindled in circumference over by over.[40] In one article he referred to a match between Union Street and Summer Place which, imaginary though it may be, suggests some knowledge of the family history.[41]

He did claim to have bowled to Crawford, a future England player, when at Repton.[42] That is plainly not true: Cardus did not play cricket at school,[43] and it is a sure bet that public school Repton's fixture list did not include a match against the urchins of Manchester.

Moving onto formal cricket, the most detailed information we have is the scorecard of a two-day midweek match played at Pendleton, near Manchester, on 10 & 11 May 1910.[44] This is included not in his autobiographical volumes but in the 1977 edition of *Cardus on Cricket*, the scorecard being in handwritten form and accompanied by Cardus's cartoons of some of the players involved. Cardus was playing for Captain Rose's XI, who defeated G.P. Dewhurst's XI by an innings and 82 runs. Cardus's performance was quite remarkable, his bowling figures being 5–52 and 7–59 as Dewhurst's team were dismissed for 151 and 130 whereas Rose's team scored 363–6 (Cardus did not bat).

The result did not reflect Captain Rose's team being mismatched against inferior opposition: quite the opposite. Five of Dewhurst's team had first-class cricket experience, although those careers were largely nearing the end (*see* Table 3). Three other team members are recorded on the Cricket Archive website as having represented their public schools. These included Dewhurst, a businessman who had played for Rossall School at cricket but was better known as a footballer: he had one match for Liverpool and indeed appeared in an international match for England against Wales in 1895.

In contrast, it is not clear that anyone in Rose's team had first-class experience. One possible exception is A. Crowther, who was the top scorer with 170: he may have been the individual who played in one first-class match for Yorkshire in 1905. It has not been possible to identify who Captain Rose was. However, one of the players was C.C. Fleming, presumably Cardus's employer, who incidentally had passed his 50th birthday and scored a respectable 39 batting at no. 3. On the face of it, Cardus's performance was highly impressive.

Some further information about Cardus playing cricket is available from *Second Innings*.[45] He was an off-spin bowler with limited batting ability. Half a mile from his home was Rusholme cricket club, where he fielded at net practice, but it was a club for the gentry rather than Cardus's class. His first match, which he remembered vividly, was in a team representing a theological training college in Whalley

Table 3. Dewhurst's XI

		A	B	C	D	E	F
1	W.B. Burns	2			0		0
2	A.F. Spooner	1	23	Lancashire	18	1906–09	18
3	H.D. Stanning	1	28	Lancashire	33	1906–08	33
4	F.H. Hollins	0	32	Lancashire	35	1898–1927	34
5	H.G. Smoker	1	29	Hampshire	31	1901–07	31
6	T.A. Higson	1	36	Lancs, Derbys	29	1892–1923	25
7	W. Birchenough	2	17	Eton	0		0
8	W.L. Winser	2			0		0
9	R.H. Stanning	1			0		0
10	G.P. Dewhurst	1	38	Repton	0		0
11	W.H. Sell	0	28	Rossall	0		0

Source: *Cardus on Cricket* and Cricket Archive website

Key

A = number of times dismissed by Neville Cardus in the
        match
B = age
C = main teams played for
D = number of first-class matches played in career
E = period of first-class career
F = number of first-class matches played before Rose/
        Dewhurst match

Range, Manchester. Assuming the information provided is correct, this appears to be the Lancashire Independent College, now the British Muslim Heritage Centre. It is not clear what connection he had which led him to play there. Cardus said the team played in a league on Saturday afternoons, and on his debut he took 9 wickets for 14 runs. He went on to say that over the season he took some 60 wickets for 80 runs but was almost always on the losing side, as the poor pitches led to his team conceding many extras, and the batsmen were unable to reach the required totals.

The Lancashire College team played in the Manchester and District Sunday School League, together with non-league friendlies. The club had its own ground adjacent to the college, and the members had built their own pavilion.[46] Since Cardus was at Shrewsbury in 1912 and played for some other team after Lancashire College, the season he played for Lancashire College was 1910 or earlier. It is not possible to tell which year it was from the MG; although it published a scorecard of a match played by the College in each of 1908, 1909 and 1910, Cardus did not play in any of these particular games.

It is, however, possible to confirm Cardus's comments about low scoring. Taking 1910 as an example, Lancashire College had a team in each of the first two of the four divisions. The MG reported abbreviated scores of league matches in the first division for four weeks, in which the average runs per wicket was under 5, consistent with what Cardus reported. This doubtless reflected the quality of the pitches. It would not be a surprise that, in this environment, he could produce some outstanding bowling figures. It should be admitted, though, that the quality of the cricket in the Sunday school league would have been quite modest, even in the top division, and Cardus wished to stretch himself by playing in matches of a higher standard.

In the following year Cardus played on better pitches,[47] though for what club he does not disclose, just that his bowling was not as successful as before. It has not been possible to trace a reference to Cardus in the scorecards of Manchester and district matches reported in the MG and some local newspapers. This suggests that he was still playing at modest club standard.

There is one other reference to add: playing for a boys' club Cardus shared a century partnership with friend Eric Brindley; the match was won after it seemed lost.[48] However, given that Cardus admitted "I did not bat seriously"[49] and that there are doubts about whether Eric Brindley existed, it would be wrong to rely on what was written. Perhaps it was what Cardus wished had happened.

Cardus was to be a cricket coach at Shrewsbury School in 1912. Although he wrote, "When I arrived at professional status, playing for clubs here and there and at Shrewsbury",[50] it is unclear whether he played professionally for clubs before that. If so, it may amount to no more than a collection from spectators for a good performance.

Hence, although Cardus said that he was recruited on the strength of his bowling averages in Manchester club cricket,[51] no such records have been found. John Arlott wrote that Cardus's appointment at Shrewsbury School was "on flimsy qualifications", implying his record was indeed modest.[52] The truth again proves elusive.

Playing cricket: professional status at Shrewsbury School

The summers of 1912–16 occupied Cardus as assistant cricket coach at Shrewsbury School. When recruited in 1912 this brought a weekly income of £2.10s (£2.50), on top of which there were tips and perquisites. The senior coach that year was 47-year-old Walter Attewell,[53] to whom 24-year-old Cardus was very much the junior. Attewell had played five first-class matches, one for Nottinghamshire in 1891 and four in the United States in 1894. Unfortunately, Cardus, in *Autobiography*, called him William Attewell, referring to him playing for the Players against the Gentlemen and visiting Australia: this William was Walter Attewell's cousin, who played for England as well as Nottinghamshire.[54] The misunderstanding is explained later:

"… my senior was Attewell. I have since been told he couldn't possibly have been *the* [italics in original] Attewell, but more likely his brother Walter. He never spoke to me as though he were not the one and only Attewell, born at Keyworth."[55]

We read in *Autobiography* of a change in senior coach in 1913. Cardus had the year wrong – it was 1914 – but the man was right: Ted Wainwright, who was similar in age to Walter Attewell, being 49 years old in 1914.[56] The new coach was also vastly more experienced than Cardus, having had a first-class cricket career that spanned 1888–1902, playing for Yorkshire, and five Test matches for England. Cardus reckoned that he "could spin the widest off-break I have ever seen".[57] Indeed, Wainwright may have helped Cardus achieve turn from his own bowling (see the comment from Richard Keigwin in Chapter 8).

Cardus recalled his time at Shrewsbury fondly when writing about an Old Salopian, Bland, playing for Nottinghamshire:

"He knows what it is to walk down the avenue of limes to the river, to call out 'Boat!' to the ferryman, to climb the hill, to walk through the gate near the little chapel, to come suddenly upon the playing fields stretching to the west."[58]

One incident is worth mentioning: Cardus had to have his shoulder blades massaged by a Dr Whincup.[59] It is good to report that this looks to be the truth as, in the 1911 census, we can trace Frank Whincup, a surgeon working in Shrewsbury.

Wisden recorded that Shrewsbury probably had a better season in 1912 than their results showed, including innings defeats to Rossall and Uppingham. They had a moderate season in 1913, winning four and losing four matches, while drawing three. Thereafter, an improvement was clear: the next year was "splendid", winning five matches, losing one and drawing five. The slimmer wartime volumes of the following two years had no specific report on the school, although they look to have competed well.

The good results for the school appear to have reflected the impact of Wainwright. His first year at the school in 1914 coincided with what Sale described as "the turning point of Shrewsbury's fortunes"[60] and he was still there in 1917, when Shrewsbury were unbeaten in school matches and, according to *Wisden,* were "one of the sides of the year", this after Cardus had departed. Wainwright was to die in 1919, aged 54, and two articles in the MG that year are worth recording. One, in May, expressed the view that Wainwright's work "was so admirable that the team rapidly developed from mediocrity into one of the best amongst the public schools."[61] His obituary in October included, "He was rather more advanced than most professional coaches in schools in that he strongly advocated back-play."[62] It is reasonable to think that these items were written by Cardus, paying tribute to the coaching skills of his superior. In Cardus's instructional articles for club cricketers in the MG in 1922 there are two references to Wainwright, who may have helped improve the understanding of cricket of not only the Shrewsbury boys but also his assistant coach.[63]

In summer 1914 Cardus also took on a role as secretary to school headmaster Dr Cyril Alington. This finished in summer 1916 when Alington accepted a post as head of Eton. Cardus was invited to join him but was unable to do so because of uncertainty about whether he might be required for the war.[64] Although he had originally been rejected by the army because of short-sightedness, he could have been called up for re-examination.

In *Close of Play* Cardus mentioned several boys at Shrewsbury, "I have seldom seen or known better since" and added that none of them went into county cricket.[65] However, one of those listed did attain county standard: Miles Dempsey appeared twice for Sussex in 1919. Another of those mentioned, Donald Boumphrey, was in a Wales team that played a first-class match in 1928; and his younger brother Colin, who was in the Shrewsbury first eleven in 1913–15, appeared for the Royal Air Force in a first-class fixture in 1932. Four other boys at Shrewsbury in Cardus's time who went on to play first-class cricket have been traced: Harold Miles (23 matches for the Army, MCC, Free Foresters, Europeans and the West), Bill Blaxland (19 for Derbyshire), Hubert Rhys (10 for Glamorgan, Free Foresters and Wales) and Reginald Phillips (1 for Wales).

It was when county cricket resumed after the war that Neville Cardus would also realise the impact of his cricketing years at Shrewsbury, benefitting the writing of someone who had originally learned the game by reading the Badminton Book of Cricket in the Free Library at Rusholme.[66]

Chapter 6

INTRODUCTION TO MUSIC, THE ARTS AND WORK

───── ❧❧❧ ─────

Early interest in theatre and music

Cardus was like many other children in that his first visit
to a theatre appears to have been to see a pantomime. He
thought his first show was *Robinson Crusoe,* with Vesta
Tilley as the principal boy, and that he was not more
than 12 at the time.[1] Newspaper references indicate
that there was such a performance of *Robinson Crusoe* at
the Prince's Theatre at Christmas 1895,[2] when Neville
was aged seven. Pantomimes were a theme of Neville's
childhood and his memory appears more accurate than for
early cricket matches. He mentioned seeing *Aladdin* with
Ada Reeve as the principal boy, G.P. Huntley as Widow
Twankey and Horace Mills as Abanazar: this appears to
be the performance at the Prince's Theatre at Christmas
1900.[3] *Cinderella* was the offering at Christmas 1902, with
Eugene Stratton, Tom Foy and Malcolm Scott in the cast;
this was at the Comedy Theatre and Cardus was earning
money selling chocolates.[4] And George Robey was seen
playing *Mother Goose* in the Christmas 1904 pantomime.[5]

There was also "proper" drama. Since Beatrice worked
at the Comedy Theatre, as did Neville, it is not surprising
that Neville told us that it was his aunt who "took me to
my first theatre; it was called *The Swiss Express* and, what
is more, I saw it from a box."[6] The production was a farce,
with brothers Renard, but it is not possible to deduce when

Neville was first present as this was a regular production in Manchester, commonly at the Comedy Theatre. Neville also remembered Henry Irving at a "farewell appearance" at the Manchester Theatre Royal; that would have been in the period 5 – 10 December 1904 and indeed either 6 or 10 December if he saw *The Bells*, which he seems to remember.[7] Also in the area of drama, Neville wrote that he had "seen Shakespeare acted vividly, but badly I suppose, by touring companies dominated by Osmond Tearle."[8] However, there is an inconsistency: he wrote that he was aged 17 before he came to know Shakespeare,[9] which was after Tearle died in 1901. A more definite reference is that he enjoyed the music in the interval of a play, *David Ballard*, in a production of Miss Horniman.[10] This was reviewed in the press in September 1908; Neville Cardus was aged 20 at the time.[11]

Cardus's early interest in music was focussed on the music hall and musical comedies.[12] The first chapter of *Conversations* is devoted to the music hall, the disappearance of which he regarded as a great loss.[13] He recalled watching the Pelissier Follies at a theatre in the Midland Hotel, Manchester; the cast included Fay Compton.[14] She was married to the theatre producer, Harry Pelissier, whose company was based in Manchester in 1906,[15] their performances at the Midland Theatre continuing in January 1907.[16]

In 1907 Cardus had an experience that he regarded as a "miracle". He was at the Prince's Theatre for Edward German's light opera, *Tom Jones;* his reference in *Autobiography* is that he attended on 7 April and then returned "night after night".[17] The review in the *Manchester Guardian* was very favourable,[18] and not only did Cardus admire it but it led to him realising that he could remember music without effort.[19] He was also to refer to the incident in a report on the Lord's Test of 1930.[20]

Trying to find the first Hallé concert that Cardus attended is not straightforward (as might be expected). He wrote in 1957 that it was an event in 1907, conducted by Richter, although there are no further details.[21] Later, he referred to it being a concert when Sir Charles Santley sang "Oh ruddier than the cherry" from Handel's *Acis and Galatea,* together with "It is enough" from Mendelssohn's *Elijah*, this in winter 1908.[22] There was a performance of *Elijah* on 23 January 1908 when Santley sang, though no other work was scheduled for the concert.[23] What Cardus has been more definite about is that, on 3 December 1908, he heard the premier of Elgar's first symphony, conducted by Hans Richter with the Hallé at the Free Trade Hall.[24] It is therefore reasonable to conclude that he began his Hallé experiences in 1907 or 1908.

Cardus never studied an instrument but he did have some voice training.[25] He heard Francis Harford, reckoned to be one of the finest singers of the day, sing the *Dichterliebe* cycle of Schumann; press reports indicate that this was in October 1910.[26] The outcome was that Cardus tried to become a lieder singer and, following some lessons, a number of engagements came his way.[27] After about a year, problems with his larynx and problems with his teachers led him to give up his career as a singer.[28] It might be regarded as rather limited musical training for a music critic. Incidentally, the timing is consistent with Cardus accepting that his love of music meant that he had only limited memories of cricket in 1908–12.[29]

There is an odd episode to which Cardus devotes three pages of *Second Innings*: he visited, for supper, the home in Victoria Park, Manchester, of Max, a German professor of music at the college of music in Manchester.[30] This would have been Max Michael Mayer, born in Vecha about 1860, who gained British naturalisation in 1900 after having been in the country for five years. He lived in Addison Terrace, built in Victoria Park in 1848–50 and where Charles Hallé lived in 1848. It is now a listed building. He later moved to West View, also in Victoria Park, and now a mosque; he died on 26 October 1931.

Cardus is sketchy about the detail of this incident. In addition to referring to the professor merely as Max, he does not say when the visit occurred. Indeed, it has to be questioned whether it took place. Would a shy young man have visited Mayer, nearly 30 years older than Cardus, living in far superior circumstances, and a well-respected member of the music profession who advised Otto Klemperer about a musical career?[31] The episode may reflect Cardus idealising about what he would have liked to have happened rather than reality.[32]

Early work

Autobiography provides a lengthy list of jobs that Cardus had, starting from his first wages as a pavement artist at the age of ten. [33] He helped with the family laundry, delivering washing. Add in driver of a joiner's and carpenter's handcart, selling newspapers, helping with ladders, boiling type in a printer's works, messenger boy, office boy and handy lad. He sold chocolates in the Comedy Theatre, this before it was closed in 1903 (it later reopened as the Gaiety Theatre). He sold flowers at Easter outside an inn in Northenden, Cheshire,[34] which may link with his grandparents (and possibly Cardus himself) living in Rose Cottage, Northenden. There is also a musical connection: he was paid for singing in concerts.[35]

One clue to the timing of these jobs is that Cardus remembers that, when pushing his handcart, he saw a poster telling of the death of Dan Leno, a music hall comedian and actor.[36] That death took place on 31 October 1904.[37]

Noticeably better was the job which began in December

1904, in an insurance office in 64 Bridge Street, Manchester: Cardus was working for brothers Hugh and Christopher Fleming.[38] Hugh was the senior partner in a firm of ship and insurance brokers; they were agents for the United Dutch Marine Insurance companies.[39] They had been in the business for some time. Hugh and Christopher were aged about 54 and 42 respectively in 1911, both bachelors living with their two sisters and a servant in an eight-roomed house in Stretford. Cardus's weekly income began at 8 shillings (40p) and had advanced by 1911 to £1. A bonus was that the work was not too demanding: he could spend some time furthering his studies and, on occasion, going to Old Trafford to watch cricket. He was to continue working there until 1912.[40]

Insurance was not what Cardus had in mind for a career. He has told us how, about 1908, he used to go and stand opposite the MG building in Cross Street, Manchester, late on Monday nights, and imagine the senior staff at work.[41] Some of Cardus's stories reflect not what happened but what he wished would happen. However, in this case, his imagination would turn into reality: he would come face to face with these people when he began work for the MG in 1917.

Early writing on music; and the name "Neville" emerges

What prompted Cardus's career as a music writer? He wanted to be an artist when he was aged 17 or 18 but realised he wasn't good enough to make the grade.[42] Hence, "I developed an itch, a great desire, to write about music." He read the work of music critics Ernest Newman in the *Birmingham Post* and Samuel Langford in the MG.

Before the MG, Cardus had another newspaper job: as a music critic on the *Daily Citizen*, a daily eight-page Labour paper that paid him a penny a line.[43] He recalled that this followed his departure from Shrewsbury in 1916 and that his first notice was of a Hallé concert that included Elgar's *Falstaff*. He rued the loss of remuneration as his 80 lines of text were cut down to 22. In the first month he reviewed 10 concerts at about 3 shillings (15p) each but the job lasted less than three months. In a letter to George Popper he expressed satisfaction about his work in this role.[44] The newspaper's readership may not have appreciated the subject matter; Cardus opined that this "was the age in which music was definitely not for the masses... Music was not yet a common possession; a Hallé concert was a privilege hard to share."[45] Incidentally, Cardus indicated that he had joined the Independent Labour Party, although it is not clear when this was or for how long.[46]

The facts of his work for the paper are somewhat different, and perhaps more impressive. Appendix 1 summarises the notices that Cardus wrote (the titles given by the newspaper are not very imaginative).

Cardus's contributions began not in 1916 but rather earlier. His *Who's Who* entry indicates 1913; it was actually 3 November 1913.[47] He reviewed a promenade concert on 1 November with Hallé conductor Michael Balling. The article was 48 lines long. Although Cardus was later to claim that he had never written out of regard for public demand, or with a public or an editor in mind,[48] this piece was drafted in a way that he presumably felt would appeal to the newspaper's Labour readership:

"Mr Balling's appearance at Saturday's promenade concert in the Free Trade Hall, Manchester, occasioned considerable enthusiasm from a large and frankly 'popular' audience; indeed, one could scarcely have wished for a more convincing testimony for the appreciation which the Manchester 'man in the street' has for the Hallé conductor's efforts to democratise the city's musical life."

Sadly, he went on to say that the programme was not quite of the kind calculated to bring the best out of Balling.[49]

The *Falstaff* concert was the fifth of his notices, on 28 November 1913, and it had 46 rather than 22 lines. In the first month to 1 December there were five contributions, i.e. half of what was indicated in *Autobiography*. However, the job lasted nearly six months instead of three: there were 29 contributions, the last being on 21 April 1914. In May Cardus would have been off to Shrewsbury, so the ending of the contract reflected his summer employment on cricket business.

The articles were typically 40–50 lines long, and the range of concerts included appearances by Elgar and Rachmaninov. Altogether more impressive than the reader of *Autobiography* might think.

Interestingly, Cardus's contributions were signed J.F.N., though without any indication of what the N stood for: presumably not Newsham. This may be the beginning of Neville as (part of) his name. That N was the most important letter was suggested by two of his notices, on 4 and 6 February 1914, being bylined just N., but thereafter it was J.F.N. again. Why did John Frederick become Neville? According to John Arlott, Cardus was very conscious of the difference, for a writer, between the names Fred and Neville.[50] So perhaps the move into writing prompted the change of name, with the N in the *Daily Citizen* being the start. Later on, we see a letter to friend George Popper on 20 May 1916 that is signed "JFN",[51] although other correspondence continued to use "Fred". A lecture at Shrewsbury on 9 June 1916 was by "J.F.N. Cardus".

The *Daily Citizen* was not his only appearance in print. Cardus's entry in *Who's Who* showed that he had contributed to various musical journals in 1912–14. Presumably he made several submissions but only one was published: an article, just over a page long, on English composer Granville Bantock, which appeared in *Musical Opinion*.[52] Although *Autobiography* put the date as 1910, it was 1916 as reported in *Conversations* and as mentioned by Lamb and Hilton.[53]

While Cardus had some positive comments about Bantock, he felt that the composer had limitations. There was an early mention of Boswell, who was to feature several times in his writing over the years, and he was the author he wanted to accompany him on a desert island (*see* chapter 12):

> "Is Bantock greater than his art? There are men, we know, who express their genius in the business of everyday life, in their conversation and action, while their created works are but pallid reflections of their superhumanly vital selves. Bantock may be such a man, – the pity is we have so few Boswells about."[54]

The *Musical Opinion* article, in December 1916, is important for another reason: the name Neville appears. The author is named as J.F. Neville Cardus. The move to Neville took place gradually; appendix 3 documents the names by which Neville Cardus was known.

There is no indication at all of why Neville was chosen. If speculation is permitted, it is worth adding that one of the cricketers he admired was John [Jack] Crawford, whose middle name was Neville. He was one of *Wisden's* five cricketers of the year in 1907. As *Wisden* was one of the books that Cardus read,[55] perhaps this is how he came across the middle name and why he admired it.

From Shrewsbury back to Manchester and the MG

Cardus returned to Manchester in 1916 and needed to find work.[56] He mentioned being a casual labourer, although no details are forthcoming.[57] He provided more information about a different role: "I was driven to the worst of the period's resorts for the down-and-out respectables – I became an agent for a Burial Society which specialised in policies covering funeral expenses amongst the poor".[58] This involved calling on the inhabitants of back-to-back tenements, collecting premiums on policies and selling new policies, neither of which he did well: he gave up the work in December 1916.[59]

Cardus revealed in *Autobiography* that, feeling "shipwrecked and sinking", he wrote in December 1916 to C.P. Scott, editor of the *Manchester Guardian*. We know that, some years before, Cardus had imagined the staff working at the newspaper. His application was clearly highly ambitious, with little formal education and only modest achievements in his life to date. Yet he had made strenuous efforts to improve his knowledge, and he was clearly keen to write. Why not set your sights high when near at hand were the headquarters of one of the most prestigious newspapers in the country; indeed, one that had grown from a small provincial weekly to a newspaper with a world-wide reputation?[60]

Cardus continued; knowing that he was not yet ready for a job as a writer, he asked for work in the counting-house and enclosed specimens of his work.[61] He indicated that Scott replied by return of post, inviting him to his house in Fallowfield for an interview. The episode is described in detail, including the questions Scott asked, and the furniture in Scott's house, with particular mention of paintings by Francis Dodd of Scott's two sons, Laurence (who had died some years before) and Edward.

The following day, according to Cardus, Scott suggested that he work at Scott's home, in a "semi-secretarial" role, for example by providing verbal summaries of books and periodicals. Cardus accepted this, although the arrangement provided no remuneration and ended after a month when Scott wrote that he was "congenitally incapable of using a secretary. I fear then that I am wasting your time."

Cardus's narrative then recalled, in the middle of March, a letter from Scott inviting him to see head reporter Haslam Mills for an interview, which took place on the second Monday of the month (12 March).[62] The dates aren't quite right as we have Scott's letter, dated 20 March, and the interview was obviously after that. One of the questions concerned whether Cardus commanded shorthand, which he admitted he did not. The outcome was nevertheless favourable, which was an impressive achievement for a loner who had a very limited formal education and little published writing. *Guardian* historian David Ayerst referred to the description of events in *Autobiography*: "Cardus has worked up his interview with the elegant Chief Reporter into a conversation piece which Mills would have appreciated."[63] We might guess that Cardus already had an ability in conversation, perhaps with his confidence boosted by his wide range of reading, which persuaded the MG to offer a job. Indeed, the reputation he was to have as a conversationalist may have enabled Cardus to make the most of the opportunities over his lifetime.

The "semi-secretarial" work is intriguing. Working for and at the home of the editor of a great newspaper, even for a month, looks like a very positive result, and surprising, given Cardus's career to date. It would be valuable to have some corroboration of what happened. To help us, we have a copy of the first page of Cardus's letter to the MG dated 13 January 1917, and the letter from Scott dated 20 March inviting Cardus for an interview with Haslam Mills.[64]

It is possible to identify two errors in what Cardus wrote, although they are minor and do not necessarily invalidate the episode of semi-secretarial work. First, the 13 January letter seems to have included some of his previous work;

and he did not seek a writer's job, instead asking for a post among the proof-readers or in the general offices. This therefore appears to be the letter that Cardus dated in *Autobiography* as December 1916. Second, the paintings of Scott's sons were completed in 1920 and could not have been seen by a visitor to Scott's home in 1916/1917.[65] Cardus presumably saw them on a later visit.

To make sense of what happened, we need to add in some further correspondence. Since Scott's letter of 20 March starts, "I was away last week or would have replied sooner to your letter", this implies that Cardus wrote a further letter in the first half of March.[66] It has not been traced.

Scott's letter of 20 March included, "I think you said you had some shorthand, and I daresay you could improve it." How did he come to write this, bearing in mind that this is inconsistent with Cardus's admission in his interview with Haslam Mills? It is unlikely that Cardus's letter in the first half of March indicated a knowledge of shorthand, as Scott presumably had the letter in front of him when replying and would have been more definite than "I think you said". The shorthand claim may have been in the 13 January letter, though would have had to be later than the first page which we have. But it would surely have been reckless of Cardus to claim, in writing, a skill he did not have. The other possible source is that Cardus did carry out unpaid semi-secretarial work, in the course of which there was a perhaps vague but verbal and misinterpreted suggestion about shorthand. Indeed, Scott's use of "I think you *said* [italics added]" would then relate to words that Cardus spoke. Further, since the unpaid work involved verbal summaries of published work, there would have been no need for practical testing of shorthand skills at the time.

There is no mention of this unpaid work in Cardus's

other writings or in *Conversations*. However, the analysis of the available correspondence, incomplete though it is, makes it quite plausible that Cardus did undertake some unpaid work for C.P. Scott before joining the MG staff. Further, it could have helped Scott decide to arrange an interview for Cardus.

Before the offer of the real job working at the newspaper he loved, there was more pain. Cardus wrote that, from the end of January to March 1917, he "eked out a subsistence wage" and continued to study.[67] He did not, however, have to wait long for his fortunes to change, as we shall see in the next chapter.

Chapter 7

THE *MANCHESTER GUARDIAN* AND A CRICKET WRITER

Working for the *Manchester Guardian*

It is Neville Cardus's work for the *Manchester Guardian* which propelled him to fame as a writer on cricket and music, both for the newspaper and elsewhere.

The date was 26 March 1917 when he started work in the reporters' office, with pay at 30 shillings (£1.50) per week.[1] He recorded that his first assignment, on his first day, was to report on a lecture by Mrs Swanwick on population and militarism. The lecture had been arranged by the Manchester branch of the Women's International League and took place at the Lower Mosley Street Social Club. An article headed "The birth-rate in peace and war" appeared the following day; such articles were not credited.[2] The training programme at the MG clearly wasn't lengthy! To be fair, Cardus did write that, at the MG, he was given tutorials "as thorough and as wide-ranging as any that an undergraduate has had at Oxford or Cambridge... the best university in the world".[3]

Initially, Cardus's work for the MG was "ordinary humdrum anonymous work... I had to do all the routine work of a reporter."[4] In *Full Score* Cardus wrote that C.P. Scott "used me as a reporter covering local government, outbreak of fire, and as reviewer of music-hall performances; so that in turn I coped with Manchester City Council committees, law courts, George Robey, Beethoven, Sir Thomas Beecham, Gracie Fields with an occasional Test match as a sort of side-line."[5] Not all the truth, though: the first Test that Cardus reported was in 1921, when he was already established as a cricket reporter.

Only some articles in the MG were credited but, fortunately for Cardus, these included music notices. Cardus had been enthusiastic about music hall in his youth, and he was sent to report on a Manchester music hall, which he described as "a secondary affair, outside the city";[6] it was at the Ardwick Empire. This led to the first time his work was credited in the MG by the appearance of the initials N.C. It was on 10 April 1917, when his contribution was the third of three items under the heading of variety halls, the focus of his article being Mr Ernie Mayne. This first appearance of "N.C." was a notable step in confirming the name by which Neville Cardus was to be known for the rest of his life. It had taken many years to come; indeed, when he first went to the MG, he was still known as Fred.[7]

Cardus was lucky that he was able to combine work with pleasure by continuing to report on the music hall. One performance that made an impact was by Little Tich (real name, Harry Relph) at the Manchester Hippodrome: he referred to it in *Autobiography* and went on to describe it to Daniels.[8] This appears to be the notice published by the MG on 27 August 1918.

In 1918 Cardus was promoted to the "Corridor", taking charge of the Miscellany column and the back page article, while occasionally writing the fourth leader.[9] Cardus also did dramatic criticism. In *Autobiography* he mentioned visiting Liverpool for the stage version of Arnold Bennett's *Sacred and Profane Love*.[10] His report appeared on 16 September 1919, with three long paragraphs before concluding that the company at the Liverpool Playhouse acted the play in a competent way. "N.C." appeared at the end. Work was strenuous as Cardus was also working for C.P. Scott in a semi-secretarial role, calling on him at home most mornings.[11]

The range of Cardus's work included book reviews, and *Autobiography* includes an excerpt from his comments on Percy Scott's *Fifty Years in the Royal Navy*, which MG readers saw on 7 November 1919.[12] Later in the month, his name also appeared: Neville Cardus was the name at the foot of an article on music, "A Farewell".[13] His workload is illustrated by N.C. also offering his views on Christmas books for children on 1 and 16 December 1919, covering 30 and 29 books respectively.

The beginning of Cardus's writing on cricket

The year 1919 was a good time to be writing for the MG; its circulation of 70,000 had never been higher and profits were rising.[14] It was then that Cardus started writing on cricket, as county cricket resumed after the war. It was an unusual cricket season in at least one respect. Some had felt that there would be insufficient interest in cricket to sustain interest over the three days traditionally allotted to county championship matches, and Lancashire's proposal for two- rather than three-day matches was accepted. Since the hours of play were extended to 11.30 to 7.30 on the first and 11.00 to 7.30 on the second day,[15] this meant the cricket writers finished work later than previously.

Cardus showed how he began reporting on cricket in June – apparently by chance – in *Autobiography*:

> "In March 1919, I suffered a breakdown, and after I returned to my job, W.P. Crozier suggested one day that I might recuperate myself by sitting in the air one or two days at Old Trafford... I might write reports on a match now and then, suggested Crozier. So I went one Monday morning to Old Trafford and described

the first game there since 1914. It was understood that this open-air contribution would not interfere with my usual work on the paper".[16]

He had written in 1936 about the start of his cricket writing career, and this is broadly consistent. Crozier suggested he sit in the sun in the day to assist his recovery after a breakdown and work at night as leader writer. A little later, Cardus was at the Lancashire v Yorkshire match and wrote:

"Then one day Parkin – the one 'jazz cricketer' of that time – ... took nine wickets in most sensational fashion. I was so thrilled that I went off my head and wrote about two columns about it. The 'Guardian' published it, it pleased the public and I became a cricket writer by sheer fluke. It had never been in my mind to be a cricket writer. I had trained myself for musical criticism."[17]

Similarly, Cardus related in *Conversations*: "I had not been well, and the news editor, a wonderful man named W. P. Crozier, asked if I would like to convalesce in the sunshine at Old Trafford and write one or two cricket reports. One or two!"[18]

This accidental introduction to cricket-writing appeared in Hart-Davis's introduction to *The Essential Neville Cardus*[19] and in *His Own Man*.[20] And it is accepted in a history of the *Manchester Guardian*:

"For with the revival of the game in 1919 a young reporter whose role on the paper was undetermined and his future unsuspected, was rather casually sent to cover a county match. Within a week Neville Cardus had found his place on the paper".[21]

What is not quite correct is some of the detail above. It

was not a Monday in June when Lancashire's first match took place; instead, a Wednesday in May. It was against Derbyshire and began on 19 May. The MG contained a preview of the match in its 19 May issue, which may well have been written by Cardus, but there is no credit. The same day also saw a brief item about former Shrewsbury School coach Wainwright recovering from an operation. Presumably it was Cardus who contributed this, although not credited.

Cardus's first cricket match report, Lancashire v Derbyshire at Old Trafford, appeared on 20 May, although without any credit. It was about 880 words long. Much of the report was standard fare, but it did include reflections about this being the first county match since 1914:

> "It was indeed easy to feel the sentimental aspect of the occasion. One came into the enclosure from the dusty town, and there were for many an old cricket lover strong tugs on the heart as they again saw the soft green splashed with the spring sun and the red pavilion and the county flag streaming in the wind."

The report of the play on the second day of the match, which Lancashire won, finished with the initials N.C., so we can say that 21 May 1919 was the first cricket match report for which Neville Cardus received the credit. The piece was about 760 words long.

However, this was not the first article on cricket by Cardus that the MG published. On 27 January 1919 there was an item headed "An old cricketer", who was a character called William, based on the Shrewsbury coach, thought (erroneously) to be William Attewell. The author was shown as Neville Cardus, this being the first time his name appeared as such in the paper. Then, on 31 March 1919, the MG included a review of *Wisden* (then called *Wisden's*), credited to N.C. This concentrated on just two points: those cricketers who had lost their lives in the War, and the editor's comments on the way the championship was to be conducted with two- rather than three-day games. The article included a reference to cricket as art and finished with a musical connection when commenting on the shortening of matches:

> "one would like to stress that cricket, of all pastimes, is an art… We ought not to fundamentally alter a great game to satisfy a mere popular 'stunt', any more than we ought to introduce violent syncopations into a great symphony in order to bring it into line with the current passion for 'jazz'".

This was followed by an article credited to N.C. on 5 May, which previewed the new cricket season. Here he doubted the significance of the change to two-day matches: the reduction in total playing time was only from 18¼ to 15 hours. There were also two artistic references:

> "Cricket, like the arts themselves, are [sic] dominated by the factor of personality… a groundsman, … a true artist, he beholds in a beautiful wicket, an end in itself".

A further article by N.C. was published on 12 May, headed, "Style in cricket, the effect of modern bowling". This was a thoughtful piece reflecting on the tendency towards what he called "merely efficient batsmanship" at the expense of style, and the "googly craze", regarded as erratic, and inhibiting attractive batting. Cardus added references to art and music when describing what had been wrong with cricket in 1914:

> "What cricket lacked was the batsman whose play was stamped with a really individual manner, rich in scoring strokes to be identified with a batsman's name

as the sweep of the artist's brush or the curve of a composer's melody."

These four articles on cricket that predated Cardus's reporting the match at Old Trafford throw doubt on the idea that his first match report was by chance. There is certainly a case for thinking that Cardus had been identified as a writer on cricket, with a plan that the articles of a general nature that he had written would be followed by reports of actual matches. Crozier knew that Cardus was fond of cricket and had coached at Shrewsbury.[22] What was new was crediting the author of Lancashire cricket reports with his initials; it was not the custom pre-war. It was an innovation that was to serve Cardus well.

The unfolding of the 1919 season

After the home win against Derbyshire, Lancashire had three successive away matches. Cardus was not yet travelling to away fixtures, which gave him the opportunity to play cricket for a Manchester Press XI on 4 June, when Lancashire were at Northampton. Cardus's next match report was on the Roses contest against Yorkshire at Old Trafford on 9 and 10 June, preceded by a preview on 7 June: "Nothing in cricket is better than this – the game, the scene, the crowd." The opening day went well for Lancashire, and Cardus's article was some 770 words long. It was the following day when Lancashire bowler Cecil Parkin took 8–35 in the second innings, added to 6–88 in the first, and Lancashire won with just five minutes to spare. Cardus told Daniels that this stimulated him to write 1500 words, which MG editor C.P. Scott was insistent should be published without cuts, despite the chief sub-editor claiming that there was no room.[23] Cardus then said, "Not long afterwards I became cricket correspondent of the *Manchester Guardian*."[24]

The outcome was that Cardus reported on all of Lancashire's 12 home championship matches, all at Old Trafford, with one possible exception. That was the last home match of the season against Northamptonshire (27–28 August), when there was no play on the first day until 4.30pm and none at all on the second day, and the reports were not credited. In any event, Cardus would have been preparing his review of Lancashire's season, published on 29 August. His verdict was that his team's season was, on paper, not brilliant, but that, "The victories over Sussex and Notts at Old Trafford were in themselves sufficient to make the season memorable." Cardus's watching and reporting on cricket appears to have been a more than satisfactory use of his time.

Cardus also reported on Lancashire's three-day first-class match against the Australian Imperial Forces at Old Trafford (June 12–14), and one away fixture: the Roses match against Yorkshire at Bramall Lane, Sheffield (August 4–5). The latter meant that it was later possible to issue *The Roses Matches 1919–1939*, a collection of his articles for the MG which covered all the inter-war contests between the two counties.

Cardus claimed, in 1922, to have seen another match or, at least, innings in 1919 when, on 1 August, Jack Crawford made a brilliant 144 not out for Surrey against the Australian Imperial Forces at The Oval.[25] However, he was not credited in the match report in the MG; the two previous days N.C. had been at Old Trafford for the fixture with Sussex and, at the time, he had not reported on any match outside Lancashire. Indeed, in his article for the MG on 4 August, Cardus referred to the view of Crawford's innings by London critics, which implies he did not see it himself and that the comment he later made was wrong. Perhaps it was a case of he wished he had seen it.

Cardus had certainly made an early impression with his

writing. There was a possibility of him writing for another newspaper as well as the MG, but on 18 June 1919 C.P. Scott refused to grant permission, although was glad that the quality of Cardus's writing had been quickly respected.[26]

The birth of "Cricketer" in 1920

From the following year, Cardus's writings on cricket appeared under the pseudonym Cricketer. The initiative for this came from MG news editor W.P. Crozier, whose secretary, Madeline Linford, thought of the name.

Cardus provided two descriptions of events! In *Second Innings* he recalled that Crozier argued that the public did not remember initials and asked Cardus for a suitable alternative to N.C.[27] In *Conversations* Crozier is remembered as saying that N.C. already appeared in his notices on the arts pages, so something different was required for cricket reports.[28] Cardus did not come up with any suitable ideas, and Cricketer was suggested by Madeline Linford, who overheard the discussion. This was what was adopted.[29]

Who was Madeline Linford? Cardus included her in his list of the first film critics,[30] and described her as "a very gifted girl".[31] It is of interest to ask why: her talents went beyond inventing pseudonyms.[32] She was a remarkable person, who started work with the MG in 1913 as an assistant in the advertisements office before becoming secretary to Crozier. She became the first editor of the newspaper's women's page in 1922, which role she had for 17 years. Until 1944 she was the only woman on the editorial staff; she retired in 1953. She also wrote a biography of Mary Wollstonecraft and two novels. Gifted indeed!

Cardus had begun the summer with a preview of the season in the MG on 19 April 1920. This appeared under his name, Neville Cardus; since the previous practice had been to use his initials, this may have been a mistake.

The name Cricketer made its debut on 27 April 1920, under an article, "The opening practice at Old Trafford, Lancashire's prospects", commenting on events at the ground the day before. If the introduction of the pseudonym was meant to distinguish the cricket writer Cricketer from the music writer N.C., execution of the new policy left something to be desired as the item also had a credit to N.C. at the foot of the article. The same thing happened when Cardus wrote about Surrey cricketer Bobby Abel on 3 May.

It was 10 May when readers saw an article by Cricketer without N.C.; indeed, two such articles, one on Sir Jack Hobbs, the other, a report of a league match where Cardus had seen Oldham beaten by a Rochdale team that included two of his favourite county cricketers, Cec Parkin and Jack Crawford. There was still a relapse into old ways the following day, when the article headed "Club cricket" was credited to N.C. with no mention of Cricketer. The article, which reflected on the nature of club cricket rather than being a match report, expressed unhappiness that the Rusholme club had become defunct. It is 12 May when the editorial team have got their act together, as from then on the reader is treated to articles by Cricketer without mentioning N.C.: the article that day was a preview of Lancashire's first county match of the season, against Leicestershire at Old Trafford.

Over time many will have come to realise that N.C., Cricketer and Neville Cardus were one and the same person. Sometimes the MG helped this process: for example, the report of a cricket match in which he played referred to Neville Cardus as Cricketer of the *Manchester Guardian*.[33] Similarly, when the newspaper reviewed *Days in the Sun* in 1924, it referred to author Neville Cardus as Cricketer.[34] Cardus was also a frequent speaker at meetings in Manchester on both cricket and music, where publicity and introductions could help clarify that the speaker named as Neville Cardus was in fact also known as Cricketer and N.C.

Cardus starts travelling: reporting cricket in 1920

The year 1920 was important not only for the introduction of a pseudonym. It was when Cardus "was asked by the 'MG' to write on cricket every day, and to travel the country from Old Trafford to Lord's, from Sheffield to Canterbury."[35] While his heart would still stay with Lancashire, he was becoming a national cricket writer rather than a local one.

This change was apparent early on. After writing about Lancashire's first match, at home to Leicestershire (12–14 May), he missed the next game, away at Northampton (15–17 May); instead, he was present at Sheffield on the Saturday (15 May) to report on Yorkshire v Derbyshire, although he admitted to leaving before the end of the day.[36] Thereafter, he did report on Lancashire's next four matches, two away (Derbyshire at Chesterfield and Yorkshire at Bradford, i.e. not far from Manchester), and two at home. He did not go to Southampton to see his county play Hampshire but we see the range of acceptable travel increased as he went to Leicester for Lancashire's visit on 5–8 June. After a home game against Northamptonshire we see that range increase further as Cardus reported on Lancashire's matches against Nottinghamshire (Trent Bridge), Kent (Tonbridge) and Middlesex (Lord's). It is worth recording that, on the face of it, his first visit to Lord's was on 19 June 1920, and he commented,

> "The Middlesex batting was vastly disappointing to those of us from the North of England who had so often been assured by London critics of the game that only at Lord's on a June day could we come to

understand what was brilliant batsmanship."[37]

Nevertheless, Middlesex beat Lancashire by an innings, with Patsy Hendren scoring 183 not out.

There followed two matches at Old Trafford, against Derbyshire and Warwickshire, on which Cardus reported. The next fixture was against Hampshire, played at Aigburth, Liverpool: Cardus was author of an article on the first day (Saturday) but then left for London to see the Varsity match. This was to be another disappointment at Lord's. He was present for the first two days of what was to have been a three-day contest but which was extended to four as there was no play on the first day. Neither, as it turned out, was there any play on the second, leading him to begin his report,

> "For the want of something better to do during these last two incredibly wet days at Lord's, I have been trying to understand why that place so forcibly recalls Charles Dickens's 'Bleak House'."[38]

Rain curtailed play on the third day as well but Cardus wasn't there. He had gone to Old Trafford, where it turned out to be dry for the first day of MacLaren's benefit match against Kent.[39] Lancashire won easily in two days. It is not clear if Cardus was present for the next visitors, Essex: there was play only on the second day, when the published article was not credited.

Cardus also visited Lord's for the Gentlemen v Players match, noting that 19 of the 22 cricketers involved were from southern counties, and not one from Lancashire, despite their being second in the championship.[40] This was to be the second victory by an innings that Cardus witnessed at Lord's, with the Gentlemen dominant. He did not miss seeing Lancashire as they were not playing at the time.

From London, Cardus proceeded to the Saffrons

ground, Eastbourne, where Sussex hosted Lancashire. He clearly enjoyed his travels:

"Eastbourne is not a thousand miles away from Manchester but for all that the place seems in another hemisphere to the grimy man from the north. Here you may live under an Italian sky, a sky rich with the blue of a Brangwyn picture. To-day this lovely cricket ground was a study in blue and green."[41]

Cardus then reported on all of Lancashire's remaining matches, except those against Worcestershire. He missed the away match at Amblecote in order to be at The Oval, where Surrey were entertaining Yorkshire; they were fifth and second in the championship table respectively. The crowd on the first two days numbered about 20,000 and he wrote:

"It would seem that all London is talking about this game; wherever one goes, in tube, train, 'bus, café, the topic of conversation is still the same."[42]

His report on the third day conveyed infectious enthusiasm (if not precision about the result: Surrey's margin of victory was 31 runs):

"This great match has had a most amazing finish. Surrey won at ten minutes past five by thirty odd runs after a day's play which swung this way and that until the vast crowd hung on to every movement of the cricketers breathlessly, and emerged from the agony at the end rather limp with nervous exhaustion."[43]

Cardus may have watched the final home match of the season against Worcestershire on 29 August to 1 September, but the MG was not published owing to a printers' strike.[44]

Cardus's Test match debut as writer in 1921

Although 1920 had seen Cardus extend his horizons, one thing was missing. There were no Tests in 1919 or 1920, so it was the Australians' tour of England in 1921 that provided the first opportunity for him to report on a Test match. Unfortunately, he had been ill since New Year's Day 1921,[45] which had meant far fewer articles from him in the MG in the first four months of the year, in comparison with 1920. Luckily, he was recovered for the opening of the Ashes series at Trent Bridge, Nottingham.[46] His first article, on the prospects for the two teams, appeared on the first day of the match, 28 May 1921. However, his contributions to the MG were more limited than they might have been as, although it was meant to be a three-day match, England lost by 10 wickets on the second day.

The second Test was at Lord's and produced another big victory for Australia (by 8 wickets). Cardus commented,

"For the Test match manner Lord's is very becoming. Last week's big game played anywhere no doubt would have left some fine impressions. But because it all happened at Lord's the sense of greatness comes into one's impressions. The momentous is in the air at Lord's; the place is murmurous with history."[47]

He had to report a further heavy defeat at Leeds, where Australia won the series and retained the Ashes. However, there was a true home fixture to look forward to: the fourth Test at Old Trafford (July 23–26). The MG explained special preparations for the match, with extra trams, trains and car parks arranged, special stands erected, the Culcheth Military Band to be present from 9.30am and the caterers prepared for an attendance of 30,000.[48] Sadly, these efforts were in vain as rain prevented any play on the first day. While an article in the MG described the repeated pitch inspections the author was "G.P." rather than Cricketer.[49] Cardus did report on the second and third days' play, with England having the advantage of a draw. One incident of note was that the England captain had displayed his ignorance of the laws when trying to declare his side's first innings illegally. The person involved was Lionel Tennyson, who Cardus had earlier described as "the grandson of a great English poet, and at the moment there is a fitting air of the poetic about this cricketer."[50] Cardus was later to criticise his captaincy on the final day of the last Test match, at The Oval, when the draw left the series 3–0 to Australia.[51]

Chapter 8

CRICKET DEVELOPS

———— ❧ ————

Neville Cardus's "scoop": MacLaren's "England XI" defeat the Australians at Eastbourne

One incident in Cardus's cricket reporting career stands out in particular: a "scoop" when he defied the MG news editor W.P. Crozier to watch a match of apparently no importance, a decision which turned out to be remarkably prescient. The 1921 Australian touring team, led by Warwick Armstrong, were unbeaten going in to a match at Eastbourne on August 27–30 against an eleven organised by A.C. MacLaren, called "England XI" in the press. The team included five men aged 24 or less and three aged 39 or more.

Cardus told what happened in *Autobiography*.[1] MacLaren had asked him to come to Eastbourne. This led to a disagreement with Crozier, whose view was that the Eastbourne contest was of little interest and would last only a day; instead Cardus should be at The Oval, where Surrey were hosting Yorkshire in a match important for the championship. Cardus won the argument, with a premonition that MacLaren would achieve something in what would be his last appearance in English cricket. Only local reporters were present at the match in addition to himself.

The first day at Eastbourne was a disaster for the home side: all out for 43, the Australians replying with 174 and the England XI 8–1 in their second innings. Cardus bought the MG and "went hot and cold to see a long column about an anti-climax; my deputy was given pride of place for his account of Lancashire at Leyton."[2] On Monday morning the score deteriorated to 60–4. Cardus was expecting to catch the train for The Oval match. But there followed a turnaround: Aubrey Faulkner's 153 enabled the England XI to reach 326. Needing 196 to win, the Australians were 25–1 at the end of Monday and then bowled out for 167 on the Tuesday, a winning margin of 28 runs for MacLaren's team. Cardus shared his excitement with readers with an enthusiastic report (chapter 1).

However, Cardus was wrong to claim that the MG gave precedence to the Lancashire match. In Monday's paper, one article summarised all the cricket matches taking place, with Middlesex v Surrey taking priority,[3] MacLaren's XI and the Australians second, and Lancashire at Leyton third. However, the Eastbourne match was the subject of a separate article, by Cricketer, and this was longer than the summary of all matches.

The MG missed the monetary impact of the Australians' defeat that was highlighted in the *Dundee Evening Telegraph* with the headline, "Australian cricketers lose £15,000 by the Defeat". It explained that each player would have received £1,000 if the team had finished the tour unbeaten.[4] The tourists were later to lose another match, against C.I. Thornton's XI at Scarborough.

Incidentally, what was not known at the time was that MacLaren was to play first-class cricket again, for MCC on their tour of Australia and New Zealand in 1921/22.

Cardus as cricket correspondent

Cardus had started off writing about cricket in traditional mode, dutifully recording the events of the day, although there were references to the arts and music from the outset.

He adopted the practice of reporters in the press box of keeping their own record of the play, there being none of the statistical support available today.[5] The printed report of the second day's play in the second match on which he had reported, against Yorkshire in 1919, included 17 overs of Parkin's bowling analysis as in the scorebook.[6]

We may believe that Cardus was not a man for facts and figures. However, later on, several of his articles still included plentiful statistics.[7] But he did attack the preoccupation of cricket with numbers and records, urging that the game should be an expression of personality.[8] His view of the scoreboard was that it was secondary to events taking place on the field;[9] it did "not get anywhere near the secret of Woolley. It can only tell us about Bloggs."[10] Similarly, he was negative about statistics: if they "don't tell us the truth, what is the use of them?"[11] Yorkshireman Emmott Robinson's cricket was described as "of a kind that could never be estimated by averages."[12]

It was MG music critic Samuel Langford who encouraged Cardus to concentrate on the characters playing cricket rather than their statistics.[13] The scoreboard became less important to Cardus: "I wanted to concentrate on the field of play… I began to see cricket as something more than a game."[14] In some cases this would lead to an absence of facts that the reader may well expect: for example, in "Spooner at Old Trafford", about his innings in the 1920 Roses match, Cardus does not tell the reader how many Spooner scored (62).[15] Such an approach played to his strengths, of course. Musical references were common. His county's speciality was not quick scoring: "Cricket, like music, has its slow movements, especially when my native county of Lancashire is batting."[16] However, after a while, he felt he was becoming too literary, so "I even reacted against the romanticism in my own cricket writing."[17] Nevertheless, "the humour of English character kept creeping in".[18]

It was certainly true that there were some slow movements in Lancashire's play.[19] In the Roses matches of 1919–39 their scoring rate averaged but 2.06 runs per over. Yorkshire in these contests managed 2.43 runs per over. However, even this was less than the typical rate of about 2.7 in the county championship over this period.[20] The slow play may have helped provide plenty of time for Cardus to concentrate on his impressionistic writing.

Fortunately, runs would be in more abundance elsewhere. One of Cardus's favourite grounds was Trent Bridge: in 1922 he described the pitch there as "Lotosland for batsmen, a place in which it has always seemed afternoon and 360 for 2 wickets."[21] There may have been some deterioration when, forty years later, the score was set at 350–3.[22] But the character of Nottinghamshire's headquarters was clear enough from phrasing that obviously wasn't literal truth but pleasingly different.

The characters in his writing led to stories. In 1939 Cardus wrote an article in the MG on the debut of Lancashire wicket-keeper Bill Worsley, summoned from the coal pits to take the place of the county's injured first-choice keeper.[23] The conversations between Worsley on the one hand and Walter Brearley and Archie MacLaren on the other demonstrate the humour involving the newcomer in an unaccustomed environment and his experienced colleagues. Brearley is taken aback when, having offered to buy a drink for Worsley, the new keeper from the mines chooses "creem de month". Worsley then surprises MacLaren with his standing so close to the stumps for the fast bowlers, and exasperates him by celebrating his catches with the practice in the Saturday afternoon leagues of throwing the ball in the air and catching it with a one-handed jerk behind his back.

The words are naturally made up, and relate to Edgbaston in 1903, long before Cardus ventured outside Manchester.

Nevertheless, it makes enjoyable reading, although the details of the batsmen caught by Worsley are not wholly accurate.[24] In his article, Cardus is hesitant about Worsley's name; but this uncertainty is gone when the story is repeated, and indeed expanded, in *Autobiography*.[25] Story first, facts second, but the context is such that many readers will accept that and enjoy it.

In 1932–33 the 'Bodyline' Ashes series took place in Australia, but Cardus wasn't there.[26] This could be linked to the financial difficulties of the MG: sales revenue fell as subscription rates were dropped in the face of fierce competition, and advertising revenue reduced by about a third during the financial crisis of 1929–31. However, other papers made offers for Cardus to cover the tour, and the MG could have shared the cost. Cardus wrote that he declined to travel because he feared an unfriendly atmosphere; his motto was "anything for an easy life". But his record as a music critic suggests otherwise. Further, it was reported as early as 13 May 1932 that Cardus would not tour, this well before the touring team was chosen and when the bodyline idea was developed (Cardus thought that comments from South African batsman H.W. Taylor during the rain-affected match between England and the Rest (27–29 July) were influential). So, a non-cricketing explanation may work best: he didn't want to spend several months without his mistress (see chapter 9).

Early on, using reports from Australia, he wrote that Larwood "has no need to brutalise his natural rhythm and style by bowling at a batsman's body on the leg side… By attacking the batsman's body, on the leg side, nearly all of cricket's greatest strokes are put out of action."[27] Cardus was also writing on the series for *The Observer*, under the Neville Cardus byline. His views appear to have developed after more information about the tour became available.[28]

A match of a different nature that Cardus reported was

when Lancashire women played the Australian women tourists in 1937. The Australians:

"gave a clever and invigorating account of themselves, to the joy of a good crowd. Not for some time has so much animation and satisfaction been expressed at Old Trafford as we heard yesterday: the play must have convinced the most stubborn die-hard that women cricketers can be as skilful and as natural as women lawn tennis players or women hockey players. Comparisons with men are irrelevant."[29]

When in Australia in the previous winter, Cardus had been positive about the future of cricket for women, who he believed had "graceful tendencies".[30]

Cricket provided opportunities for friendship. Cardus wrote of a weekend spent at the London home of playwright J.M. Barrie, so strange that he carefully checked his memory and assured readers that he was not exaggerating.[31] The basics are, however, sound. In *Autobiography* it is dated June 1926, when Cardus arrived from Birmingham, where he had seen bowler Root baffle the Australians. Cardus described Barrie's butler, Thurston, whose talents he found included speaking several languages. The Saturday was spent working at Lord's. On returning to Barrie's home he saw Barrie's sister, Maggie, and referred to her as Margaret Ogilvie. In the morning she said she had been in communication with Cardus's mother "on the other side".

The start of the weekend can be traced to Friday 4 June, when Fred Root had taken 7 wickets for 42 runs for the North in the Australians' first innings. Barrie's biographer confirms the butler was Frank Thurston, who was familiar with Spanish, French, Latin and Greek; he had an "enigmatic and, some thought, slightly sinister personality."[32] On the following day, Cardus was watching the Test trial at

Lord's.[33] Barrie did have a sister, Margaret, but Ogilvie was the maiden name of Barrie's mother, who had died in 1895.[34] More of a puzzle is her night-time communication as Cardus's mother was alive in Manchester. Cardus does not draw attention to this point, although Brookes does.[35] Cardus's family was still an enigma.

Cricketer gains recognition

It did not take Cardus long to make a name for himself as cricket writer; indeed, C.P. Scott recognised this early on (chapter 7). By the end of 1920 "'Cricketer' had won appreciation throughout the cricket world."[36]

In 1922 the MG published nine articles by "Cricketer" on batting, bowling and fielding, intended to help the club cricketer.[37] It is perhaps a surprise that someone of such modest ability as a cricketer as Cardus should attempt to advise others, though it is fair to assume that he benefitted from watching Wainwright coach at Shrewsbury. Following many requests that it received, the MG decided to publish the articles in book form, and *The Club Cricketer* appeared for sale on 22 May, the author shown as "Cricketer". It pre-dated another milestone, the first book where Neville Cardus was named as the writer. This was *A Cricketer's Book*, published by Grant Richards on 28 June of the same year. It was largely based on articles that had appeared in the MG; *The Times*' reviewer appreciated the writing and choice of words.[38]

Cardus was a frequent writer for *Wisden*, and was named as the author of the article about Lancashire in the 1927 edition which celebrated the county's 1926 championship victory. It was unusual for contributors to be credited at that time; the inclusion of his name may have been accidental. Articles attributed to Cardus appeared in the editions from 1951 to 1975, with the exception of 1962 and 1973. His death occurred shortly before the 1975 volume appeared on the bookshelves; the dust jacket acknowledged "sadly, his final article for *Wisden*".

Acknowledgement as a leading cricket writer also came in the offer to write about cricket in some general publications. In particular, Cardus's article on W.G. Grace in Massingham's *The Great Victorians* was praised as "not only the best in the book but also the most intimately Victorian".[39]

Cardus was a keen conversationalist, which may have led to his being an early contributor to broadcasting. Cricket commentaries on the radio in England began in 1927, but the MG refused a request from the BBC in April for Cardus to report on three matches.[40] This meant that he missed the chance to take part in the first broadcast of a Roses match, on 6 June 1927, when that role was given to Stacey Lintott, a *Daily Mirror* journalist.[41] Cardus's first broadcast was not much delayed, however: it was from the Manchester station of the BBC, and not a commentary but a talk, merely entitled *Cricket*, on Thursday 4 August 1927, 7.00–7.15pm. The *Radio Times* described the speaker as Cricketer of the *Manchester Guardian* and mentioned his work on music.[42]

Overseas radio work also came Cardus's way. In 1931 he made broadcasts to New Zealand, claimed to incorporate the longest direct conversation that had been conducted: 12,000 miles between Manchester and Wellington.[43] When the Ashes series was taking place in England in 1934, he gave "Test match radiophone talks", broadcast for Australian listeners.[44]

Cardus's books also had an overseas audience, although there was already a recognition that the writing could not always be relied on as the truth. An Australian reviewer of *Days in the Sun* wrote, "The cricket essay is a thing cultivated in England, and here Mr. Cardus mingles fancy with fact. The latter is preferable."[45]

The Leeds 1929 incident:
not Cardus's finest hour[46]

This incident refers to the third Test match in 1929, between England and South Africa at Leeds. At the end of the second day's play (Monday 15 July), South Africa in their second innings were 116–7 and only 14 runs ahead of England. Cardus finished his report in the MG with, "The remainder of the match can have little purpose save to provide the scorers with details necessary for making up their accounts."[47] The *Times* correspondent wrote, "it looks very much as if the players, and some spectators of high consideration, would be able to catch conveniently early trains to-day."[48] Cardus, who would later confess to finding the day-to-day reporting of cricket to be wearisome, decided to absent himself from the final day's play.

What happened on the Tuesday was that South Africa staged a great recovery. Owen-Smith reached 129 out of South Africa's total of 275 and while England scored the required 184 for victory they lost 5 wickets in doing so. Indeed, when the fifth wicket fell with the total at 110 the result looked in some doubt. The game ended shortly after 4pm.[49]

Cardus has provided us with two explanations of his absence. According to *Full Score* (1970) he left Leeds for London on the Monday in order to spend Tuesday with his mistress, "Milady". They passed the time wandering around Barnet.[50] On returning to London around 6pm Cardus was horrified to learn of the delay to England's victory, went to his club and consulted the tape messages for information on the day's play:

"From these useful details and statistics I composed a column of 'eye witness' descriptive writing. I then consulted the Bradshaw railway guide, saw that a train from Leeds arrived in London at about 9 o'clock, so

I timed myself dramatically to rush into the office of the *Manchester Guardian* with my report."[51]

A lesser-known version of events was given in the Australian press in 1936, when Cardus wrote:

> "Little use would it be for a writer to travel next morning all the way from Manchester to see two rabbits dismissed in an over and so I did not go to Leeds. I went for a walk in the country and when I got back to Manchester in the late afternoon, I saw newspaper posters: 'South Africans' great recovery' and 'Owen-Smith's superb innings.' … I did not go into my office: I retired to the privacy of my club. I asked for the Press Association's report. And from the bare bones of its description I wrote my column and breathed again."[52]

Is the correct answer the 1970 version, when Cardus was using his new-found freedom after the death of his wife in 1968 to talk about his mistress (who had died in 1937)? Alternatively, is the 1936 report correct; we know that he went on weekend rambles in Derbyshire[53] and that he was a member of the Old Rectory Club in Manchester?[54] This would imply that, in 1970, Cardus changed and elaborated his story to make it more interesting.

A clue to the solution is found in his reference in 1970 to going to his London club. The 1936 *Who's Who* entry informs us that Cardus was a member of the National Liberal Club, to which he was admitted in 1931.[55] He was also a member of the Savage Club, which he joined in 1934.[56] There is no suggestion in any of his writing that he had joined another club by 1929 and subsequently left it. This therefore implies that the 1970 description of events is untrue and that the more mundane version from 1936 is what we should rely on.

Cardus later drew attention to some important words

towards the beginning of his report:

> "The reader will note that in the bogus report from Leeds, the operative sentence is: 'The South Africans kicked back from a position so hopeless that few of us even took the trouble to be present at Leeds until we scented the battle from afar.' I admire yet the audacity of that sentence."[57]

The MG article did, though, include "Leeds, Tuesday", which hid the fact that the author was elsewhere.

Cardus did not suggest his resourcefulness on this occasion should be an example to young reporters. But providing a bogus report for his readers as a result of shirking his responsibility in order to spend a day walking in the country would not be regarded as Cardus's finest hour.

Perhaps Cardus had this incident in mind when, the following year, he wrote, "You can never take your eyes away from a cricket match for fear of missing a crisis."[58] In *Autobiography*, he relented and was satisfied with impressions: "In a quarter of a century of criticism of music and drama and cricket I have gradually evolved a sound guiding principle – not to write about any event unless I have been there to see or hear it; at least it is as well to give the reader the impression that one has been, so to say, in the vicinity."[59] Readers might welcome better confirmation that Cardus was where he should have been.

Playing cricket in later life

Cardus's writing about cricket for the MG didn't stop him playing cricket for some years. We can find out more about his playing ability from eight matches in 1919–22 in which Cardus played and where the scores were reported in the MG (Table 4). On five occasions he was playing for

Table 4. Playing record of Neville Cardus in matches reported in the *Manchester Guardian*

Date	Home team	Total	Away team	Total	Cardus's batting Bat order	Runs	Cardus's bowling Wickets
4/6/1919	St Bede's College	74–6	Manchester Press (midweek team)	130–4 dec	4	4	1
4/6/1920	Manchester Guardian	88	Sir F.R. Benson's XI	64	10	10	3
29/7/1920	E.F. Stockton's XI	121–4d	Manchester Guardian	67	5	1	3~
22/9/1920	Cheetham Hill	56–9	Manchester Guardian	54	10	5*	1
25/9/1920	Cheetham Hill	153	Mr H.D. Nichols's XI	105	10	0	4
28/7/1921	Sir E.F. Stockton's XI	162–5	Manchester Guardian	117	9/12	0	0
15/9/1921	Manchester Guardian	156–9	Messrs Reiss Bros	137	10	3	2
23/9/1922	Romiley XV	113–9dec	Neville Cardus's XI	183–5	dnb		0

~ 3 for 31 in 15 overs

Table 4

Venues: St Bede's College (1919), Old Trafford (4/6/1920, 29/7/1920, 28/7/1921), Cheetham Hill (22/9/1920, 25/9/1920), Withington (15/9/1921), Romiley (1922)

Notes: In the 28/7/1921 match the *Manchester Guardian* team had 12 men.

Neville Cardus played for the team that is underlined.

Source: *Manchester Guardian*, dates immediately following matches, except 27 September 1920 for second match at Cheetham Hill and 25 September 1922 for match at Romiley.

the MG, while another team was that of H.D. Nichols of the MG. One of the opposition teams was led by Sir Frank Benson, a 61-year-old actor. E.F. Stockton was MP for Manchester Exchange in 1922–23. Overall, Cardus averaged 3.83 with the bat and took 14 of the 63 wickets that the opposition lost.

Cardus recalled that he bowled Sir Frank Benson "for thirty-five stylish runs"[60] although, in the match above in 1920, Benson scored just eight runs and was bowled by one of Cardus's team-mates. For the fixture against Romiley, Cardus had assembled a cast which included one batsman who had an England cap, J.T. Tyldesley, and another, Herbert Sutcliffe, who would receive one a couple of years later.

One further match can be added. When in Australia in 1938 Cardus was persuaded to appear, on 2 March, for the midweek team of Melbourne Cricket Club against Ringwood in a half-day match at the Melbourne cricket ground. The Melbourne captain, Hector Donahoo, encouraged Cardus to bowl, which he did for an hour and 20 minutes, taking 2–75. Ringwood scored 176 and Melbourne 99. As regards batting, "Mr. Cardus did not figure among the leading scorers."[61] A photograph of Cardus bowling in the match is reproduced in *The Elusive Mr Cardus*.

Even later in his lifetime (age 62!), Cardus was due to captain the Authors against the National Book League in 1950 but the match was rained off.[62]

Cardus has several references himself to his playing career, although the truth cannot be guaranteed without corroborating evidence:

- a match against a team that included Worcestershire bowler Robert Burrows; Cardus hit two fours to win the match;[63]

- he played in a friendly match at Old Trafford and was stumped by Duckworth, thought to be his first stumping at Old Trafford;[64]

- he captained a *Manchester Guardian* XI against a team captained by A.C. MacLaren at Old Trafford in about 1923. Cardus was proud of his first ball to MacLaren, which nearly bowled him but was pleased that the former England captain hit three sixes off his bowling;[65]

- he bowled Rusholme out, which gave Cardus great satisfaction; there is no mention of when this was (it may have predated his spell at Shrewsbury);[66]

- he played for Sir John Squire's team at Taunton, albeit with the match starting without anyone recording the score;[67] and

- he bowled a few overs at Perth in October 1936, possibly not in a formal match, for the first time in four years.[68]

In addition, *The Elusive Mr Cardus* refers to county cricketer Richard Keigwin being impressed by Cardus's bowling in the garden of W.G. Grace's nephew at Thornbury in 1939 ("very good slow off-spinners… It was extraordinary how much he turned the ball").[69]

Cardus had a highly optimistic assessment of his ability. In 1928 he wrote to his friend Harold Timperley suggesting, presumably with tongue in cheek, that they could both have won places in the England team on their 1906 form.[70] In 1956 he asserted that he played in good class cricket and supposed "that as an off-break bowler I was about as good as Fred Titmus of Middlesex was when he was eighteen years or so old."[71] When Titmus was aged 17 in 1950 he played 25 first-class matches, taking 12 wickets at an average of 30.83; rather less well next year, taking part in 7 first-class games, with 4 wickets at 44.25. This is still a rather more impressive performance than taking some wickets for a works team! Writing in the *Guardian* in 1974 Cardus referred to the urchins playing cricket on wasteland in Manchester and said that the group produced one who could have played for Lancashire as a bowler but preferred to write about cricket.[72] That sounds like a dream that an urchin might have.

It is worthwhile revisiting what Cardus wrote about his bowling in the pre-Shrewsbury years. This was before he had the benefit of watching professional coaches Attewell and Wainwright in action. How reliable is the assertion that he took nine wickets in the first innings he bowled in a club match? The poor pitches in the Sunday school league mean that, while some exaggeration may be present, impressive bowling figures are not impossible even if Cardus was not repeating such feats in every game. What about his 12 wickets in the two-day match for Captain Rose's team against a team including five batsmen with first-class experience? That is rather more challenging. Given Cardus's appetite for making up stories and exaggerating his cricketing ability, is this an elaborate joke? If this two-day match were true we might have expected some mention in his writings, but this is not the case. Indeed, all we have is a scorecard and accompanying cartoons in the 1977 edition of *Cardus on Cricket*; they were not in the original 1951 edition nor in the predecessor book, *The Essential Neville Cardus*, in 1949. Therefore, the information was not published in Cardus's lifetime. We know that there was a mischievous element in Cardus. It may have been a match that he wished had taken place rather than did take place.

Chapter 9

NOT ONLY CRICKET

Neville marries Edith King

There was a significant personal milestone for Neville Cardus in 1921: his marriage. His wife was Edith King, whom he had known for around five years or more.[1] Edith was a schoolteacher, and it is said that Cardus married her because she helped him so far on the road to literacy.[2]

Edith was born in 1881 in Mossley, which was then in Yorkshire, although has since become part of the borough of Tameside in Greater Manchester. Her father was John Thomas Sissons King, who had been born in Leicestershire. In 1879, in Manchester, he married Fanny Jane Walton, a Mancunian. John King was a schoolmaster, later becoming a headmaster, and it was perhaps this influence that led Edith into an educational career. After attending Stockwell Training College in London, she became an art teacher in Manchester.

Edith's name was something of a puzzle. Her birth certificate shows her as Edith Hannah King, consistent with the censuses of 1891–1911. But, on the marriage certificate, Hannah has become Honorine, a name derived from Latin as "woman of honour". Since her husband was named as Neville (both John and Frederick having disappeared), both parties had enjoyed a change of name before they were married. The marriage certificate also has a third Christian name for Edith: Walton,[3] which had not been referred to on the birth certificate or on censuses and is not on Edith's death certificate. Walton was her mother's maiden name.

How old was Edith? We find that Neville Cardus was not the only one with question marks about his age. The marriage certificate said 33 (and 31 for Neville). This was plain wrong: she was 39 (and Neville was 33). Did they both know the truth?

Edith's age continued to present problems. There is a four-year error in the 1939 Register, where she claimed to have been born in 1885; and also on her death certificate, where her age at death was shown as 82 but was actually 86. More remarkable is the information on the list of passengers on the *Stratheden* returning from Australia to London in 1955, where she claimed to have been born in 1889, a little over eight years after her true birthdate. Was Edith a pioneer of anti-ageing cosmetics?

The strange afternoon of the wedding day

On Wednesday 15 June 1921, two days before the wedding day, Lancashire began a three-day match against Leicestershire at Old Trafford. Cardus, using the pen name Cricketer, reported on the first day's play in the MG of 16 June. The articles on the two succeeding days had no byline, and were presumably filed by a colleague or other correspondent. Cardus was to be married on 17 June, and it is good to know that the MG allowed him time off!

The wedding, on the Friday, provided the basis for a Cardus story. He related that, in the morning, he was watching Lancashire at Old Trafford, with Hallows and Makepeace opening the batting, then took a taxi to the register office, later returning (with Edith!) to Old Trafford to discover that Lancashire's score had moved on by just 17 runs: Makepeace 5, Hallows 11, and a leg-bye.[4] That this isn't quite true is explained in *His Own Man*, with cricket enthusiast Geoffrey Copinger having found that Hallows and Makepeace did not play together in this match.[5] From Cricket Archive we find that Lancashire were batting on the Friday; Hallows opened and carried his bat throughout the innings, scoring a century, so he would have been batting in both the morning and afternoon, though his fellow opener was Walker Ellis, not Makepeace. Cardus must be the only cricket writer to report a leg-bye scored while he was away getting married: it makes it sound a good story but likely too good a story to be true.

Cardus was, however, soon away on business again. The day following his wedding, he was in London watching Lancashire's match at Lord's, his report being in the issue of 20 June.

Edith and Neville: not a typical marriage

Where did the newly married couple live? Neville was living with his uncle Robert at 154 Moseley Road; Edith had been at Victoria Park, Manchester. Robert died three months after Neville's wedding and it is not clear how long Alice, his widow, continued to live at their home (she was elsewhere in Manchester at the time of the 1939 Register and her death in 1974, not having remarried). Slater's Directory shows Robert Cardus to be at 154 Moseley Road in 1922, reflecting a delay in updating records. In 1923 and 1924 the entry at the address is Frederick Cardus. Why Frederick rather than Neville? Perhaps he was continuing to use Fred as a resident, not writer. Maybe he thought that his terraced house was not befitting a (now senior) journalist and it was preferable to be incognito using his old name, Frederick.

In 1925, the directory shows the house being occupied by Wilfrid Sharples, telephone fitter. Neville Cardus had himself had a telephone fitted: in 1925 he was in the phone book, at 2 Barnsfield Avenue, Withington.[6] It was a semi-detached house more appropriate for his status. He and Edith remained there until their time in Australia after the start of World War II. In the 1930s Neville would spend more time in London; he reckoned to be there for about 15 days a month.[7] In 1939 he was on the electoral register at the National Liberal Club in London.

In the 1930s Cardus had a lover (Barbe, also called Milady) and his later writings indicate a fondness for female company although details are, not surprisingly, unclear. When Neville went to live in Australia in 1940 he found a flat where he not only lived but carried out his writing so when Edith came to Australia a year later she took a separate flat nearby, not the usual relationship for a married couple. It was a marriage without children and it is worth drawing attention to Cardus's comment, "Edith was a great spirit and character born for sisterhood not marriage."[8] *Autobiography* contains a remark that, "I married the good companion who is my wife".[9] In 1970 Cardus wrote, "My wife and I remained great companions over a period of half a century, but we never shared sexual communication... until I had reached my fortieth year, women scarcely existed for me, except as sisters, a companion-wife or as aunt."[10] Not a typical marriage.

Cardus's reporting on serious music

To revert to work: Cardus had trained himself as a music critic and, with the MG, he was soon to become an assistant to "S.L.", the newspaper's senior music critic Samuel Langford, whom Cardus called "the most searching, most thoughtful and wise writer on music of his time."[11]

The story of Cardus's first contribution to the MG on serious music is told in *Autobiography*.[12] It was in 1920, and the second of two concerts given by Russian operatic tenor Vladimir Rosing. The first concert had been reviewed by Samuel Langford who, Cardus wrote, "was much too deeply immersed in the style and musical form of German Lieder to see eye to eye with Rosing's and Moussorgsky's methods." C.P. Scott, who was a friend of Rosing, decided to send the tickets for the second concert to Cardus, whose review duly appeared on 13 January. Cardus added, "I felt rather awkward about it… I don't think Langford took it very well at the time."

This is not the whole story. It was back in 1919 when Langford had reviewed four concerts with Rosing.[13] The following extract is clearly favourable rather than negative:

> "We had not heard Rosing before, but for us the question whether Rosing is really a beautiful singer, and not merely a dramatic one, was settled completely in his favour".[14]

In January 1920 there were two Rosing concerts but Cardus reviewed both, not just the second. They took place at the Midland Hall in Manchester on 12 January and in Rochdale, arranged by the Rochdale Chamber Concert Society, on the following day.[15] Cardus was certainly not uncritical: at Rochdale, his view was that Rosing "was hardly in his best voice and the low-ceilinged room was also against him."[16]

We can start to make sense of what happened by noting Langford's whereabouts on those two days. He was watching Beecham conduct *Parsifal* and *Tosca* at the new Queen's Theatre in Manchester; for *Parsifal* it was the first performance in England outside London.[17] That is where we would expect the senior music critic to be. Hence, the decision to give Cardus the tickets for Rosing was not necessarily a decision by Scott thinking that he would prefer the review by Cardus; rather, a logical decision based on Langford being occupied on more important music business elsewhere. The postscript in *Autobiography* is that

Scott told Cardus that he was pleased with the notice of the Rosing concert and nominated Cardus as Langford's deputy.[18] That may well be the case, though the context that Cardus provided is misleading.

The following year, the name Neville Cardus in full appeared as the author of an article, an unusual event. This was an appreciation of singer Jenny Lind on the centenary of her birth.[19] In view of Cardus's many mistakes about ages, it is right to confirm that he had the centenary correct: Lind had been born on 6 October 1820.

Ballet also featured in Cardus's reports. In *Full Score*, Cardus mentioned another example of his early work, devoting over two pages to his review of Russian ballerina Tamara Karasavina dancing at the Palace Theatre, Manchester. This was published on 19 April 1921.[20] It is intriguing that, the day before, the MG published a review by none other than Langford of a concert featuring Vladimir Rosing.[21]

Neither was the Hallé forgotten. On 5 December 1922 Cardus was at Rochdale Town Hall, where he reviewed a concert by the Hallé under Hamilton Harty.[22] This may well be his first review of a Hallé concert; none earlier has been traced.

Cardus's music work took him further outside Manchester than Rochdale: the first time he travelled abroad was to Vienna. At the Vienna State Opera he heard Wagner's *Die Meistersinger* and Richard Strauss's new opera, *Die Frau Ohne Schatten*. N.C.'s report in the MG, on 4 January 1924, called the performance of the latter superb, but it "provoked much less applause and animation than a Tuesday noon concert will produce in Manchester any week." He went on to say,

"It is certain that had this performance of Richard Strauss's opera been given in Manchester the crowd would have behaved in the hearty, gusty manner of a crowd at Old Trafford after a quarter of an hour's 'jazz' batsmanship by Parkin."

Parkin was Cec Parkin, the Lancashire and England off-spinner. He was described as eccentric in character, and "[a]s a batsman he was useful at times and showed good style, but his average of 11.47 denotes uncertainty to a high degree."[23] He could doubtless produce an attractive and perhaps eccentric 15 minutes of batting.

The above was an exception to the normal rule which Cardus expressed: "I have never known 'Cricketer' to invade the preserves of 'N.C.', music critic of the *Manchester Guardian* – which is a curious point."[24]

Cardus as senior music critic

Samuel Langford died on 8 May 1927 (in another of his timing errors, Cardus referred in *Autobiography* to the death in May 1926).[25] Cardus contributed a lengthy appreciation in the MG on 18 May and edited a volume of selected writings of Langford, with an introduction that mentioned his immense love of conversation,[26] something that Cardus listed in *Who's Who* among his own interests. The annual announcement of and comment on the forthcoming season of Hallé concerts in the MG, previously the province of S.L., was, on 17 September 1927, the work of N.C. The first concert of the season, on 20 October, was devoted to music of Wagner and N.C., as he was, of course, credited, remarked that conductor Sir Hamilton Harty had worked hard to broaden the appeal of the concerts, and that there was a vast and enthusiastic audience.[27]

Cardus was able to see some celebrated performers, and *Full Score* has a short chapter on pianist and former Polish prime minister Paderewski, who Cardus said he last saw play at a concert in Manchester on a Saturday in

October 1928.[28] That was 20 October, and Cardus is quite correct in recalling three of the pieces that were performed, namely the *Études Symphoniques* of Schumann, the Ballade in G minor by Chopin and the A flat Sonata of Beethoven's opus 110.[29] However, he did see Paderewski again. This was on 17 October 1931, at a concert organised by Brand Lane.[30] The age-old problem of ages was again apparent. Paderewski's age at the 1928 and 1931 concerts was given as 62 and 72 respectively,[31] whereas he was 67 and 70.

There followed a concert where there was an odd incident. Cardus wrote that he had to leave a concert early and while his notice described the playing of Chopin's Ballade in G minor as in the pianist's "own aromatic manner" or similar words, the problem was that the planned work had been replaced by the Ballade in A flat.[32] The concert was on 10 November 1928, the pianist was Joseph von Pachmann, and the phrase used was "his reading was all aroma".[33] Cardus was again having difficulties with ages: he referred in the MG to Pachmann being in his 81st year (right) and also "at the age of 81" (wrong).

Cardus was sometimes scheduled to review a concert where it turned out that he was unable to attend but made arrangements to ensure that he could still submit an article.[34] Arthur Bullock, from Prestwich near Manchester, sometimes covered Hallé concerts for Cardus around the late 1920s/early 1930s: Cardus would write the review on the basis of his familiarity with the orchestra and the pieces being played, but needed someone to be present in case something unusual happened of which he ought to be aware. On one occasion when the weather was foul Cardus decided to stay at home and sent in his review as usual. Unfortunately, he had no back-up that night and he was not to know that the weather had led to the concert, in Yorkshire, being cancelled. Cardus was fired by the MG but soon taken back.

Cardus enjoyed the Salzburg festival, his first visit being in 1931. He arrived by about 23 August, the rain following him from England.[35] He heard Bruno Walter conduct *Das Lied von der Erde*, played by the Vienna Philharmonic Orchestra, "as though every note were familiar speech." The same orchestra provided the highlight of the festival, with a concert of symphonies by Haydn, Mozart and Brahms under Sir Thomas Beecham, who "revelled in all the exquisite shades to which he was able to help himself."[36] This was also the first occasion when Cardus met Beecham.[37]

The year 1932 saw an increase in Cardus's responsibilities in London. Following the retirement in 1931 of Eric Blom as the MG's London music critic, Cecil Gray was appointed to this position. He was asked for fortnightly articles on London music, though not confined to critical treatments of performances. However, problems with Cardus soon arose, with Gray complaining in October 1931 that, after he had reviewed a concert conducted by Richard Strauss, Cardus also reviewed the same concert in the following day's newspaper.[38] Concerned that an unpleasantly competitive atmosphere may develop, Gray met Cardus and the issue appeared to have been settled. However, that was not the case. There was an occasion when Gray issued notices of concerts of music by Schönberg and then Stravinsky, followed by an article covering both composers.[39] However, Cardus also had an article on the same pair.[40] This was despite Gray having told Cardus what he was preparing. Although it was thought that Gray was exceeding his brief, Cardus appeared to be contributing to the problems: Gray confided that he found it difficult to work with Cardus. The outcome was a decision that Cardus should cover both London and Manchester music, with Gray ceasing to work for the MG.

Horowitz was a pianist that Cardus admired, writing

that he first saw him in May 1931.[41] In fact it was two years later, the concert taking place on 5 May 1933.[42] Cardus's notice, part reproduced in *Autobiography*, gave his view that he was ready to believe that Horowitz was the greatest pianist alive or dead.[43]

While Cardus benefited from the Hallé being a major professional orchestra in his home city, relations were strained from time to time. He was in trouble with Hamilton Harty on several occasions, and the Hallé once made a deputation to the MG, demanding that he should be removed.[44] Thomas Beecham wrote to the Hallé in 1937 refusing to conduct any concert to which Cardus was invited, the reply being that the invitation was sent to the newspaper, which could decide which critic to send.[45] Cardus indicated that he was unaware of this at the time,[46] although a letter he sent to W.P. Crozier suggests he may have known.[47] Beecham also twice withdrew Cardus's press tickets for Covent Garden.[48] One comment about Beecham's conducting reminds us that the author was Cricketer: "On one occasion he [Sir Thomas] achieved the best square-cut since Macartney retired. But he should try to get nearer to the ball, and over it, while making his leg-glance."[49]

Cardus's approach to music criticism was subjective, which was something that "You can't get away from"; he did not believe there were objective tests of criticism.[50] He admitted that he did not share what later became the contemporary approach to music criticism, which he regarded "much as an analytical chemist regards the contents of his test tube."[51] It was later said of Cardus that "his richly descriptive style is not altogether in tune with the more technical, analytical approach to music criticism that prevails today.[52] However, the merit of his work could still be appreciated: "In his concert notices he avoided technical jargon, cultivating instead an elegant, witty and urbane style that gave audiences an insight into the spirit of the composition and performance."[53]

On a lighter note Cardus referred to the best misprint in an article by him, when the "banal duet" in *Otello* was replaced by "canal duel".[54] On the cricketing side, there was an unfortunate telegraphing error when Woolley, Chapman and Carr appeared as "primitive" batsmen; the word should have been "punitive."[55]

Cardus's other writing

Cardus was a prolific author, whose work went beyond the MG. He wrote books, not only on cricket, but also on music, together with his autobiographical volumes; Hilton has compiled a valuable summary.[56] The Neville Cardus Archive at Old Trafford has more detailed information. Many of his books are collections of articles originally published elsewhere.

An early example of his music-related work was an article on Thomas Beecham in 1919 for a magazine, *Voices*, edited by Thomas Moult, with whom he corresponded for several years.[57] Later examples were articles published in *Tempus*, on music in Australia (1948) and period music (1952). He wrote a book on the first five symphonies of Mahler, a composer he much admired, although a planned further volume, covering later works, was never completed.[58]

One magazine which Cardus did not end up writing for was the *John O'London's Weekly*. He wrote that he attended an interview to join the staff of the magazine, not yet launched, in the spring of 1919, the first time he had visited London.[59] The first issue of the weekly was 2 April 1919.[60] The timing of the interview may have been before the spring: leaving the interview Cardus saw a poster announcing the murder of Rosa Liebknecht: this was actually the murder of both Rosa Luxemburg and Karl Liebknecht,[61] which took place on 15 January 1919.

"Milady": Hilda Elizabeth Ede, with whom Neville Cardus had an affair

It is right to mention an important part of Cardus's personal life: about eleven months after the death of his wife, he went public in the *Guardian* about a mistress. His article, headed, "The most beautiful woman I know", attracted several letters expressing how readers were moved by it, and MG Women's Editor Mary Stott wrote that everyone she met, both inside and outside the office, was commenting on it joyfully.[62] A year later, in *Full Score*, he devoted a chapter to her, entitled "Milady", as she was called by England cricketer C.B. Fry. We find in *His Own Man* that she was a married lady, Hilda Elizabeth Ede, known as Barbe.[63]

When did the couple first meet? This is difficult to say: the oft-found problem of contradictions in Cardus's writing is not made easier by the sensitive nature of the subject. The *Full Score* chapter specifies 8 October 1928;[64] the *Guardian* article, 8 October 1929. Cardus's notebook implies 1930: "After 1929 … I had time to fall in love. A letter reached me one morning in August 1930… addressed from a cottage in Dymchurch".[65] A later comment in his notebook in 1949 is thought to suggest September 1930 as the first meeting.[66]

Both *Full Score* and the *Guardian* include a remark by Cardus that, when he first heard from Barbe, he had been occupied with Lancashire v Yorkshire at Old Trafford when the Canterbury cricket festival was taking place,[67] which is consistent with a first meeting in 1928 or 1930. The two sources indicate that they met at the bookstall at Charing Cross station, linked to Cardus being in London for a Kreisler recital.

There are some reasons for thinking that 1930 may be the solution:

- no Kreisler recital has been traced around any of the dates in question, raising doubt over the accounts in the *Guardian* and *Full Score*;

- the notebook may be more reliable as it was private and, although not contemporaneous, written nearer to the time in question;

- it is consistent with Cardus referring to knowing her for seven years,[68] since Barbe was to suffer an early death, in 1937 (although in view of Cardus's problems with years and ages this should not be regarded as definitive);

- his Roses match report in the MG in 1930 did, unusually, refer to the Canterbury festival,[69] possibly because the letter he received referred to it and it was on his mind; and the August Roses match was at Old Trafford in that year.

In *Full Score* Cardus indicated that the relationship was consummated at the Charing Cross Hotel after they had heard Sibelius's Symphony No.7 at the Queen's Hall.[70] Cardus did report on such a concert: it took place on 9 October 1933.[71] Unfortunately, this does not help date the first meeting, as while Cardus wrote in *Full Score* that it was two years after they first met,[72] his notebook revealed: "Even after I had loved and known Barbe Ede four years, I was still unawakened, a virgin."[73] Another contradiction!

The year 1930 would not be the solution for the first meeting if we believed that Cardus's absence from the final day of the Leeds Test match in 1929 was due to his spending the day with Milady. However, the conclusion that he went walking in the country allows us to think that 1930 is the most likely year that the affair began.

The liaison involved Barbe accompanying Cardus to Salzburg, Vienna and Paris as well as in London and elsewhere.[74] Brookes indicated that passions cooled over time, with Edith becoming aware of the affair and attempting to contact Barbe's husband, Elton Ede, to help limit the potential damage.[75] Cardus also discovered that Barbe had other extra-marital relationships; it was a bitter-sweet relationship.

Barbe and Cardus did have something else in common: both were cricket journalists, Barbe working for the *Kent Messenger*. That paper, unusually, had a report on the Lord's Test of 1931, headed "Kent woman at the Test match": written by Barbe and presumably arranged to give Cardus and Barbe an opportunity to meet (and get paid at the same time!).[76] When Cardus first visited Canterbury to report on a match for the MG, in 1934, Barbe was also there, working for her local paper.[77] Barbe went on to cover the women's Ashes Tests of 1937 for no less than the MG;[78] one suspects that Cardus helped arrange this. The third such Test was at Maidstone, starting the day after Kent (men)'s match with Lancashire at the same ground, which Cardus had covered on the first day. This timing may well have given the couple the chance to spend time together.

Barbe suffered from asthma and died in Gravesend at the age of 44, on 17 September 1937.[79] That she and Cardus had remained in touch is evident from Cardus's letter to his publisher Rupert Hart-Davis, indicating that he had telephoned her on the day before her death: "she was full of life and laughter. I had arranged for her to go through the proofs of *Australian Summer*."[80]

It is useful to learn more about Barbe Ede.[81] She was born Hilda Elizabeth Huggins in Gravesend on New Year's Day 1893, so she was 11½ years younger than Edith, Cardus's wife. Her parents were Henry and Elizabeth Anne Huggins. The 1901 and 1911 censuses showed the family living in Gravesend, and they had a domestic servant. The father's occupation was journalist although he was a soap manufacturer by the time Barbe married.

Barbe married Ernest Elton Ede in Cheriton, Kent on 23 April 1917. He was then age 25 and serving in the Royal Navy. He had several occupations. His death certificate referred to him as the retired chief accountant for merchant bankers. However, he had a further role that brought him to the notice of the public: he was a journalist, being cricket correspondent for *The Sunday Times*, for whom he was writing from 30 October 1932. Might Cardus have had some input to this appointment?[82] Ede's writing included favourable comment about the contribution of his wife's lover to Thomas Moult's collection, *Bat and Ball*,[83] and in 1937 he called Neville Cardus a "good judge", though went on to dissent from Cardus's view that leg-break bowling was unimportant in England.[84]

Elton Ede continued writing on cricket for *The Sunday Times* until 1956, although he ceased to report on Tests from 1948 (when Cardus worked on the newspaper for two years). He had re-married in 1941 and died in 1969 (on 27 September; he was still alive when Cardus revealed in the *Guardian* the existence but not the name of his former mistress).[85]

Chapter 10

EXTENDING HORIZONS
IN THE LATE 1930s

<hr/>

Austria and Australia:
Neville Cardus's music and cricket 1936–37

Cardus was accustomed to going abroad to report on concerts, but it was only in 1936 that he was able to travel overseas for the purpose of cricket. It is instructive to examine his workload over 1936–37 when he went to the Salzburg Music Festival, a favourite of his, followed by his first journey to Australia, where the MCC tourists would be battling for the Ashes.

In 1936 the Salzburg Festival started on Saturday 26 July. However, Cardus had a busy cricket diary in England, which restricted the time he could spend in Austria. He was at Trent Bridge on 11 August, reporting on Nottinghamshire's draw with Lancashire,[1] but then appears to have missed Lancashire's home match with Glamorgan.[2] His next appointment was at The Oval, where England were playing India, or "All India" as they were called, in the third and final Test match of the summer. England won by 9 wickets on the last day, 18 August. The match wasn't over until nearly 4pm and it was then a case of heading to Salzburg.[3]

Also on 18 August, the MG announced that, "Mr Neville Cardus, 'Cricketer' of the 'Manchester Guardian' will go to Australia this autumn as Special Correspondent of the 'Manchester Guardian' to describe the tour of the

English cricket team and in particular the series of Test matches." Cardus was also to report for the *Melbourne Herald* and the South African *Argus* group of newspapers.

Cardus clearly appreciated the splendour of the Salzburg festival, and his article published on 28 August included, "I have been present during the last few evenings at performances which for beauty of conception and general finish of technique could not easily be excelled in this world". He was especially complimentary about Toscanini: "The ideals set up by Toscanini are so high that only a genius such as his own could reach out to them – with rich resources of execution at his disposal." This piece was credited to "Neville Cardus", as was a further article, appearing on 5 September, which also praised Toscanini: "first of all, a great and pure musician; secondly, he is a consummate orchestral director and technician; then, and thirdly, he is an artist." This did not prevent criticism, though, Cardus's view being that Toscanini's interpretation of Schubert's C major Symphony was entirely wrong: "wonderful music but not Schubert." Cardus was a busy man; on the same day (5 September) his preview of the forthcoming Hallé season appeared, this being credited to N.C.

Cardus had not been back in England for long when he was packing his luggage into a taxi to Waterloo station for the journey to Australia, the first time he was to cover an MCC cricket tour. Unfortunately, he left his umbrella in the taxi.[4] The MG saw the team at the station en route to the ship, and noticed that "Neville Cardus at his window raised his monitory fingers and gave a slightly reassuring gesture."[5] What that gesture was and why it was only slightly reassuring is not explained. They boarded the *Orion,* bound for Australia, on 12 September. They were to arrive in Fremantle on 13 October.[6]

On 31 October, Cardus wrote to W.P. Crozier, editor

of the MG, that Australians were cricket-mad and he was a celebrity. The press clearly thought very highly of him, as exemplified by this article in the *Newcastle Sun*, for which he was to report:

> "Cardus's Shrewd Insight Of The Game
> Neville Cardus, whose stories of cricket are acknowledged to be the finest in the language, will have a greater and happier audience than any cricketer ever had, and he is unique in that he is always in form. 'The Sun' has been fortunate enough to induce him to brave the perils of the sea and the sickness thereof and to forsake his beloved music for six months to make the trip to Australia on the Orion, in its interests."[7]

Similar praise came from the *Melbourne Advocate*:

> "Mr. Neville Cardus, who will be a member of Sir Keith Murdoch's team while in Australia, always plays to the point. This Trumper of the pen can score from any part of the dictionary... he is always in form, being able to turn a flashing phrase, no matter how deadly the bowling may be. His well-flighted metaphors are always impeccably accurate, and he has an uncanny paragraphic length. Cardus always bowls along to a full stop; but he punctuates his deliveries with astonishing correctness... He is one of the few whose word-play would not improve with more use of the cut."[8]

Cardus's first article on the tour for the MG appeared on 17 October, headed "M.C.C. team's first match in Australia. Hats, rain, overcoats and cheap wickets". The day at Perth brought back memories of Manchester, although Australia's rain was said to be pure and undefiled, a natural element, not a chemical or dye. It didn't help that Cardus had left his umbrella in the London taxi. The article was credited to Cricketer. Oddly, the report of the next day's play was by a special correspondent. The article on MCC's victory on the third day was, however, credited to "Neville Cardus (Cricketer)" and this was how his reports appeared for the remainder of the tour.

Perth was not awarded a Test match until 1970 so Cardus's first Test down under was at Brisbane. His preview, published in the MG on the day the match started, 4 December, was dated 15 November, when he was in Sydney. Publication schedules then quickened up; he was able to report on most of the first day's play – up until tea – on 4 December for publication on 5 December. The Test matches started well for England, who won twice, but Australia, with Bradman dominant, recovered to take the series 3–2.

Before he left, Cardus received a letter from the Hill barrackers of Sydney, who appreciated the ability, fairness and style of his reporting.[9] Cardus featured not just in print but also on the radio, giving daily reports on the Test matches.[10]

The Australian press recognised that Cardus was a writer on music as well as cricket, and indeed that music was his real passion; he liked to be known as the music critic of the MG[11] and was described as one of the most eminent music critics in England.[12] Although music criticism was not the object of the stay in Australia, he did go to a performance of *Lilac Time* in Perth. His review in the *West Australian* on 21 October 1936 led to an open letter of complaint:

> "… we do think it is like your superior cheek to write of having gone to His Majesty's on Tuesday night 'resigned to the worst.' 'And the worst always occurs when indifferent artists try to do their best' you added fatuously… If you came out here to write cricket for the 'Manchester Guardian,' why don't you stick to cricket and Manchester?"[13]

Later musical experiences were more favourable. He applauded a production of *The Bartered Bride* ("Your opera students were up to the best London standard for such productions")[14] and praised a young pianist, Vina Barnden.[15]

Cardus did not cover the tourists' matches in New Zealand; he was among the passengers on the *Orontes* when it left Sydney on 10 March, bound for England.[16] His book *Australian Summer* includes, in addition to the detail on the Test matches, his views on the experience, concluding, "Heavens, how I shall miss Sydney this winter, when the cold dark days surround us in England!"[17] As events turned out, he was to be in Sydney in the following winter.

On 22 April Cardus arrived back in Southampton. Although he had expressed the view to Crozier that he would not want too much cricket reporting in the summer,[18] he was present at Old Trafford on 1 May 1937 to report on the first day of the county season, when Derbyshire were the visitors: it was only "mildly interesting".[19] There was a continuation of the practice adopted in the winter of the author being shown as "Neville Cardus (Cricketer)".

Salzburg and Sydney again: 1937–38

It was a busy time when, later in 1937, Cardus was off to Salzburg again. He was met by weather that was unfortunately familiar to him: rain.

Rain appeared to be a feature of Cardus's life. It stopped play in his story of an early match at Old Trafford after MacLaren had opened the batting. Recall that rain meant no play was possible on the first day of Cardus's first Test at Old Trafford for the MG in 1921, while the next Tests there in 1924 and 1926 were also rain-affected. But it would be unjust on Manchester not to add that rain also prevented two days' play in Cardus's first Varsity match at

Lord's, that it followed him to his initial visit to Salzburg in 1931 and that it interfered with his first day's cricket in Australia in 1936.

The August 1937 instalment of rain in Salzburg was depressing: "Since I arrived in Salzburg last week every day has been wet – driving mists of drenching rain."[20] It had a consequence: less play, more work:

> "This article was begun shortly after breakfast: there was no alternative for any of us but work, so dreadful was the rain. I now write the finishing sentence after lunch, at three o'clock. It is raining harder now, and even the traffic on the bridge across the river is quiet."

On returning to England, Cardus was at The Oval on 11 September for the challenge match between championship winners Yorkshire and Middlesex. The good news was that it wasn't wet. The bad news was that it was bitterly cold: "so cold that Hendren at third man blew his fingers and swung his arms like a coachman in Charles Dickens. The excellent crowd wore overcoats and comforters."[21]

Then ill-health meant that Cardus had to cut short his concert-going in the winter. The last Hallé concert he reviewed was on 9 December, when Sir Thomas Beecham was conducting. Cardus sailed to Australia on the *Oronsay*, leaving London on 18 December, bound for Sydney. It was reported that his visit was to improve his health,[22] and the MG confirmed this,[23] although in *Autobiography* the motivation was referred to as cricket.[24] He planned to return to England in March with the Australian cricket touring party. Such a long absence may have been more than what was needed to improve his health: in a letter to Crozier on 17 January he said,

> "I am already cured. But I must have been in a dreadful state – to have envisaged the voyage at all [to Australia]! Now I am aching for work, & for

my friends. Apparently I've been through a sort of crisis…"[25]

Was the crisis a result of overwork? Cardus had experienced long spells of ill-health before. He missed a year's schooling and he had a breakdown before starting to report on cricket at Old Trafford in 1919. His illness in 1921:

> "was as though a garden rake were being clumsily and impatiently drawn through my bowels. For a year or two I had often known terrific pains in the stomach two or three hours after a meal… The cause of the trouble was poor and insufficient food and a nervous system agitated by the fact that C.P. Scott was using me as one of his secretaries."[26]

If work and a poor diet had been the source of the problems in 1921, it may have been the cause of ill-health at other times, including 1937. The year began with Cardus, in Australia, remarking, "I am nearly at breaking point! Murdoch's papers have treated me like a galley slave. I am part of a press gang, hurried to death over every sentence for the next edition!"[27] Not only was the work arduous but the travelling was worse.[28] The work in the Salzburg rain in August added to his woes. On the face of it, things came to a head in the autumn.

Australia was a logical choice for recuperation after Cardus's favourable experience the previous year. He arrived in Sydney on 26 January 1938. Also on board had been one Helen Chambers with her husband and children. A *Sun* (Sydney) journalist reported, "she and [Neville Cardus] found each other immensely diverting, I gather, as they are both riotously amusing conversationalists."[29] We know that Cardus was fond of the sound of his own voice. Fortunately, others were too, and while in Australia he made a number of radio broadcasts on both cricket and music. The music programmes were not formal affairs:

> "Advantage is being taken of the presence of Neville
> Cardus, in Australia on a visit, to furnish listeners
> with talks on music and musicians of a newsy
> character. Two of these gossipy sessions are on this
> week's programmes, and they are of a nature to
> interest, as well as the musical world, all who love
> to hear about the men and women who are making
> good. The title of the first talk is 'The Worthwhile
> Composers of Today' — Wednesday at 9.45pm over
> 3AR, relaying to 2CO and 3GI. The second talk is
> labelled 'You'll Enjoy Some of These — The Celebrity
> Artists Coming'."[30]

Cardus was frequently quoted in the press with his views
on music and, more commonly, cricket. He emphasised
that the purpose of his visit was for his health rather than
as an unofficial spy for the English team.[31] One admission
was his preference for Tests played to the finish, although
such a view was uncommon in England.[32] He thought that
the odds were six to four on Australia in the Test series of
the summer, provided it was dry; even if the weather was
wet, it would be a surprise if England won.[33] As it turned
out, the series finished 1–1 with the game at Old Trafford
abandoned without a ball being bowled and the two other
matches drawn.

Celebrity Cardus was also asked for his views on music;
he expressed his belief that,

> "Australia's best form of musical development lay
> along national lines. The media best suited to this
> were the development of local talent in the direction
> of lieder singing and chamber music in the home.
> The geographical position of the country was an
> advantage as well as a drawback, said Mr. Cardus,
> because there was no chance of a glut of music and

artists, such as was tending in England to make a commodity of music."[34]

Although on holiday, Cardus still wrote occasionally for the MG on cricket. For example, he commented critically on the choice of the Australian tour squad in an article written in Sydney on 4 February, but not published until 26 February.

Cardus returned to England and indeed the press had a photograph of the Australian tour party leaving Melbourne on the *Maloj*a on 8 March, together with Cardus and another English journalist, William Pollock.[35] They stopped off in Fremantle; the Australians played (and beat) Western Australia at Perth on March 18–21. Cardus, together with the Australian Test team, arrived back in London on the *Orontes* on 20 April.

Back in England

Cardus was on duty from the beginning of the cricket season in 1938, seeing the Australians at Worcester. He was among 11,000 in the crowd: "For Worcester cricket the occasion was momentous", although the acute congestion spoiled the graciousness of the place.[36] Naturally, his schedule for the year included the two Roses matches. Sadly for him, both were won by the side from east of the Pennines. Indeed, Yorkshire won 13 of the contests in 1919–39, with only five victories for Lancashire. Another disappointment was the Ashes Test at Old Trafford, completely rained off (it was a four-day match): "The field was an archipelago… The groundsmen became amphibian… At one time I received the impression that they were dragging the river for a body."[37]

This was the one year in the inter-war period when Cardus reported on more matches at Lord's (eight) than in Lancashire (six, including the abandoned Test). His diary for 1938 included several visits to Lord's for fixtures he was familiar with. Gentlemen versus Players was there: he saw this six times in the 1920s, nine in the 1930s. The Varsity match was also on the agenda: three times in the 1920s, seven in the following decade. And, of course, the Lord's Test, not missed since he was first there in 1921. Indeed, he was on duty at all the inter-war home Tests, except for the Oval Test of 1929, when he was at Trent Bridge for "a match that is certain to affect the county championship critically" (Nottinghamshire v Lancashire).[38]

In the English cricket seasons from 1919 to 1939 he reported on 576 matches for the MG: see Appendix 4. Of these, 270 were in Lancashire, although the proportion from his home county fell from 53% in 1919–29 to 39% in 1930–39. He covered home matches for all 17 first-class counties except Glamorgan, although he did visit Cardiff for the Test Trial in 1932.

Not all his work was on grand matches or at prestigious venues. In 1931, when there was a gap in the fixture list of Lancashire, Cardus saw their second eleven play against Northumberland at Werneth, near Oldham. It was a friendly place, although the cricket field was "not a beauty spot" and he lamented that "many of the chimneys were not sending out the smoke of prosperity."[39] The quality of cricket was some way short of first-class and he didn't watch beyond the first innings, although a highlight was seeing the son of Cecil Parkin in the home team.

His staying power was also limited when Lancashire were batting slowly at Edgbaston in 1939 and Cardus "… relieved the afternoon's tedium by watching a game going on outside the ground".[40]

There were times when the MG needed a deputy for its cricket correspondent, for example, when the Salzburg music festival was taking place. Cardus arranged for C.L.R. James to take this role in 1933–35, and his articles, often covering Lancashire, were credited accordingly.[41] James, from Trinidad, was to become famous as a historian and Marxist.

Cardus had reported on an average of 30 matches a year in the 1920s, though this figure was down to 26 in the 1930s. Hamilton wrote about 1937: "[Cardus] seldom went to Old Trafford again; or, indeed, anywhere else. He barely covered more than a dozen matches from May to mid-September. Most of these were at Lord's".[42] The facts are that Cardus's name appeared above reports of 26 matches that season, of which 11 were at Old Trafford and 6 at Lord's.

The beginning of World War II: Neville Cardus's story

The 1930s come to an end with Cardus in England and in *Autobiography* we read of his experience at Lord's on the eve of World War II:[43]

"On the Friday morning [1 September 1939] when Hitler invaded Poland I chanced to be in this same Long Room at Lord's watching through windows for the last time for years. Though no spectators were present, a match was being continued; there was no legal way of stopping it... a beautifully preserved member of Lord's stood near me inspecting the game. Suddenly two workmen entered the Long Room in green aprons and carrying a bag. They took down the bust of W.G. Grace, put it in the bag, and departed with it. The noble lord at my side watched their every movement; then he turned to me. 'Did you see, sir?' he asked. I told him I had seen. 'That means war,' he said."

On checking the records we find that a match had been

taking place at Lord's but it was over in two days, when Middlesex completed their defeat of Warwickshire on the Thursday. Hence no match was taking place on the Friday in question.

On the Wednesday Cardus had been at Old Trafford, reporting on the first day of Lancashire's match with Surrey. He missed the second day, reported by a special correspondent. This was, he wrote, to make arrangements with his wife in connection with the wartime evacuation; then he was taking a holiday at Buxton, staying at the Palace Hotel[44] (the third day's play of the Lancashire match was cancelled). Cardus did write elsewhere that he was in London on Sunday 3 September, walking in St James's Park, although the account is fanciful;[45] even if true, it doesn't explain being at Lord's on the preceding Friday instead of the contemporaneous evidence that he was to be at Buxton.

In *Full Score*, Cardus repeated his story, confirming that the match was between Middlesex and Warwickshire, adding, "Nobody was present to watch it, excepting a few elderly faithfuls… Now happened the incident I have described elsewhere. Nobody has believed that actually it did happen, yet it is true."[46]

There is one other possible interpretation of events. The MG reported that on 29 August the valuable oil paintings of cricket scenery and celebrities in the Lord's Long Room were being taken down, together with other relics of the game, for removal to a place of safety.[47] The process may have taken more than a day: a photograph of the removal of Lord's cricket treasures was included in *The Times* of 31 August. At around the same time the Middlesex v Surrey match was taking place on 26–29 August.

So, did Cardus attend this match and was it at this earlier game when he saw W.G. Grace's bust removed? In 1941 he did write, "In 1939 I attended the match between

Middlesex and Surrey, which began on the eve of the outbreak of war. The place was sad".[48] Three factors suggest this is not the right answer.

First, the reports in the MG of matches played on 26–29 August have no mention of Cardus, so we conclude it was highly unlikely that he was present at the match. It is possible that he was there in a personal capacity but as he was not a member of MCC it is not clear that he would have been permitted to enter the Long Room.

Second, on the Saturday of the match there were around 8,000 people present[49] and while the numbers would have been lower on the Monday and Tuesday it would not seem consistent with Cardus's remarks regarding few people being at Lord's.

Third, in the article where Cardus claimed he was at the Middlesex v Surrey match, he told a story not about the removal of the bust, but rather explaining that he was in conversation with an old man who was making a comparison with 1914.[50]

The only further point to add is that Cardus was at Lord's for the Middlesex v Somerset match which finished on 25 August and he did comment, "Lord's was almost empty this morning…"[51] However, there is no evidence that this was when the bust was removed and Cardus certainly did not suggest it.

In conclusion, the story of the removal of W.G. Grace's bust is a good one but, despite the protestation that it was true, it appears it was only a story: there wasn't a match at Lord's that day and Cardus wasn't there as he was on holiday.

Chapter 11

A CELEBRITY IN AUSTRALIA
1940 TO 1947

━━━━ ⟨∞⟩ ━━━━

Cardus visited Australia on seven occasions, and Table 5 summarises his time there. We now turn from September 1939 to Cardus's decision to return to Australia, this time for over seven years.

Table 5. Neville Cardus's visits to Australia

From	To	Reason
October 1936	March 1937	MCC tour of Australia
January 1938	March 1938	Holiday for health reasons
February 1940	May 1947	Lengthy stay
November 1947	March 1948	Continuation of stay after visit to England summer 1947
January 1949	April 1949	Continuation of stay after visit to England summer 1948
October 1950	March 1951	MCC tour of Australia
November 1954	March 1955	MCC tour of Australia

Following the outbreak of war, Cardus wrote in *Full Score* that his two occupations, as music critic and cricket writer, were gone; he could not continue drawing his salary from the MG with self-respect.[1] He asserted that, a week or two after the incident of the removal of W.G. Grace's bust, he heard his last concert in London for nearly a decade: Beecham at the Queen's Hall.[2] In fact, this was rather later, on 16 November,[3] and there followed several concerts in Manchester on which he reported. These included, on 24 December, a performance by the Hallé of *Messiah* with Malcolm Sargent conducting.[4] It is only fair to add that he felt that using the Paramount cinema for Hallé concerts left something to be desired;[5] it was used owing to the unavailability of the Free Trade Hall (taken over as a store[6]).

Cardus decided to go to Australia, to which he was becoming accustomed, and the announcement in the MG was on 10 January 1940:

"Mr Neville Cardus, the well-known writer on music and on cricket has been granted leave of absence by the 'Manchester Guardian' in order to visit Australia. Mr Cardus will write in the 'Melbourne Herald' and its associated papers mainly on music; and also on cricket which it is expected will continue in Australia with its usual intensity. He will take an advisory part in the musical direction of the Australian Broadcasting Commission.

Mr Cardus is already well known to a large Australian public both from his work in the 'Manchester Guardian' and from his articles in the Australian press during the last M.C.C. tour in Australia. He will contribute to the 'Manchester Guardian' on cricket and music as they are played in Australia during wartime."

Australia offered music and cricket in a way that England did not, and Cardus was doubtless encouraged by his positive experiences of Sydney. He described the time when he bought his ticket:

"But one December day when I was walking down Haymarket, my eye was attracted to a poster in many colours. This poster extolled the pleasures of air-travel. It depicted a 'plane fashioned out of silver and gossamer. More fascinating still, it depicted a bevy of alluring girls exquisitely dressed, all leaning negligently on the wings, drinking cocktails – all presided over by, apparently, the Blessed Damosel leaning out of the gold bar of heaven. I immediately went into the office of the company which displayed the poster and bought a ticket."[7]

It is fair to think that events were not quite as described!

In early January 1940 Cardus went to Australia by flying boat, the first time he had ever flown.[8] An inconvenience was that the sea plane did not fly at night so each day the passengers had to get off the plane in order to sleep ashore. They stayed at a different hotel each time, although this gave the opportunity to stop off at places including Calcutta and Singapore. It was 11 February when he arrived in Darwin, Northern Territory.[9] The press soon sought the views of Cardus, who said he regretted that so many leading English cricketers were being called up for the war.[10]

Although Cardus's contract was with the *Melbourne Herald*, he quickly found that writing about music for an evening paper did not work, and transferred his allegiance to the *Sydney Morning Herald*. What was the programme for the first concert he reported on for his new employer? In *Full Score* he recalled that it was a hackneyed collection of pieces such as Weber's *Oberon* overture, an early Schubert symphony and Beethoven's Symphony No.5.[11] Cardus was consistent in *Conversations*, when he recalled that the programme included the works by Weber and Beethoven, "and some other work that I'd heard a thousand times."[12]

However, the earliest review traced was on 18 March, when Cardus heard the third symphony of Brahms, the second symphony of Sibelius and Franck's *Symphonic Variations*. He admitted that he was both pleased and disappointed by his experience.

The original commission from the *Melbourne Herald* had been for Cardus to cover the concerts of Sir Thomas Beecham. It was only on 11 June that Beecham arrived and, shortly after, he was interviewed by Cardus on radio, although without any preparation and with Beecham not at his best, the outcome was some unsatisfactory disconnected dialogue.[13] Cardus turned out to be very positive in his appreciation of the concerts conducted by Beecham and indicated that he was talking, lunching and dining with him for three or more months.[14] He wrote that Sir Thomas did remarkable things with the Australian orchestras: "I have never before known him perform transformation acts as remarkable as these upon the orchestras of Australia. Audiences have roared their delight".[15] Overall, Cardus was pleasantly surprised by the amount of music that was played: "Music flourishes in Australia at the present time as never before. At least the public appetite for concerts increases even if the standards of performance occasionally waver and wobble."[16]

Cardus became well known for his broadcasting, especially his weekly series on Sunday evenings entitled *The Enjoyment of Music*, which appears to have been first broadcast on 13 October 1940.[17] He also gave radio talks for children, the feedback from which gave him much pleasure.[18] Cardus was, however, unaware that he needed a licence to own a radio, and he was fined £5; he may have been less than impressed by his being described as art critic and radio announcer in the press report of the case.[19]

He was known in Australia for his dual role as writer on music and cricket, and wrote as Neville Cardus when writing on each subject. Indeed, he could speak on both subjects to the same audience:

> "Neville Cardus, famous cricket writer and music critic of the 'Manchester Guardian,' is swiftly establishing himself as a landmark in Melbourne's cultural landscape. With Test cricket in eclipse because of the war, Cardus is using the other string to his bow in a performance to which most of Melbourne is listening… Yesterday he spent lunchtime talking to Melbourne University graduates about 'The Bat and the Baton.' Epigrams aplenty enlivened the meal. Here are some sample 'Cardus-isms':
>
> Bradman is the Toscanini of cricket: he bats with the same sort of ordered science. He does not impose himself too much on the game… A batsman can make a cricket match an allegro or a funeral march."[20]

Cardus's recollections in *Full Score*

Full Score has a chapter devoted to Cardus's stay in Australia from 1940 to 1947. This was supposedly "largely fantasy" according to Muriel Wayland, née Cohen, a pianist whom Cardus admired.[21] It is therefore of interest to investigate some of the incidents that he described: true or not?

Cardus was involved in a controversy about the use of the German language during the war. He mentioned that there was correspondence in the *Sydney Morning Herald* concerning whether German should be used in coaching lieder at the Sydney Conservatorium of Music, the prestigious music school.[22] While this issue did arise in the newspaper's columns,[23] Cardus's contribution was on the related subject of whether it was appropriate for songs to be sung during the war using the German language.

He had already written an article on 1 March 1941 criticising those who thought that it was everybody's duty to drive out German art and music from their life. Later that month came news that at the August 1941 Sydney eisteddfod no singer would be allowed to give a German song in the German language, a ruling with which he strongly disagreed in a letter to the *Herald* on 27 March. This brought a response from Roland Foster, professor of singing at the Conservatorium and proponent of the "no German" policy; he argued that the war was not only with Hitler and Goering but with a nation. Cardus responded on 3 April, quoting Churchill in support of his argument and saying that as a matter of logic Foster should object to teaching the German language in Australian schools and universities. Foster pointed out on 7 April that no objections had been raised to the decision that the French and Italian languages should also not be used in songs at the eisteddfod. Cardus added a further short letter to the *Herald* on 9 April to finish the correspondence on the subject. When the eisteddfod went ahead in August not only were all songs sung in English but the term "lieder" was replaced by "art songs".[24] The Sydney eisteddfod was suspended for the remainder of the war and resumed in 1946.

In 1941 Edgar Bainton conducted the first public performance of the symphony he had composed, and Cardus wrote in *Full Score* that he praised it in his notice. He had felt, though, that Bainton would do better if thoroughly acquainted with the score, a comment that the *Herald* sub-editor thought illogical as the conductor was also the composer.[25] The sub-editor had the last word, as the comment did not appear in the notice as published.[26]

Schubert's *Trout* Quintet was the subject of a recital in 1944 by the daughter of an Australian politician. Cardus wrote in *Full Score* "to the effect that she changed it to an

Australian schnapper, a toughish fish in home waters."[27] It is possible to trace that the notice concerned a recital by Gertrude Concannon, whose father James was a member of the Australian parliament.[28] The actual words included in the review at the time were, "'The Trout' of Schubert was changed into a Flounder."[29]

Full Score then related the consequence of this incident, namely a question asked in Parliament by Senator Lamp, "How much longer are the people of Australia to be pestered with Neville Cardus?"[30] That indeed happened, and Lamp was urging the Postmaster-General to stop Cardus's broadcasts with the Australian Broadcasting Commission. The Postmaster-General replied that Cardus was only employed casually by the ABC in giving a weekly broadcast, the last in the series to be on 8 October.[31]

Cardus recalled, in *Full Score*, the transformational effect of conductor Eugene Ormandy arriving in Sydney round about 1944, and described his performance of Brahms' second symphony as "polished 'to the nines'".[32] It is possible to date the concert in question: it was the conductor's first concert in Australia, on 10 June 1944. Cardus's review in the *Sydney Morning Herald* demonstrated clearly how much he admired it, remarking that Ormandy's impact on both orchestra and audience was electrical.[33] No memory failure on this occasion.

Marjorie Lawrence was described by Cardus as "the greatest artist of song and opera produced so far from Australia".[34] She toured internationally and, having contracted polio in 1941, her only visit to Australia in the 1940s was in 1944.[35] In *Full Score* Cardus praised her singing the *Liebestod* from *Tristan and Isolde*.[36] This can be identified as a concert at Sydney Town Hall on 7 October 1944 when Cardus's comments were indeed positive, referring in the *Sydney Morning Herald* to her singing with rare vocal splendour.[37]

The admission in *Full Score*, "I became notorious in Sydney",[38] illustrated Cardus's reputation as a harsh critic. One example of an unfavourable review, from 1940, concerned Australian-born composer Miriam Hyde, whose work *Heroic Elegy* he regarded as "the sort of sincere, mild stuff which a gifted student in a not particularly gifted advanced class in London could turn out on any occasion without excessive provocation."[39] Miriam Hyde's obituary indicated that she had a robust response: she set up the Australian Composers' Guild.[40]

Cardus's musical criticism could be stinging, although his views would not always be shared by the concert audience, which may have contributed to the view that he was severe in coming to a verdict. He made disparaging comments in *Full Score* about Georges Thill, a singer known for his gramophone records, suggesting that he needed a new needle.[41] The concert in question took place at Sydney Town Hall on 22 August 1946, when Cardus wrote that he would have preferred a softer needle.[42] Not one to mince words, he went on to claim that there were at least three Australian-born tenor singers capable of "a finer vocalism and a finer sense of atmosphere and style than Georges Thill conveyed at his concert." He felt he was a better judge than the vast audience, which "applauded without much discrimination his most painfully nasal tones, his harsh unimaginative top notes, and his wooden out-moded 'vocalism'."

Humour was an alternative way to convey a message and, in *Full Score*, Cardus gave two examples from his reviews.[43] First was a recital by pianist Paul Schramm, who was giving numerous recitals at the time, and Cardus suggested that instead of counting sheep to get to sleep, he could count concerts by Schramm; "and when I reach 57 the chances are that I'll be jerked into acute wakefulness, and find myself at a Schramm recital." This is indeed what Cardus wrote in the *Sydney Morning Herald* of 26 September 1946. The review brought forth a reply from Schramm in the form of a letter to the editor, accepting the humorous spirit in which the review was written:

"Sir, – I have read Mr Cardus's report on my recital, and wish to express my gratitude for pointing out shortcomings. I shall give my attention to these points and hope to gain better artistic results in future. I have been very amused by his introduction to the critical part of the report. It is true Euston M. Greene puts on many recitals for me. Probably he does this because he still can make them pay. I cannot see any other reason for it. We went into consultation about Mr Cardus's sleepless nights. And as we both wish him sincerely a good many restful occasions, it was decided to stop giving concerts in Sydney before reaching the ominous figure 57 – and finding him again at a Schramm recital. He will have to 'count sheep' again.

Paul Schramm"[44]

The second humorous example also relates to Paul Schramm although he is not specifically mentioned. Cardus explained in *Full Score* that he wrote his notice of a concert including Beethoven's Symphony No.5 using terms applicable to the English Grand National: "At the first fence the second horn fell, at Becher's Brook the first trumpet and third trombone fell... Also ran, Beethoven."[45] The concert took place on 5 November 1946, the date when the race for the Melbourne Cup was staged. However, the work was Beethoven's Fifth Piano Concerto, with Clive Douglas as conductor and Paul Schramm as pianist. According to Cardus they broke all records for pace, and the newspaper headline was "Cup Influence On Tempo Of

Orchestra".[46] Schramm had been born in Austria and his activities had been restricted during the war so it was only 1946 when he moved to Sydney to revive his international career.[47]

In *Full Score* Cardus discussed, in glowing terms, two concerts with Israeli pianist Pnina Salzman, one on the day that saw the end of the war, and a later performance of Beethoven's *Appassionata* Sonata.[48] The first recital in her series which Cardus reviewed was on Wednesday 9 May 1945; the other was at a concert later that month; in both cases the reviews were indeed outstanding.[49]

Another incident in *Full Score* is where Cardus gave career advice to Peter Finch, Charles Mackerras and Joan Sutherland and, in each case, failed to recognise their potential for worldwide recognition.[50] The reference to Joan Sutherland came after she sang in Eugene Goossens' opera *Judith,* at the Sydney Conservatorium. However, the performance concerned was on 9 June 1951, when Cardus was back in England.[51] It is not possible to check whether the advice to Finch and Mackerras was truly as stated. However, the information about Sutherland confirms that Cardus could embellish the facts to improve a story, even a story he told against himself.

Cricket in Australia

Cricket was not the main object of the stay in Australia, but Cardus was still thinking about Lord's, writing in the MG, "Heaven, am I ever going to walk into the Long Room on a hot day escaping from the sun; am I ever again going to feel the shadiness and dignity of the Long Room as I see around me all the pictures and relics of the game's history?"[52]

The Australian chapter of *Full Score* makes no mention of the cricket that Cardus saw. Arriving in 1940 he was, however, in time to see and report on the final match of the first-class cricket season, between New South Wales, Sheffield Shield winners, and the Rest, played at Sydney on 8, 9 and 11 March.[53]

There was some first-class cricket in Australia in 1940–41 but it was not a priority for Cardus, whose job on the *Sydney Morning Herald* was music critic. Thereafter, the worsening war situation meant that no such cricket was played in Australia from 1941–42 to 1944–45. The first Tests after the war were in 1946–47, against England. Cardus reported on all five matches for the *Sydney Morning Herald*, writing a column headed "As Cardus sees it". The series included matches at Adelaide, Brisbane and Melbourne as well as two at Sydney. His reports also appeared in the MG, where they were shown as being by Neville Cardus, and in *The Times* where they were credited to an unnamed special correspondent.

Cardus's cricket reports generated a more favourable reception than his music reviews if the letter below published in the *Sydney Morning Herald* is representative:

"Sir, – having wholeheartedly disagreed on many occasions with the forthright and, seemingly to me, almost bigoted denunciation and 'wipe-offs' contained in the music criticisms of Neville Cardus, it gives me considerable pleasure to have been forced into a revision of my estimate of that critic's perspicacity and integrity as revealed by his sparkling and amusing cricket commentaries…

One sincerely wishes that there were Test cricket to be 'Cardus–ized' every day in the year. He brings to the too–often prosaic pages of the daily paper a zest and sparkle as refreshing as the tang of vintage champagne. He gets into one's nose and one's hair, but delightfully. His audacity is of Elizabethan magnitude, his shafts and flighted barbs of wit more diverting than any comic strip.

I am sorry if this is a bit of a rave, but it is a pity that only Test cricket can give us this truly amazing and amusing Cardus. Someone ought to think of something to keep him in the daily Press the year round.

Lawrie Brooks"[54]

Edith and the lady friends

Edith followed Neville to Australia, though only in 1941. It was on 25 October that she sailed from Liverpool to Sydney on the *Port Alma*, citing Australia as her intended country of permanent residence.

Edith lived separately from Neville in Sydney, allowing him to concentrate on his writing. They kept in close touch, although Edith's photo album from Australia had few pictures that included her husband. She occupied herself with art and drama, and was a speaker at a number of functions.[55] Edith wrote in 1944, "I am doing much painting and helping the University Drama."[56] She was registered as an elector in New South Wales in 1949, giving her occupation as artist.

Cardus kept in close touch with Edith in Sydney. However, he believed that Australian girls and women revelled to show their femininity[57] and was not short of other female company. It is known that he had been friendly with artist Joan Morrison. Claude McKay wrote, "When Neville Cardus first came to Australia he succumbed to the naughtiness of the Morrison girl and requested specimens of Joan's original drawings."[58] Cardus regarded her highly as an artist: "She has depicted the Australian girl in all her grace as no other artist has succeeded in doing."[59] In *Full Score* he wrote that when in Australia he was involved with three women.[60] They are not named (no surprise). Angus McLachlan, former news editor of the *Sydney Morning*

Herald, thought that Cardus's "relations with [attractive young women] rarely went further than comradeship."[61]

Return to England 1947

Why did Cardus return to England in 1947? In an article in the *Sydney Morning Herald* he said he wanted to find out how music was reviving elsewhere and to renew standards.[62] He wrote in *Second Innings* of his need for spiritual refreshment from London.[63] In *Full Score* he added a further reason: William Collins were publishing his autobiography.[64]

He left for England by flying boat on 29 May 1947.[65] He was, however, embarrassed when the previous week the Australian press learnt of a letter that Cardus had written in 1945 to his friend and theatre critic James Agate, who had included an extract from the letter in a book published in 1946.[66] The letter was said to have achieved the prominence of the Zinovieff letter.[67] The extract included:

> "I am sick of Australia… I have not heard ONE witty remark from an Australian in five and a half years. Dein bin ich, Vater! – rette mich! [Thine am I, father! Rescue me!]
>
> Ever, Neville"

It was reported that Cardus wrote this when he was upset after listening to a very bad musician.[68]

The letter to Agate presents a different picture from Cardus's comments in *Conversations* that the period 1940–47 represented "seven of the most wonderful and happy years I've ever known" and if he were allowed to repeat two periods of his life he would choose his first five years with the MG and every day of his seven years in Australia. He added, though, "Mind you, there were moments when I wanted to get away."[69]

Chapter 12

THE METRONOME YEARS AND SETTLING BACK IN ENGLAND

Cricket in England 1947

Cardus went back to England but his stay would be only temporary. For a few years he was "travelling backward and forward between England and Australia with something of the air of an angular metronome".[1]

Cardus no longer wanted the routine day-to-day reporting of cricket.[2] He did, however, write for the MG – as Neville Cardus rather than Cricketer – on three of the Test matches against South Africa. He was living in London, based at the National Liberal Club. His visit to Lord's in June was an emotional one:

> "The native returned to Lord's on Saturday to find that the passing of time and change and transition have left the place the same and even more delectable… The native came home sometimes with a lump in his throat."[3]

In July, Old Trafford had a chilly wind and slow South African batting to greet Cardus on arriving back at his home ground: "On a severely cold day a large crowd at Old Trafford submitted willingly to an amount of austerity such as no government would have the courage to impose on the most long suffering of people."[4]

Cardus had seen England win twice, but the further Test he saw, the final match of the series at The Oval, was drawn after a magnificent defensive performance by the visitors on the final day.[5] England ended up 3–0 winners of the five-match series.

Music in England 1947

A highlight of Cardus's concert-going for the MG was his visit to the inaugural Edinburgh Festival: he was impressed by the quality of the music and found the organisation of the festival to be excellent.[6] Particularly pleasing was the Hallé Orchestra. Conscious of the appearances at the festival of several performers with an international reputation, Cardus wrote that, "John Barbirolli and the Hallé not only stood up to this challenge boldly: they confronted it with assurance and plenty. They lost no time in making a contribution of distinction."[7] This was also the first occasion when he heard the voice of Kathleen Ferrier, satisfying him "beyond reasonable expectations."[8]

The metronome in action:
return to Australia 1947–48

His return to Australia was by flying boat, arriving in Darwin on 30 November 1947 on his way to Sydney.[9] He could read reviews of *Autobiography*, which the advertisement by publishers Collins in the *Sydney Morning Herald* called the "Best reviewed book of the year".[10]

Cardus's primary role was as music critic for the *Sydney Morning Herald*. He recognised how important his opinions could be; after all, he wrote that, in Australia, "music criticism is almost as illiterate as dramatic criticism."[11] He was conscious that he had been accused of unkindness to young Australian artists but was happy to promote the promise of lieder singer Eleanor Houston based on a rehearsal he heard.[12]

The talks on music that Cardus gave on radio started again on 11 January 1948.[13] They continued to be well received; his broadcast on Mahler (also on the BBC Third Programme) was "a notable contribution to musical criticism interspersed with records of Mahler's music... certainly made us feel more friendly towards him".[14]

Cardus said that he would treat cricket as pleasure,[15] although the press still had an appetite for anything he said on the subject, and picked up his praise of Bradman as "the brain and the vertebrae of Australian cricket, its government and executive."[16]

In England again: summer 1948

Cardus left Sydney on 10 March 1948 to travel on the *Strathaird* to England.[17] The attraction was the Ashes series, the last Tests in which the visitors would include Don Bradman, with whom Cardus had a good relationship; "[h]e is as good as a batsman as Bach was as a composer".[18] The Australian cricket touring party were on the same boat.[19] Lord Beaverbrook had attempted to recruit Cardus to report on the Tests for the *Sunday Express* but too late;[20] he had already agreed to write for *The Sunday Times*. England were soundly defeated 4–0 in the five-match series.

However, it was music that was on Cardus's mind: he had said he was looking forward to a rest in London when not writing the music column for *The Sunday Times* or engaged in another autobiography.[21] Writing the music column was based on the verbal promise from W.W. Hadley of *The Sunday Times* that he would succeed Ernest Newman as principal music critic on his retirement, expected to be on his 80th birthday (November 1948).[22] But he had jumped the gun as Newman didn't retire. Beaverbrook arranged for Cardus to become music critic at the *Evening Standard*; Cardus was sceptical as to whether working for the evening paper would work out; it didn't, and he resigned.[23]

Cardus's autobiography was adapted for and broadcast on radio,[24] and there were other radio appearances.

It appears that Edith stayed in Australia: she was scheduled to give a talk in the series of Arts Council lectures, "Before the curtain rises", on 1 September 1948.[25]

Return to Australia 1948/49

Cardus complained that, in London, the true devoted sense of art was not fashionable, and questioned whether the critic could do anything worthwhile; "So I am going back for a while to Sydney, to a land where, in all things, the future is – if the Irishism is permissible – in front and not behind."[26] Although "for a while" suggested that his commitment to Australia was less than wholehearted, the ship's passenger list recorded his country of intended permanent future residence as Australia. Health may also have played a part in the decision to return. Cardus wrote to a friend Franzi, that he hadn't been well in England and "so I am going back to get my strength back in the sunshine."[27]

It took Cardus just one month to get back to Sydney. He was on the maiden voyage of *Orcades*, leaving London on 14 December 1948. The passage to Fremantle, in 22 days, was a record.[28] He arrived in Sydney on 14 January 1949.

Cardus was able to see the birth of a new newspaper: the *Sunday Herald*, a sister to the *Sydney Morning Herald*. He wrote regularly for it and, in the first issue, focussed on some Australians making an impression in London's musical life.[29] His positive approach here contrasted with a comment made earlier in the month that composition of music did not exist in Australia, which was not well received.[30]

Controversy arose following publication of a new book, *Of Musical Things*, written by a musical sociologist

Dr Alphonse Silbermann, lecturer in music at Sydney Conservatorium. It contained some strident criticism of Neville Cardus in particular who, it was argued, lacked relevant technical knowledge. One newspaper headlined its review, "A sour note for Cardus".[31] Cardus used the *Sunday Herald* to reply, arguing that musical criticism is a skill in itself requiring the ability to write intelligently and fairly.[32]

Australian broadcasting continued to feature Cardus. *The Age* (Melbourne), in its review of radio programmes, highlighted on 19 March 1949 that, for musical people, his *Music Critic on Holiday* should be the best bet for the week. His role in Australian music life was illustrated by he and Edith being guests at the Music Lovers' Club in Sydney on 8 April 1949.[33]

Cricket was not forgotten: Cardus reported that he saw a considerable amount of grade cricket (high-class club cricket) in Australia in January and March and was particularly impressed by the quality of the bowling.[34]

Making a home back in England: 1949

Cardus returned to England in spring 1949. His publisher Rupert Hart-Davis provided this description, "In person he is slight, lean and spectacled: in character, ascetic, unbusinesslike and diffident."[35] There were again comments in Australian newspapers that he had accepted the position of music critic at *The Sunday Times*.[36] It is not clear how this came to be reported; Newman was continuing his job there, notwithstanding having turned 80 in 1948. When back in England Cardus's view was that Newman was "scholarly and witty as ever".[37] Elsewhere, readers were told that Cardus had been offered a musical appointment in London, meaning less time for cricket in the future.[38] No specific music role was, in fact, lined up.

The passenger list for the *Strathaird*, which left Sydney

on 16 April 1949, showed that Neville Cardus was travelling back to England, now his country of intended permanent future residence.[39] Cardus arrived in London on 21 May. He based himself at the National Liberal Club.[40] Edith travelled later, leaving Sydney on the *Orcades* on 28 January 1950; this followed the last of many farewell parties, at the home of Elizabeth Ogilvie.[41]

In the summer of 1949 Cardus completed his second (and final) year's work on cricket for *The Sunday Times*. He was now very much a Lord's man, which was where he reported on 15 matches, including 2 Tests, over his two-year stint for the paper in 1948–49. Over the river he was at The Oval on 4 occasions, including 2 Tests. Visits to the North were infrequent: just for the 2 Tests at each of Old Trafford and Headingley (where he also saw a Roses match). A Test and a county game at Trent Bridge and Kent v Surrey at Blackheath made up his total of 27 match reports.

Australia 1950–51: a tour for both cricket and music

Although Cardus had no intention of making his home in Australia, he was back there for the MCC tour of 1950–51. Not only did he plan to watch the Tests; he also wanted to attend the concerts that Sir John Barbirolli was giving.[42] Cardus travelled with the MCC tour party on the liner *Stratheden*, leaving London on 14 September and arriving in Fremantle on 9 October 1950.[43]

Hallé conductor Sir John Barbirolli was to conduct concerts organised by the Australian Broadcasting Commission as part of the Commonwealth Jubilee celebrations. Barbirolli was also enthusiastic about cricket: he claimed to be the only person of Franco-Italian parentage (although he was born in England) who had such an interest.[44] It was reported:

"Test cricket has lured Sir John Barbirolli... to Australia, when earlier invitations failed... He could not find the time to visit Australia as guest conductor before. But this year he was told a tour would be arranged so that he could see two Test matches, with rehearsals at night. Keen cricket fan Barbirolli found this irresistible."[45]

Cardus was again broadcasting on music on radio with weekly sessions of *The Enjoyment of Music*. Indeed, the *Age* (Melbourne) reported, "The brightest musical spot was the last of the Neville Cardus Enjoyment of Music sessions on Tuesday night from 3LO, which gave a close analysis of the Delius violin concerto".[46]

The Test series was won 4–1 to Australia, although Cardus felt 3–2 would have been a better reflection of the performance.[47]

Cardus returned home on the *Strathaird*, which left Sydney on 3 March.[48] He was with other journalists and those members of the touring party who did not go on the New Zealand leg of the tour.[49] Arrival in London was on 9 April.

Music in 1951 and thereafter

Following the retirement in 1951 of Granville Hill as the MG's principal music critic, there was an opportunity for Cardus to rejoin the employer with whom he had grown up, in the role of London music critic.[50] He learned of his duties in a meeting on 12 October 1951; in addition to concert reviews there were to be fortnightly general articles, which would be his *Music Surveys*.[51] It was somewhat earlier that he had started writing again for the newspaper, with Cardus admitting on 16 July that, "It's a great pleasure to be writing for the old paper again; but I'm nervous as a beginner".[52] On 20 July his review of a book on Viennese music appeared, with the byline Neville Cardus. His notices from the Edinburgh Festival that were published on August 28 and 30 were shown to be by N.C.: the pieces featured were the fourth symphonies of Bruckner and Vaughan Williams. His first London review was of a concert at the Royal Festival Hall on 9 October, when Vladimir Horowitz played Rachmaninov's Third Piano Concerto.[53] This, like subsequent work, was attributed to Neville Cardus. The series of *Music Surveys* began with a piece on Hugo Wolf on 1 December 1951; the last was on 1 April 1958 entitled "The critic and his readers".

Being based in London didn't mean he was restricted to London, especially when haunts of old beckoned. Although he only had fleeting visits to Manchester after 1939,[54] Cardus travelled to his home city for the reopening of the rebuilt Free Trade Hall on 16 November 1951. Barbirolli conducted the Hallé and Cardus wrote that there were "tumultuous and moving moments".[55] He was abroad for the reopening of the Vienna State Opera in November 1955.[56] Cardus was pleased that his London diary led him to attend a concert at the Royal Festival Hall by the Hallé in 1960, where he was able to report that the orchestra had "recovered from recent technical failings and is itself again."[57]

Test match reports in England: 1953

Disagreement arose over the appointment of Cardus to report for the MG on the Ashes Tests of 1953.[58] In 1952 Cardus had received an enquiry from elsewhere about covering the series but wished to know if he would be able to report for the MG, which he would prefer. Editor A.P. Wadsworth sought the views of sports editor Larry Montague who, back in 1946, had expressed the view that, in Manchester, Cardus's name was "mud" and had written a letter to Cardus that Wadsworth found tactless.

Montague's view in 1952 was no more favourable. He admitted he was prejudiced: partly because of Cardus's revelations in *Autobiography* about his mother (who was a respected neighbour of his) and partly because of his actions during the war, when Cardus left England for less troubled Australia. There were other reasons, including the problem of having a separate cricket correspondent who would be excluded from the Tests. Montague's criticisms continued, at least some of which appear based on fact:

"… since the war he has not even been writing good Cardus. There is a continuous yearning for the beautiful, allegedly beautiful that is to say, past, which has become almost nauseating. I know from watching him that he does not watch the cricket properly even during Tests on many occasions. I have gathered from cricketers that he is now considered rather a sad joke by many of them. His lack of consideration for his own sports staff was excellently illustrated by his failure to cover or report that he could not or would not cover matches he had contracts to cover early this season… I know that every member of the present sports room would be most reluctant to have to work with a man whom they trust in no way either as a journalist or as a private individual."

Wadsworth ignored Montague's personal likes and dislikes and had a different approach to Cardus's writing: "The M.G. has built up a certain style of cricket writing. Impressionist if you like and distressing to the academic soul. Our readers have liked it. They may be stupid but there it is." Cardus was in for the Tests.

As luck would have it, the series had a momentous end. In the MG of 20 August 1953 Cardus applauded England regaining the Ashes at The Oval after a wait of 19 years (the previous four matches of the series had all been drawn).

His article, headed "A rare old day for England", appeared on page 1 and was followed with further coverage on page 2, "Last taut hours at The Oval".

A final visit to Australia: 1954–55

MCC were touring Australia in 1954–55. Cardus had envisaged going there to report for the MG who, unaware of this, had arranged for their cricket correspondent Denys Rowbotham to cover the tour.[59] As it happened, Cardus was ordered by two specialists to spend the winter away from England to help cure his sinus problems. So, he did go to Australia, travelling to Sydney on the *Oronsay*. This departed from London on 13 October, arriving in Fremantle on 4 November and Sydney on 11 November. Edith joined him, leaving London on 8 December on the *Orsova*. At the Tests Cardus provided occasional reflective offerings for the MG, while Rowbotham wrote the day-to-day reports.

At the outset of the tour Cardus had forecast that England would beat Australia, "given the will".[60] They went on to win the five-match series 3–1. Cardus missed the Australian victory at Brisbane; he stayed in Sydney.[61] Notwithstanding his optimism, Cardus wrote that this was one of the most surprising Ashes series victories; he had been disappointed by the weakness of the Australian side.[62]

How much of the Tests Cardus watched is open to question. MCC tour manager Geoffrey Howard wrote, "I don't think he saw a ball bowled in any of them – perhaps a little at Sydney but that is all [emphasis in original]."[63] Cardus, incidentally, wrote that he also saw some state cricket and Saturday club matches.[64]

Although Cardus anticipated also reporting on the Tests for the *Sydney Morning Herald*, most of his writing for them and the MG was on music, on which subject he was also heard on the radio.[65]

The attractions of Australia were lessening. He wrote that, "the main atmosphere of an Australian concert-hall or theatre is one of a provincial 'social' self-consciousness". [66] He complained that cricket crowds were "noisy, unreflective, hearty, familiar, with too many children about", this also being his main complaint about life in Australia, where he thought graciousness and charm were rare. [67]

It is not surprising that there were to be no further trips to Australia. Cardus left in the second week of March on the *Orsova*, arriving in London on 11 April 1955. Edith had already made her own way back to England, arriving in London on 21 March on the *Stratheden*. The metronome could be laid to rest.

Neville Cardus: recognition of his life

In the Queen's Birthday honours in June 1964, Cardus was appointed CBE; he was described as journalist and writer. In the New Year's honours 1967 he was knighted for services to cricket and music. One comment was, "… surely he was knighted for having become something of a national treasure. That is the usual reason." [68] Cardus enjoyed the recognition even if later than ideal: in 1958 he wrote, "It is really a pity I haven't been knighted – it would have been much easier for people to meet me." [69]

Among many other honours, two were especially valued as they reminded Cardus of his childhood life in Manchester. [70] These were the Hallé concerts to commemorate his time with the *Guardian* (see below), and his presidency of the Lancashire County Cricket Club, beginning on 4 February 1971 for two years. [71]

Recognition: Hallé concerts to honour Cardus

Cardus enjoyed the two concerts with the Hallé as an appreciation of his work for the *Guardian*, although his memory for dates is called into question again. The concerts took place on Thursday 14 April 1966 at the Free Trade Hall, Manchester and Saturday 16 April at the Royal Festival Hall in London. The programme consisted of Mozart's Symphony No.34 and, for the first time at a Hallé concert, Mahler's Symphony No.5.[72] The same pieces were played in the Free Trade Hall concert on the preceding Wednesday. Sir John Barbirolli conducted the Hallé. Mahler was a favourite of Cardus, whose piece entitled "Mahler, warts and all" was published by the *Guardian* on 16 April.

Brookes explains Cardus's insensitivity in opening, in full view of the audience, an envelope that Barbirolli presented on behalf of the *Guardian*'s management: a cheque for £100 (*Private Eye* indicated that it was only £50).[73] However, the conductor also presented Cardus with a copy of his version of the score of Mahler's Symphony No.5, with his own markings and an inscription:

"On behalf of the Guardian and the Hallé Concerts Society, I have the honour and deep personal pleasure of presenting to you this score of Mahler 5; a work played for you to celebrate fifty years of service to the art of letters and music, and in particular your devoted services to the cause of a great composer and conductor. With admiration and affection from us all – John Barbirolli, April 14, 1966."[74]

Since Cardus began working for the MG in March 1917, the *Guardian* had it right in referring to "In his fiftieth year of writing about music for the 'Guardian'."[75] Unfortunately, Cardus himself wrote that the concert "chimes in with the month which completes my fiftieth year as a 'Guardian' man."[76] Completion of the 50th year would not, of course, come until 1967. It may be that Cardus continued to believe, as he had done in a letter written in 1957, that he started work for the MG in 1916.[77] There was a similar issue when Cardus wrote an article, "Fifty years with the Guardian", which was published in 1966.[78] Counting the years was not Cardus's strong point.

Desert Island Discs

A further celebration of Cardus's life was when he was on the radio as the guest on *Desert Island Discs*. In an article in the *Guardian* on 3 December 1966 Cardus had suggested that Roy Plomley, the presenter, should invite a music critic onto his delightful programme; none had previously taken part. He himself would enjoy it as a participant but he would not choose pieces that were nostalgic or familiar. He was not precise about what his eight records would be but they included, for example, an orchestral work by William Wallace, a Scot who achieved fame as an ophthalmic surgeon and who died in the 1940s; the Symphony in F by Goetz; and a work by Algernon Ashton. Definitely not familiar pieces!

Cardus accepted that such a programme would fail to give much musical enjoyment. He therefore put forward a compromise and, as a starting point, identified four choices: Schumann's *Études Symphoniques*; McCormack singing Wolf's setting of Goethe's *Ganymede*; Lisa della Casa singing Strauss's *Four Last Songs*; and the slow movement of Bach's Double Concerto.

Perhaps the *Guardian* article stimulated the BBC to invite Cardus as a guest on the programme; his appearance was broadcast on 17 April 1967. The titles of the music are listed in *His Own Man*[79] but it is useful to set out his selections more fully (*see* Table 6 *overleaf*).[80] As it turned out, they were familiar works together with some nostalgia. Only one of his actual eight had featured in the *Guardian* article, the Strauss with Lisa della Casa. Appendix 2 takes the opportunity to provide background comments on what is some of Cardus's favourite music.

The book he chose was Boswell's *Life of Johnson*. Perhaps Cardus anticipated difficulties getting to sleep on the desert island. In 1949 he recalled long before having suffered from insomnia and saying that this was the book he preferred to read to try to solve the problem.[81] There are also several references to Johnson in his writings on both music[82] and cricket.[83]

The luxury selected by Cardus was watercolour painting equipment. Possibly this recalled his wish to be an artist when he was aged 17 or 18.[84]

An omission from the choice of records was some work by Brahms, who Cardus had earlier said was the composer he would take if allowed only one.[85] Cardus was prone to change his mind and, three years later, he selected a Wolf recital of around 1950 and featuring artists Schwartzkopf and Fischer-Dieskau as a memory to take to his desert island.[86]

When Daniels later asked Cardus for one piece of music for a desert island, his first choice, if he had the right singers, was *Don Giovanni*, closely followed by the finale of Beethoven's Symphony No.4. But then, Cardus asked, what about *Tristan and Isolde*, Mozart's G minor Symphony or Chopin's piano music and remarked that it was bad enough when Roy Plomley had allowed him eight records.[87]

Daniels also asked Cardus to choose eight conductors for the desert island.[88] Four of his answers featured in his selection for the BBC: Toscanini, Furtwängler, Beecham and Walter. The other four were Otto Klemperer, Hamilton Harty, Franz Schalk and Felix Weingartner.

Table 6. Neville Cardus's choices on *Desert Island Discs*

Composer	Title	Orchestra	Conductor	Soloist
Robert Schumann	Fantasia in C major			Vladimir Horowitz
Richard Wagner	*Liebestod* (from *Tristan and Isolde*)	Philharmonia Orchestra	Wilhelm Furtwängler	Kirsten Flagstad
Wolfgang Amadeus Mozart	Clarinet Concerto in A major	Royal Philharmonic Orchestra	Thomas Beecham	Jack Brymer
Ludwig van Beethoven	Symphony No.4 in B flat major*	BBC Symphony Orchestra	Arturo Toscanini	
Gustav Mahler	*Das Lied von der Erde*	Vienna Philharmonic Orchestra	Bruno Walter	Kathleen Ferrier
Franz Schubert	Symphony No.8 in B minor (*Unfinished*)	New York Philharmonic Orchestra	Bruno Walter	
Sergio Prokofiev	Symphony No.1 in D major (*Classical*)	NBC Symphony Orchestra	Arturo Toscanini	
Richard Strauss	*Im Abendrot* (from *Four Last Songs*)	Vienna Philharmonic Orchestra	Karl Böhm	Lisa della Casa

*Choice if allowed only one record.

Social and domestic arrangements

When he moved back to England Cardus's base was the National Liberal Club although, early on, he had an interest in 73 Lyall Mews West.[89] At the club he had "an austere, somewhat ascetic kind of life", with mornings for reading and study, afternoons for walking, evenings for a concert, opera, records or dinner with a friend.[90] Asked by journalist Stanley Parker if he lived there, Cardus replied in the negative, saying he also had a flat where he had his books and records, and where his wife had some pictures.[91] He went on to say, "But I can't work in a domestic atmosphere. I must have a place with no distraction." Parker concluded that the spartan room in the club was the solution. Hart-Davis regarded Cardus as an enchanting companion but suspected "that at heart he is seldom sorry to be left alone."[92] When at the Edinburgh Festival in 1964 he admitted to speaking only about 100 words daily.[93] This recalls the solitary nature of his youth.

The flat, a "green-upholstered subterranean flat",[94] was at 112 Bickenhall Mansions, Marylebone, and this was where Edith lived. Although her husband was often away, the couple kept in close touch, communicating frequently. Neville had two addresses: he was registered as an elector at both the flat and the club, and letters he wrote to *The Times* in 1953, 1954, 1960 and 1967 had the flat as his address; in 1961 and 1965 he wrote from his club.[95] Following Edith's death in 1968 he moved out of the club and lived at Bickenhall Mansions.

There was an important gregarious side to Cardus. His friends included Else Mayer-Lismann, a music teacher who ran an opera workshop and was later appointed MBE for services to opera. Many of his letters to her are available, with comments such as, "Ich Liebe dich so sehn. I miss you more than I CAN SAY!" [emphasis in original].[96] She was known as Cardus's "music wife", while the title "cricket wife" belonged to another friend, Margaret Hughes.[97] Cardus wrote the foreword to her book, *All on a Summer's Day* (1953), describing it as the first book on first-class cricket by a woman. She later helped edit collections of Cardus's writings on cricket. Both "wives" were beneficiaries of Cardus's will.

Another pleasure was dining at the London Steak House with invited companions, recalled by Elizabeth Grice, a young journalist whom Cardus helped.[98] Another whose writing he encouraged was Australian cricketer Jack Fingleton. While Cardus was known as a good raconteur, Fingleton, along with others such as journalist John Woodcock, recognised that he could dominate a conversation and repeat his stories.[99]

Working late

Newspapers were changing. Lengthy, reflective articles became less popular. The MG changed more than many, with new editor (Alastair Hetherington), new title (*Guardian*) and the closure of its office in Cross Street, Manchester, which Cardus called "It's like the Pope leaving the Vatican."[100] Articles had to be cut so as not to exceed a new limit of 800 words.[101] He complained that his book, *A Composers Eleven,* had not been reviewed,[102] and was shocked at the (lack of) coverage of Lancashire cricket.[103] He wrote, "But I have NO FAITH in this new Editor, who is a Scotsman!!"(emphasis in original).[104]

Relationships with the newspaper that Cardus had grown up with were not good. After the death in 1958 of Harry Boardman, MG parliamentary correspondent, Cardus wrote that he had lost all interest in the paper.[105] Among the issues was the *Guardian* cutting his copy.[106] But editor and Scotsman Hetherington thought that Cardus's writing was "getting too stodgy to be borne" and the *Guardian* wanted to move onto the next generation:[107]

> "His later [music] notices were drafted at rehearsal, completed, sometimes to the annoyance of people in adjoining seats, at performance, and sent to the office in a Harrods hired car. In the end he became an embarrassment to the features department".

Cardus was working until the end, as writer on music and cricket and broadcaster. When *Playfair Cricket Monthly* was launched in May 1960, he had an article on Hammond in the first issue, this being the first of many contributions to the magazine. He never forgot his roots and, as President, made a rare visit to Old Trafford for the Roses match of 1971.[108] Later in the year, he saw his home county defeat Kent in the Gillette Cup Final at Lord's, "a famous victory, a perfect one-day game nearly converting me to a species of cricket in which the result and competitive means are everything."[109] Cardus was satisfied that Lancashire cricket still had characters.[110] A favourite was 5ft 3in (160cm) Harry Pilling: "constantly engages my sense of character and appreciation of rare skill". Statham was gifted with a "beautifully flowing action". Higgs was admittedly not born in Lancashire but was "Lancastrian by force of environment". Lancashire's innings win over Yorkshire in 1972 will doubtless have pleased the President.

Although Cardus was critical of some of the trends in cricket, in particular the one-day variety,[111] he was positive about the contribution of overseas cricketers who brightened up cricket in England.[112] He continued giving the selectors his views about the make-up of the English eleven. And only five weeks before his death he had an article in the *Guardian*, on the theme of bouncers in cricket, and in defending them he drew on several examples from cricket history.[113]

Turning to music, Cardus was pleased to contribute an article to *The Sunday Times* in 1974, on "Music to my taste", and this was followed by a piece on J.M. Barrie and *Peter Pan*, appearing only two months before his death.[114] There were occasions when Cardus had his facts wrong, and perhaps the ageing process was a contributory factor. On 7 December 1974 he wrote in the *Guardian* about the revival of Gounod's *Faust* at Covent Garden. Unfortunately, there was a case of memory failure and a correspondent subsequently wrote to say that the production that Cardus indicated was conducted by Thomas Beecham in the mid-1930s was in fact conducted by Stanford Robinson in 1938.[115] And, earlier in the year, he had stated that conductor Leopold Stokowski had changed his name from Stokes but a letter to the editor pointed out that this was untrue.[116]

Cardus's versatility was demonstrated by the appearance on 9 July 1973 of two obituaries in the *Guardian* of which he was author. They related to one of the greatest conductors of the century (Otto Klemperer) and one of the finest cricketers (Wilfred Rhodes).[117]

Broadcasting was not forgotten, either. In 1973 Cardus appeared in a 10-minute BBC2 television programme, *Times Remembered,* on 29 March 1973; and in a series of three programmes on BBC2 starting on 6 September 1973 talking to John Arlott about his life, work and enthusiasms.[118]

Chapter 13

TO BE PERSONAL...

Why was Neville Cardus so popular with readers of his cricket writing? What can we uncover about his style, which made him so memorable?

His cricket pieces were about much more than the cricket, especially in his early years. They could include the place, the ground, the players, the ambience. He would describe his time as a cricket-follower, enabling readers to relate to him. Modern jargon would call it the customer experience. It wasn't only the actual play but also the context in which it took place.

Cardus's report might start with his journey to the ground. This helped him fill the space when rain prevented play between Yorkshire and the Australians:

> "I set out to Sheffield, on a very slow train that meandered through Derbyshire and let me see places like Crowden, which I had forgotten since the old days of the sixpenny weekend trips."[1]

Travelling to Lancashire's ground in Liverpool included mention of a multi-headed dog from Greek mythology, while the approach to Old Trafford reminded Cardus of his days as a schoolboy:

> "The journey from Central Station to Aigburth is one that even on a sunny day will acquaint you with underworld gloom; a dog that I heard howling

outside Warrington might well have been Cerberus by name."[2]

"Down Warwick Road marched the eager crowd, and it was good to see that the old pilgrimage of youth goes on still – scampering schoolboys with nourishment in paper parcels tied up by string."[3]

The weather was an integral part of the occasion and, naturally, Manchester's reputation for rain meant this was a theme, so a sunny day was a welcome surprise or reason to exaggerate:

"You will see more macintoshes in 10 minutes at Old Trafford than on any other cricket field in the world in a week."[4]

"The sun shone generously yesterday at Old Trafford, and we scarcely knew where we were in consequence."[5]

"Saturday at Old Trafford was a season of Thermidorean heat of Ethiopic scorchings."[6]

What also came across was Cardus the northerner. When Yorkshireman Verity and Lancastrian Paynter excelled for England, "The English rally was glorious; character, good North of England toughness, conquered an evil situation."[7] Cardus was clear on a visit in 1920 to Lord's that this was certainly not the north of England:

"A man from the unfashionable North, carrying with him a suggestion of real industry, feels that Lord's is all the time eyeing him curiously from a safe point of vantage, and mentally putting him down as a possible Wat Tyler, or, at the most generous estimate, an ironfounder. It is hard to imagine any place in the world where class distinctions are so firmly stressed as at Lord's."[8]

He later became more comfortable with cricket's headquarters, writing in 1937, its sesquicentenary year that, "It is nonsense to speak of Lord's as no place for the common man. [It] is a good mixer", although the MCC and pavilion were understandably aloof.[9] Eton v Harrow at Lord's was different, though: "Next year I really must take the precaution of wearing a tall hat to disguise my plebeian origins."[10]

Accustomed as he became to travelling through England, a sentimental attachment to Old Trafford remained:

"… it was a joy to come back to Old Trafford again, after much journeying through the darkest interior of Sheffield and after long acquaintance with the waters of Trent. Old Trafford's plain homeliness soothed the wanderer's mind and body alike; Old Trafford's green friendly grass was a glad sight for tired eyes to see."[11]

However, he did express concern later that Old Trafford "became absorbed in the atmosphere of real industry… homely, historic, but dirty and business-like."[12]

Cardus, having been born in Lancashire, often put his home county at the forefront, particularly early on. For example, in 1920, he wrote about how Lancashire had lost to Surrey at The Oval, whereas the report of Surrey-based H.J. Henley, in the *Daily Mail*, described how the home county beat Lancashire.[13]

It was natural to describe the ground where the match was taking place, and its setting. Cardus's first foray outside Lancashire, in 1919 to Sheffield, set the scene for 21 years of reporting on Roses battles. The style, highlighting the drama of the occasion, is characteristic of a writer enthusiastic in a new role:

"The squat chimneys outside the ground loomed black against a lowering sky, and, Bank Holiday or no Bank Holiday, there was a suggestion of smoke about, and steel smelters. All these things told eloquently of the stiff energy of North-country life, making the proper dramatic accompaniment to a battle between ancient hosts whose informing spirit is the dour combativeness of hardy northmen."[14]

Cardus was acutely aware of the North/South divide. When at the Lancashire town of Nelson he noted "a few sane, homely chimneys to reassure us that we are not in the South of England or in any degenerate aesthetic parts whatever."[15] Southend was rather different:

"Southend-on-Sea is Blackpool without the Tower, and a little farther south. The cricket field is pleasant, though one or two absurd villas outside the ground offend the eyesight by their modern lack of dignity."[16]

Trent Bridge was Cardus's second favourite cricket ground, after Lord's;[17] it was "the schoolboys' happy hunting-ground" where they can "get a marvellous seat on a stand for sixpence",[18] and he recalled when "a batsman could dawdle on [the wicket] all the day long while his score mounted almost without a thought from him – his innings growing in the sun like a plant."[19] Edgbaston also scored highly:

"When I walked through the main entrance I was confronted by a charming little house with box-hedges and flowers round the door; in the window was a cockatoo in a cage, and on the gate was a sign announcing the abode of a chiropodist… Elegant garden seats assist comfort on the pavilion; there is a lawn with geraniums and tables covered with coloured umbrellas, recalling a continental café at Bondi Beach near Sydney on a Sunday afternoon when the world seems full of surf and tawny sunshine."[20]

Leicester (the ground at Aylestone Road) was, in 1920, "so redolent of the village green, one is far away from the modern gladiatorial contests set in the midst of a hoarse multitude. Here, something in the very air conjures up the ancient spirit of cricket, the Hambledon grace and companionable ease."[21] The air was not so satisfying in 1932: "Man in his zeal for wealth and world bankruptcy goes on day by day making hideous sights, carting great chunks of matter from one place to another. The Leicestershire field is now rendered an eyesore by five huge, sinister kilns which stand close to the pavilion; also there are a factory and smoking chimneys."[22] In 1939 he threatened to bring a gas mask, and on the feather-bed wicket "the chief danger that threatened the batsmen was sudden asphyxiation."[23]

Recording the personal experience as well as the match meant highlighting the conditions in the press box in Bradford in 1938: "inadequate, not to say inhumane; galley slaves were better off than the tortured souls who this afternoon have tried to make a truthful record of an event which ought really to be forgotten at once."[24]

Cardus would wander round the ground rather than stay fixed in the press box.[25] He observed the spectators, and referred to the crowd at Dewsbury as "[r]eal Yorkshire everywhere – plain, keen, humorous... friendly, open-hearted, shrewd, and in deadly earnest."[26] At Leicester he appreciated "the amenable Midland accent one heard all around".[27]

At Lord's Cardus used to write his reports sitting on the Green Bank near the pavilion: "I have sat on it for hours on June afternoons when the cricket has not been exciting", watching "Debrett in visible motion; statesmen, poets, musicians, all the arts and graces of life passing by in an unending frieze".[28] In the 1934 Test the focus was what was happening on the pitch: "And when Bradman was batting thousands of hearts were uplifted. The excitement throbbed visibly. Perfect strangers spoke to each other… Roars of delight went to the sky."[29]

His eye for detail could help Cardus provide an amusing aside (or an irrelevant distraction if you preferred): "[Derbyshire player Stan] Worthington at short leg performed one or two conjuring tricks for his own private amusement."[30]

He didn't always find the cricket stimulating, and perhaps this explained why Cardus wasn't concentrating all the time, the following example from Old Trafford:

"[W]ith the cricket not momentous but pleasant one was at liberty to sit at ease and take an agreeable part in the high and amenable social life that goes on in the ladies' pavilion. Now and again the game claimed all of our attention, but more frequently it could be watched out of the corner of the eye".[31]

If the play didn't excite, more of the writing related to context. When the batting was poor in the Eton versus Harrow match: "The less said about a deal of the cricket the better".[32]

But where the cricket was inspiring, Cardus was most certainly inspired. The imps of mischief were at work in MacLaren's XI's defeat of the Australians in 1921; and when Lancashire won the Roses match at Sheffield in 1937:

"From beginning to finish the engagement did honour to sport gallant and challenging… The match which thrilled us these last few days will stand comparison with any of the illustrious past. Given the will – and a wicket of the right kind – cricket declines to be denied or put down or reduced to mathematics."[33]

Indeed, it is important to recognise that flowery phrasing didn't (usually) mean the basics of the match were neglected. The MG allowed Cardus plentiful space so that detail could be included. He often commented on the speed of run-scoring, the examples below from when Lancashire played Kent at Dover:[34]

"Hallows was twenty-five minutes getting his first run, and with the total 24 he sent a puny stroke to short leg and was caught at leisure" (first innings).

"Makepeace and Tyldesley forced the runs excellently after Hallows had got out: 50 was reached in little more than half an hour. Makepeace scored 37 in 50 minutes – furious driving for him. Ernest Tyldesley was brilliant: not for many a long day has his cricket been so powerful, so handsome, so masterful as in this innings" (second innings).

Of course, the description of the play could still incorporate an attractive choice of words: "Hammond was lucky with one or two snicks in his preliminary minutes 'in the middle'... Hammond's snicks were more stylish than most county batsmen's best strokes; they hinted not of incompetence but of fine art frustrated."[35] This was the man whom Cardus had seen at Cheltenham in 1920 when his first innings for Gloucestershire ended with a duck: "... the boy Hammond found the umpire's [lbw] decision unpalatable, and broke no bones about hiding his emotions. Seeing that he was playing in a county match for the first time one could feel for him."[36] Cardus's second visit to Cheltenham was in 1932, when he said that the town had as many bicycles as tabby-cats, and "the College cricket field was the prettiest sight in the world this morning".[37] Hammond then made 164: his "masterpiece was in material space and time of nearly four hours' duration; in memory it will live a lifetime."

Cardus wrote in a very personal manner, often using the first person. It was *his* view of the match, the teams and the players. For example, we have him writing about one of his favourites, Richard Tyldesley, playing against Middlesex. And he didn't flinch from offering an unfavourable opinion, as illustrated by his comments on Sussex and England batsman Duleepsinhji:

> "The only bowler who caused Hendren or Hearne spasms of doubt was Richard Tyldesley. My view is that he was not given opportunity enough… Hendren at his finest could not take liberties with Tyldesley…"[38]

> "Apparently I am Duleepsinhji's evil spirit. Every time I see him bat he commits an elementary and uncultivated error. Yet most days (so I am assured) he is a perfect stylist, plus a sinuous grace all his own. All the same, I refuse to believe he is a Ranjitsinhji any more than I believe that Gandhi is a Mohammed."[39]

> Cardus was a keen supporter of "brighter cricket" and condemned negative batting, often from his home county, although he claimed to be impartial in his criticisms of slow cricket:[40]

> "I am beginning to believe that Lancashire batting is the finest anaesthetic ever yet invented, and some day I intend having a set of bad teeth out under it."[41]

The overseas players who burst into the English game in the late 1960s were a source of satisfaction. Clive

Lloyd, who had joined the Lancashire team, was "violent, Wagnerian"[42] and:

"... the most dynamic, most unpredictable batsman of the century... volcanically destructive. Yet, with all his eruptive strokes, there is, in control, a governing centre. At the heart... of the cyclone which wrecks cities and causes tidal waves, there is a calm pivotal spot, around which fury and annihilation are scientifically directed. Rare skill and personal relish, these are the infectious human properties, or characteristics, that make West Indies cricket creative."[43]

Other counties' recruits were not ignored.[44] Cardus admired "the magic of Kanhai, the spin conjurations of Intikhab, alluring to the spectator"; and "Sobers, as batsman, is entirely and easefully musical... He puts the bloom on the orthodox".

The manner in which the game was played continued to be more important than the result. In 1969 Cardus walked out of the New Zealand Test at Lord's when John Edrich and Geoff Boycott were batting slowly.[45] And while he agreed that Brian Luckhurst and Ray Illingworth did a good job for England at Trent Bridge in 1970:

"So does a plumber who comes into my flat to fix two brand new taps in my kitchen sink. But I wouldn't pay to watch him doing his 'good job'."[46]

Nevertheless, fast scoring wasn't essential. Cardus could enjoy a passionate stonewaller: Trevor Bailey was "a perpetual source of humour as he prepared suspiciously to scrutinise the bowling he had to tackle".[47] Slow play in itself wasn't wrong and could be accepted in a romantic view of tradition, as explained when watching Gentlemen v Players in 1924:

"The sun has poured down its torrents, making that delectable drowsiness come now and again which suits cricket so well. Who will complain of slow cricket on such a day and at such a match where there is no competitive championship axe to grind?"[48]

Indeed, "slow cricket by Lancashire has not seemed quite so wearisome as usually it does" when they visited Dover, "such a green and pleasant place… with June sunlight everywhere… We have been free to watch the game idly…"[49] After the visitors won a close match by 33 runs, Cardus was again in lyrical mood: "To my dying day I shall remember gratefully these afternoons in Kent, … full of the air and peaceful sunshine of imperishable England."

Cardus was known for downplaying the significance of numbers. He asked, "What do they know of cricket who know only what the scoreboard tells them?"[50] And, after summarising the statistics of Woolley's career as a batsman, he wrote that they "tell us little of his essence. We could as illuminatingly add up all the notes in the music of Mozart."[51]

Words were a different matter. Author, critic and cricket-lover Edmund Blunden praised Cardus: "the genius of this author can be relied upon for a rich and subtle evocation of the triumphant game".[52] Fellow cricket writer Robertson-Glasgow saw Neville Cardus, "slim, grey, contained; master of the rhapsodical style, cutting his sharp epigrams from the most amorphous material."[53] He could design the phrase that just fitted. Alliteration came with the lotus land that was Trent Bridge, the scampering schoolboys and paper parcels down Warwick Road, and the "somnambulistic slowness" of fast bowlers.[54] The rhyme of "hills and mills" described cotton town Nelson,[55] while "the gusto of Barlow" applied to the South African cricketer in 1970.[56]

Metaphors appeared. A.C. MacLaren was the "noblest Roman".[57] Similes multiplied. Lancashire batsman

Oldfield "performed a number of leg glances so delicious that on the hot day they affected my senses like luscious water-melons at Brisbane."[58] Literature and the arts were frequently introduced and, as Bateman wrote, Cardus "often aestheticised cricket by way of literary allusion".[59] Iddon "began with a full toss after much preparation and arm-swinging in the Charles Chaplin manner."[60] Many of his references would be unfamiliar to MG readers; did they really recognise early Greek writers Pratinas and Aeschylus when the subject was Leicestershire's match at Old Trafford?[61] Some further allusions are mentioned in the next chapter.

When it came to the players, Cardus's focus wasn't only on their skills but also their character, as Samuel Langford had taught him to recognise. He described Australian Armstrong as "of the soil, the sun, and the wind – no product of the academies."[62]

Bradman's talent was naturally appreciated: "his every stroke is a dazzling and precious stone in the game's crown".[63] But Cardus objected to criticism that the Australian was remote and automatic, saying that he "is full of blood; no other batsman today is as audacious as Bradman."[64]

Reggie Spooner "had a tuft of hair sticking up at the back of his head; out of sheer love of him my own hair to this day sticks up at the back."[65] And, "I never saw Spooner bat without seeing, as a background for his skill and beauty, the fields of Marlborough and all the quiet summer-time amenities of school cricket. He was my favourite player when I was a boy – he and Victor Trumper."[66]

George Gunn was "one of the characters of cricket… He was the wittiest batsman that ever lived; his bat was a swift rapier not used for warfare but just to tickle the ribs. He played the game for fancy's sake; he never knew where the imp of his genius was going to take him."[67]

Cardus was clear that technical skill wasn't everything: Lancashire captain Jack Bond had the gift of friendliness, and this helped him bring the best out of his team.[68]

Boycott was another whose character was intriguing.[69] Cardus concluded that it wasn't selfishness but saintly dedication. In another obscure reference he wrote that Boycott "lacked the Sir Willoughby Patterne delighted awareness of his egoism."

Cardus found just the right turn of phrase to use:

"But it is incorrect to say that Larwood is still the fastest bowler in England… He is his own walking shadow."[70]

"Oldfield lent flavour and lightness of touch to the solid pudding of the Lancashire innings".[71]

"Mitchell forced a ball to the on for three; the scoreboard whizzed dizzily and I nearly got vertigo watching the moving figures as they whirled round."[72]

The romantic style played a significant part in Cardus's writing, and the examples below from Colchester and Worcester demonstrate how he reflected on the heritage of cricket:

"a crowd that watched the cricket for a while with simple hearted interest, and then, when it got a little tired of the game, gave itself up to sunshine and a contemplation of the ring of willow trees round the field, delicate of sheen in the soft light."[73]

"Cricket seems more than a game down here in the West of England: I feel it as part of the surrounding air: the new grass, the cool, sweet wind, the trees with their May greenness, the crack of the bat, the chimes of the Cathedral telling the passing hours – all these lovely sights and sounds and fragrances are mingled together in an English scene which does the heart good."[74]

The Colchester excerpt is from 1922, in the early phase of Cardus's writing, when he was more likely to be diverted from the match itself. Hart-Davis found that Cardus was exercising more restraint, with fewer images and metaphors, by the time *The Summer Game* appeared (1929), and by *Good Days* (1934) had controlled his romanticism, though not eliminated it; youthful exuberance was less apparent.[75] The Worcester piece appeared in 1931. Diversions still appeared in later years: in 1938 he was quoting from Lewis Carroll's *The Walrus and the Carpenter*, although in this case the absence of play at the abandoned Old Trafford Test provided an excuse.[76]

In addition to several unfamiliar references in allusions, some little used words had a habit of finding their way into Cardus's writing. Readers may well have been puzzled by Lancashire's "scantling of 86 for two wickets"; "if somebody had been with me I should have apostrophised the scene" and "that outmoded romanticism contumaciously exhibited in the past by say A.C. MacLaren".[77] Sometimes an education in Latin would help those endeavouring to understand what was meant.[78]

Cardus used historical context, displaying his knowledge, albeit sometimes imperfect, as well as style. For example, a visit to Trent Bridge reminded him that he was "treading the earth once trodden by Arthur Shrewsbury and William Gunn."[79] A fixture between Lancashire and Worcestershire in 1930 brought back memories of players in such a match in the Golden Age pre-1914.[80] Another occasion when he looked upon the past favourably was in 1937, at Maidstone, one of the prettiest grounds in the land, he thought:

"nowadays Kent and Lancashire are ghosts of

themselves, or rather it would be truer to say that the ancient heroes, MacLaren, Hutchings, Tyldesley, Seymour, Blythe and Brearley, have vanished and have been followed by men of ordinary substance and prone to error."[81]

Allied to history, tradition was important. Cardus wrote lovingly on the subject of village cricket,[82] and about cricket in a relaxing setting: Northampton hosted a dull day's cricket, "Yet even in this monotony one has discovered charm. The quietness of the afternoon, the lack of the garish sun – all this has fallen in well with one's sense of living for a while in an out-of-the-way corner of the world, intimate and soothing."[83]

The amateur game was part of this tradition. The Varsity match was "cricket in the drawing room of highly civilised men and women"[84] and, playing against Lancashire, "the Cambridge cricketers handled the bat as say, violinists handle the violin – that is to say, to express something… cricket is a game, a free and beautiful game, not a matter of a real industry."[85]

Cardus was pleased to welcome amateurs to Old Trafford in 1931, and to recall earlier times:

"Delicious sunshine made the field a cricketer's heaven when the Kent team came down the pavilion, with four amateurs, a refreshing sight, reminding us of the days of Marsham, Blaker, Mason, and Hutchings. Crawley wore the pretty Harlequin cap…"[86]

One innovation, at Old Trafford's Roses game of 1933, was music being broadcast; Cardus wasn't happy and wondered whether this was only a tentative step towards mightier reforms: "say a few side-shows with dancing, and a bearded lady, and other diversions. Then, gradually, the cricket can be got rid of altogether, to the approbation of all and sundry."[87] It is fortunate that Cardus wasn't around for the music from cricket bat-shaped guitars at the ICC World Cup in 2019. He didn't object to one-day cricket if played seriously and according to the procedure for three-day cricket.[88] But he thought it ended up as crude hit-or-miss slashing and was quite different from "genuine" cricket: "If Yehudi Menuhin were to play jazz music one night, his playing of Mozart and Beethoven would very likely suffer some fineness of touch and style the next night."

What were the significant features of Neville Cardus's style? First, he didn't provide merely a formal account of the progress of the match. He would discuss what was going on around: the venue, the weather and the crowd (more so in early years); and the players as characters (more so in later years). Second, he selected words and allusions and, with humour and some mischief, designed phrases that led the reader to sit up and smile. Third, it was very personal writing, describing his own experience at the ground and how he saw the spectators and players; this would reflect his view of the history and tradition of the game.

If you were a reader wanting a succinct summary of a day's cricket then Cardus wasn't the man for you. A letter to the MG editor from the English Department of Bristol University complained that Cardus's use of the English language was somewhat obscure.[89] While many Australians applauded his writing, others had objections: "When he writes about test cricket only himself and God know what he means – and sometimes God doesn't" and "I gave up reading Cardus after two attempts to understand what he meant".[90] Even Barbe thought that some of his writing was "a bit hifalutin".[91]

Another complaint led Cardus to admit that he had a tendency to idealise what deserved to be reprobated.[92] Questions also arose regarding factual inaccuracy, an issue for the next chapter, while cricket historian David Frith thought that *Yorkshire Post* writer Jim Kilburn began to edge out Cardus as an essayist "for the simple reason that he did not indulge himself in fantasy."[93] As time went on, Cardus wasn't always favoured: Derek Birley's view was that, "though never desiccated or arid [he] could periphrase and drool with the best of them. In this mood he is a blatant purveyor of debased romantic imagery... At its worst Cardus's writing is like advertising copy."[94]

Many readers were, of course, enjoying what they read. Correspondents to the MG called Cardus a "great critic"; wrote that he was respected and admired; and that he was never dull.[95] Another applauded his criticism of Lancashire's over-cautious cricket, although an alternative view was that this was overdone.[96]

Plaudits from other writers were many. C.L.R. James felt that it was Cardus who, in his "vivid, darting style", came closest to W.G. Grace when he wrote, "The plain, lusty humours of his first practices in a Gloucestershire orchard were to be savoured throughout the man's gigantic rise to a national renown."[97] Jim Kilburn wrote that Cardus "came to cricket with a poet's eye and extracted the essence of the game for presentation in glowing prose."[98] John Arlott contrasted pre-1914 cricket writing, competent and pleasant, with what Cardus introduced, being the first to bring "the qualities of personalization, literary allusion and imagery."[99] Cardus's writing developed over the years. It became more focussed and restrained; in any event Hetherington's sub-editors wouldn't have allowed *The Owl and the Pussycat* into the sports pages. But it remained a very personal view, using the English language not only to inform but also to entertain. Sir John Major accepted that Cardus may have given reality a little help from his charitable imagination, but that didn't prevent regarding him as a gifted writer who stirred the emotions.[100]

I am not attempting a comprehensive roll call of Cardus's supporters and critics. What Cardus had was a style that suited a market, benefitting both himself and the MG. The *Guardian* official history refers to Cardus finding an appreciation among his readers that he probably wouldn't have found elsewhere; in his prime Cardus "was one of the most important reasons for reading the *Manchester Guardian*."[101] Many people bought the paper just to read Cardus.[102] While there are, naturally, detractors, the continued interest in his work is evidence of his position as one of the leading writers on cricket, indeed on sport.

Chapter 14

THE TRUTH BUT NOT
ALWAYS THE TRUTH

———— ❧✦❧ ————

Much of Cardus's writing is about people and places, cricket matches and concerts. He didn't want his writing to be exclusively factual pieces; he needed greater freedom. The constraints of facts could be avoided by inventing people and places, about which he could then write as he wished. For example, he wrote about Shastbury, loosely based on his experiences at Shrewsbury, about the made-up villages of Puddleton-in-the-Hills[1] and Ludbury,[2] and the counties of Loamshire[3] and Blankshire.[4] He created Bloggs of Blankshire as a generic professional cricketer about whom he could write.[5] Such inventions serve a useful purpose, and circumvent the restrictions of facts without deceiving the reader as these were not factual pieces but fiction designed to convey his views on cricket.

Cardus also freed himself from pure facts by the frequent use of allusions of a musical, literary or artistic nature. For example, he wrote that a characteristic innings of Lancashire batsman Johnny Briggs "raced along like a scherzo."[6] There were literary references, with a description of the cricket field at Sheffield as a blasted heath; "but, as Shakespeare knew, it is on blasted heaths that matters of grim moment come to pass."[7] Bateman quotes one paragraph in an essay on Lancastrian cricketer Walter Brearley where he mentioned no fewer than eight authors.[8] Cardus's range of interests also covered painting (Andrews' innings for Australia at The Oval in 1921 was pre-Raphaelitish[9]) and sculpture (a reference to Rodin when writing about Armstrong in 1921[10]). Of course, this is all a matter of style as distinct from a departure from the truth.

Cardus could also admit that what he was writing was his imagination, with a suitable justification. Events at Old Trafford in 1925 were out of the ordinary when Lancashire defeated Somerset in a day. After his exaggerations, he added, "Not strictly in accordance with fact maybe, but true to imagination's view of a helter-skelter few hours' cricket".[11] The reader was thereby warned that events were not exactly as reported.

It was also possible to move seamlessly from reality to story-telling. In chapter 1 of *A Cricketer's Book* Cardus was at Lord's and wrote, "It was an occasion for a reverie, and I fell to affectionate thoughts upon the great days of cricket... Maybe I dozed for a while..."[12]

The evidence we have seen is that many of the "facts" in Cardus's writing are not actually true. Bateman wrote, "With its narrative of rags to cultural riches, Cardus's autobiographical writings are a fascinating example of the fictional quality of this genre."[13] Not everyone was overwhelmed: Engel's view was,

> "The Cardus nostalgia industry, which has just stopped short of selling souvenir knick-knacks and T-shirts, has reached almost alarming proportions; for modern readers his brilliant but idiosyncratic view of the '30s has become received wisdom."[14]

It should not be assumed that there was always a deliberate intention to deceive. Lamb wrote that it was difficult to see what Cardus achieved by the untruth of his grandmother predeceasing his grandfather.[15] Nothing was achieved; it looks to be just a mistake. Indeed, ages and years presented a particular difficulty for Cardus. His problem is apparent when he attributes Lancashire's triple county championship winning years to 1927, 1928 and 1929,[16] when it should have been 1926, 1927 and 1928. He erred in the year when his aunt Beatrice died and when Wainwright went to Shrewsbury. In his notebook in 1949 he calculated the time since he met Barbe as 29 years when it appears to have been 19.[17] Paderewski's age may have been plucked out of thin air. This is on top of the issues in determining his own age. These problems may well be linked to his admission, "I had little sense of figures…".[18] He confirmed, "…. My arithmetic has been wretched since schooldays…"[19] Indeed, when Cardus criticised Lancashire's rate of scoring, one MG correspondent produced some data on cricket matches to argue that Cricketer would have found a little study in arithmetic to have been helpful.[20] It certainly appears that faulty numeracy, together with a lack of attention to detail, led to some of Cardus's mistakes.

Further, some of the mistakes may have resulted from misinformation by others. The story of Charles Peace may have come from Cardus's grandfather; the problem of his own date of birth may be the fault of an adult relative.

Of course, *Autobiography* was written some long time after Cardus's childhood, and it is not surprising that not everything was right; how many of us can remember what happened 50 years ago? I spent much of my childhood watching Lancashire at Old Trafford but, while I can recall some of the early matches I saw, I certainly could not claim to know when was my first visit to the ground. And Cardus, in Australia, was writing without the reference material that is now available at the click of a mouse. Memory failure is bound to arise from time to time.

Mistakes about musical and cricketing history also arose. The errors concerning Stokowski's name and the conductor of *Faust* were matters of fact that Cardus had wrong.

On cricket, Cardus told readers about Nottinghamshire batsman Billy Barnes scoring a century against Middlesex at Lord's in the late 19th century.[21] Unfortunately, there was no such score, although Barnes did twice reach three figures at Trent Bridge. Cardus reported Attewell telling him that he clean bowled both Ranjitsinhji and C.B. Fry on a plumb wicket at Sussex.[22] Sadly, there was no innings where that happened. C.B. Fry apparently said to Cardus that he was bowled by Middlesex bowler Albert Trott after scoring a century for Sussex.[23] Again, that didn't take place. Doubtless a review of all Cardus's writing would uncover more examples. However, focussing on mistakes should not imply all was wrong, which is quite definitely not the case.

It is still a surprise that Cardus claimed, "I've got a very good memory – in fact, I can remember my boyhood days much more vividly than I can remember what happened last week."[24] Cardus's memory was visual; writing about the inter-war Roses matches, he explained, "The panorama of these wonderful games, year after year in my lifetime since boyhood, still moves in my mind photographically."[25]

There was some recognition that memory could play tricks and matches may become mixed up. Cardus confessed, "Other shadowy pictures from the 1900's chase one another across the film of my mind, perhaps mingling together and eluding pursuit".[26] In 1936 he wrote, "Sometimes when I am looking through an old 'Wisden' I find to my astonishment that I could not possibly have been present at a match which for a lifetime my mind has seen in all its detail… The explanation is that boys used to read the cricket reports imaginatively".[27] In *Autobiography* Cardus admits that he is at times confused in his memories.[28] He noted:

> "Sometimes when I am writing these memories from long years spent in the open air watching cricket,

my pen seems as though guided by an influence which is not a conscious part of me; do you remember the old-time 'Ouija' board and 'spirit writing'?"[29]

The accuracy of Cardus's writing was questioned in connection with his obituary of Errol Holmes.[30] This referred to a match between Lancashire and Oxford University, but Ronald Mason showed that the sequence of events described as involving Holmes, his opening bowler colleague Hewetson and Lancashire batsman Dick Tyldesley did not take place.[31] Cardus responded in the *Guardian*: in his mind's eye he could still see Tyldesley bowled by Hewetson; his visual memory was clear, though we know that it was not correct.[32] The error could be another case of failure of memory, which was playing tricks; the many matches he had observed were mixed up. That would be a fair excuse for a mistake, although it would not have happened if Cardus had checked what he wrote.

Writing about the game's characters led naturally to putting words into their mouths. One of his favourites was Wilfred Rhodes:

"'They'll get out to me because I'm Rhodes,' he appears to say. And one can also imagine him saying, like La Pucelle in 'Henry VI': 'For I have loaden me with many spoils. Using no other weapon but my name.'"[33]

Here Cardus uses "appears" and "imagine", so avoiding a direct quotation. Elsewhere he attributed words directly, but as he was up to 100 yards away in the press box, readers ought to realise that what they read was not the literal truth: it was impressions that were being conveyed.

At this point it is right to introduce the idea of "higher truth". In his essay in 1933 on Nottinghamshire batsman George Gunn, Cardus had described a sweltering day at

Edgbaston, the pitch right for making runs, with Gunn and Whysall opening the batting.[34] Gunn, wearing a white panama hat, played a short attractive innings, including 20 runs off bowler Howell until:

> "Then, without a warning sign, he daintily returned a half-volley to the bowler, a gift direct into the hand. When he returned to the pavilion, his captain said: 'Good heavens, George, what were you doing to get out to a ball like that?' And George replied: 'Too hot, sir.'"

Cardus commented: "and if it is not true it ought to be; it certainly observes the highest order of truth, which is truth to character."

Of course, it wasn't true. The three named cricketers played together at Edgbaston only in 1922, when Gunn scored 25 but wasn't out caught by the bowler. Cardus was nevertheless content that he was describing Gunn's true character; after all, he thought Gunn "the wittiest batsman that ever lived… He played the game for fancy's sake; he never knew where the imp of his genius was going to take him."

Now it can certainly be argued that there are times when it is possible to illustrate a person's character by some writing that is not the literal truth, especially if that is unknown, but some representation which can be justified and consistent with what else is known about the character. Honesty would, however, require that the reader is led to understand that it is not the literal truth.

Cardus had an opportunity to explain himself when replying to the accusation of inaccuracy in his obituary of Errol Holmes: "Mr. Mason brings forward evidence that… I wandered or floated from actual fact to the higher Truth."[35] He continued, "Before I plead guilty, m'lud, I'd like to point out that I have always tried to observe truth to character." As it turned out, Mason was not a stickler for accuracy and accepted the argument for what Cardus would describe as the higher truth:

"And I can see no reason to upbraid an artist for getting mere facts wrong... Dick Tyldesley and Errol Holmes live more authentically in Cardus's manufactured story than they would have in any slavish transcript of any real incident."[36]

Another example of focussing on characters came when Bates and Parsons were batting for Warwickshire against Lancashire in 1927:

"Once a sharp slip catch appeared to be made by Richard Tyldesley, but he apparently informed the umpire that before he scooped up the ball it struck the ground. Whereat a man on the popular side cried out 'Good owd Dick!' and added proudly, 'That's Westhoughton Sunday school for thi. No cheatin' at cricket: fair does at this game – except against Yorksheer.'"[37]

This tells us about the character of one of Cardus's favourites, Richard (Dick) Tyldesley. The reader may wonder if it is the literal truth; could the journalist really have heard what the spectator said? Cardus related the incident in a further article in 1967:

"... in a match at Old Trafford, Dick Tyldesley apparently brought off a marvellous catch in the leg trap... But, as the batsman was departing pavilionwards, Dick called him back; the ball had just touched the grass. I congratulated Dick, in print, on this act of sportsmanship. Also, next morning, I congratulated him by word of mouth. 'Thanks, Mr. Cardus,' he said: 'Westhoughton Sunday school tha knows.' Did he really say it? To fulfil and complete him, to realise the truth of his Lancashire nature and being, it simply had to be said. Whether he himself said it, or whether I put the words into his mouth for him, matters nothing as far as truth, as God knows it, is concerned."[38]

Notice the differences in the story here: Tyldesley was in the leg trap and not at slip; and the key words were said by the fielder himself and not a spectator.

The story changed again, so that Yorkshire and not Warwickshire were the opponents when it was recounted in 1974:

"… [I]t was in a Lancashire and Yorkshire match, at Old Trafford, that burly Dick Tyldesley so forgot the rigour of the game that after making a sharp catch at short-leg announced to the umpire, who was about to raise his hand for dismissal, that the ball just touched the ground before the apparent catch had been accomplished. I congratulated Tyldesley, at the end of the day's play, on his sportsmanship. 'Thanks very much,' he replied in broad Lancashire accent, 'Westhoughton Sunday School tha knows.' (Did he really say it, or did I…?)"[39]

While it is presumably the contemporaneous account that is nearest to, though not necessarily, the literal truth, Cardus was content that his descriptions of what happened were the higher truth.

One of Cardus's favourite characters was a Yorkshireman: "People say I invented Emmott Robinson. I didn't. I attributed to him the words I thought God intended him to say." [40] Cardus could accept that he was making up some of the detail: "Emmott Robinson, Rhodes and Herbert Sutcliffe, were not actually the rounded 'characters' looming large in my accounts of Lancashire v Yorkshire matches. They provided me with merely the raw material, so to say; my histrionic pen provided the rest."[41]

Cardus quoted Ted Wainwright talking about a partnership between Ranjitsinhji and Fry which took Sussex, playing against Yorkshire, from 43–2 to around 392–2.[42] There was no such match where this happened, as Sengupta has established.[43] However, when the piece was reviewed in the *Spectator* there were plaudits for Cardus's approach to writing: "In the last resort Mr Cardus likes cricket because it gives the fullest expression to the versatility, character, and talent of the man behind the bat or behind the ball."[44] The impressions of players on the field were more important than accurate reporting of fact. Cardus was writing about a time when stylish amateurs would give a different impression from determined professionals; and he was conscious of a divide between the industrial north and the sophisticated south. Bateman concluded that although Cardus was "guilty of producing a fictional construction of the past, it was an historical perspective of significance" while his writings "arose from, and responded to, the cultural, socio-economic and political tensions of its historical context."[45]

A further example, from 1935, is:

> "Emmott Robinson and Rhodes liked to walk on to a Leeds wicket before a match began and examine the turf. They would press and cajole it tenderly with their fingers. 'It'll be 'sticky' at four o'clock, Emmott,' Rhodes would say. 'No, Wilfred,' Emmott's reply would be, 'half past!'"[46]

In 1936 the story was repeated.[47] It also appeared in Cardus's obituary of Emmott Robinson.[48] The idea had arisen back in 1934 when, following the early closure of a Yorkshire innings against Lancashire at Sheffield,

Cardus fancied that Robinson would have favoured a later declaration as he had a special gift for knowing at what time of day a wicket would become helpful.[49]

The description of events changed when, in 1972, Cardus was paying a tribute to Wilfred Rhodes, who was, in this version, credited with the punchline of 4.30.[50] This episode reappears in the *Spectator*, 23 August 1974, though this indicates that it occurred at a Roses match, and Cardus claimed to have been with the Yorkshiremen when they went out for the pitch inspection, perhaps a justification for knowing what was said, though readers would probably decide that it was not feasible to remember the exact words said some decades before. It is back to Robinson for the 4.30 punchline and Cardus added, "I put words into his [Robinson's] mouth that God intended him to utter." There was no MG match report in which the incident actually occurred. And whereas the literal truth should not change over time, incidents of higher truth could and did.

This last point is also illustrated by the episode about slow-scoring batsman Trevor Bailey (chapter 1). The attempt to find this story uncovers it (strictly, something very similar) in an article in 1967, but there Cardus said he had been writing about not Bailey but Yorkshire batsman Mitchell when scoring a century in the Old Trafford Roses match of 1933.[51] However, recourse to his match report at the time finds no comparison with the honeymoon couple, although Cardus did bemoan Mitchell's slow scoring:

> "Lancashire and Yorkshire matches in recent years have been notorious for dull batting, but this batting of Yorkshire was not only dull, it was ugly. When Mitchell was smothering the ball with his legs I felt a screen ought to have concealed him from the public gaze."[52]

When writing in 1953 that Australian captain Lindsay Hassett offered him his autograph "with comic wistfulness", Cardus added, "This story, if not altogether true, is entirely characteristic of [a most friendly Australian]".[53] The detail was less important than conveying the right impression. However, a later writer added, "as we know, he made up stories in pursuit of a 'higher truth'".[54]

Green discusses what he calls "Cardus's fictions": "factual truth about cricket may not altogether have been what Cardus was after."[55] He concluded that if Cardus did not exactly cook the facts, "he certainly stretched them further than the circumstances sometimes warranted... Cardus was a creative writer first and a critic second".[56] However, he goes on to suggest that "romanticised as they undoubtedly are, Cardus's characters have a firm basis in truth"[57] and, as evidence, draws attention to the face of George Gunn in relaxed mood in a team photograph.[58] In the end, the many admirers of Cardus would overlook factual inaccuracies; Green concluded, "with the thought that Cardus by writing about games of cricket contributed to the general contentment of players and spectators alike the case for the Higher Truth rests."[59]

However, "higher truth" was not always a justification for untruths. *The Times* had a leading article in 1945 on "stubborn illusions" which, among other examples, mentioned a conflict of evidence about England cricketer Tom Richardson:

> "Cricket writers are especially prone to the amiable delusion that they were eye-witnesses of some historic match at Lord's or Old Trafford which took place while they were still in their perambulators. There is still a lively conflict of evidence as to whether Tom Richardson, after his heroic failure to break the Australian last-innings defence in 1896, 'remained at the bowling crease, dazed, solitary, and frustrated' or

'legged it to the pavilion like a stag to get down two pints before anybody else.' Truth is many-sided, and the misconceptions of childhood are usually on the side of a higher truth than the truth of fact."[60]

Critic James Agate, a good friend of Cardus, wrote to *The Times* to explain that the issue began with Cardus's description in *Days in the Sun* of Richardson being led wearily to the Old Trafford pavilion at the end of the 1896 Test match.[61] This was, however, incorrect: Agate, to whom Cardus had confessed that he was not present at the match, was there to see what happened, and knew that Richardson instead legged it to the pavilion. Agate was also aware that H.J. Henley, who he thought may well have been at the match, had the same recollection: "legged it to the pavilion like a stag and got down two pints before anyone else." Agate continued,

> "Cardus, who watched the great match at the age of seven from behind the bars of his nursery window some miles away, had the secret of the higher truth. But on the lower ground he tarradiddled."

Strictly, Cardus's description of the Test does not specify that he was relying on his own observation of the game. However, Agate is right to draw attention to Cardus having made up the information about Richardson that he presented. It would be generous to classify Cardus's misconception as a higher truth when it was, on the face of it, the opposite of what happened.

There was, however, a very simple reason for presenting something that is not the literal truth: to provide a good story. The incident of the removal of W.G. Grace's bust in 1939 appears to be an untruth; no "higher truth" justification is provided; it was supposed to be true. It is best read as a delightful story. Similarly, when confronted with concerns about the accuracy of some statements in the account of his Australian stay in *Full Score*, Cardus's reply was, "Ah, yes, but they read well".[62] The same argument can be applied to more of his writing: the story of returning to Old Trafford after his wedding is an example. Making up or embellishing an incident to provide a good read appears to be a motivation for other untruths. It may be the explanation for introducing Milady into the absence from Leeds in 1929; after all, we know that there was an untruth somewhere since if the Milady story is true then Cardus's other explanation, walking in the country, is not.

The mischievous side of Cardus is apparent in one of his *Music Surveys*: he enjoyed writing about Erich Hartleibig, a controversial composer who died aged 44 from poisoning caused by eating an overripe salzgurke.[63] It was pure fiction. Not the truth but a good story, and letters from readers showed that they appreciated it. Mischief doubtless lay behind some of Cardus's other untruths.

It is not always easy to distinguish an untruth that was a memory failure from one that was a made-up story. Cardus wrote in *Second Innings* that he went to the Grand National when the Irish favourite Rathnally fell.[64] It was in 1912 but the winner was Jerry M. and not Willonyx as stated. Perhaps this was a case of forgetfulness. However, there is a marked contrast between *Second Innings'* seven pages devoted to what he explained was a brief youthful obsession with horse racing, confirming that he went to both the Aintree and Manchester races,[65] and *Autobiography*, published three years earlier, where Cardus admitted that he only attended one race meeting in his life.[66] There is obviously a mistake somewhere, and it may be embellishment in the later writing.

A different motivation for an untruth may underlie Cardus's claim, made in 1922, that he played cricket as a youth against Repton-educated cricketer Jack Crawford. This may suggest that his upbringing was more affluent than was actually the case. It was not a "higher truth"; it produced an impression rather different from reality. Similarly, his *Who's Who* entry (1936 onwards) indicated, untruthfully, that he was educated not only at Manchester but also abroad: that again, and unusually, may inflate the status of his early life. This contrasts with his later attempts to exaggerate the poverty of his childhood, with the doubtful classification of 4 Summer Place as a slum: an untruth giving a false impression in the opposite direction.

Also recall the story of Billy Clegg and probably the rest of the "Gang". This was not factually true and maybe gave an impression of Cardus's character that he wished to convey and perhaps wished had been the case. But it was out of character. It was definitely not a "higher truth".

On the face of it, Cardus's untruths did not sit easily with the famous C.P. Scott phrase, "Comment is free, but facts are sacred."[67] In *Autobiography* Cardus brought to mind an episode where Scott was reprimanding him (wrongly as it turned out), starting, "Now, as you know, the first rule on my paper is accuracy."[68]

To summarise. When Cardus was writing reports of current cricket matches or preparing his concert notices there were clearly some details that he had to get right. Cricket in particular has plenty of facts and figures and while Cardus downgraded the importance of the scoreboard in assessing a player's performance he could not afford to and largely did not ignore the basics when reporting a match.

But Cardus was prone to making mistakes. When he was reflecting on the past, his memory could and did play tricks on him. Trying to remember facts about his family life some 50 years ago cannot have been easy. When recalling past cricket matches, he was confused by the multiple images in his mind. At times his recollections were plain wrong, and in some cases he may have been misinformed by others. The problem of memory failure was compounded by carelessness and inadequate checking, together with, in some cases, a lack of attention at the cricket match (or concert) he was supposed to be writing about. Readers relying on Cardus for an education in cricket history need to exercise caution.

A particular problem was faulty numeracy. We frequently find errors in years and ages, both Cardus's and other people's.

Cardus's writing is not judged by factual accuracy alone. It was his style that attracted readers. He enjoyed introducing musical and other allusions. He went on to develop a close interest in, indeed an affection for, the characters of cricket. To Cardus, cricketers were real people, not merely individuals who scored this number of runs or took that number of wickets. That led to stories, and many stories there were. Dissecting some of them enables us to pick holes and reveal inconsistencies. Cardus would admit that he sometimes deviated from the actual truth. The words that he attributed to players in the middle of a cricket field or elsewhere were not literally true, and it is fair to think that Cardus did not believe his readers would regard them as so. He could argue that he was not trying to deceive. He would say that rather than being literally true, he was being true to character, which he regarded as a higher truth.

However, there were also times when he described incidents that were just not true and could not be regarded as higher truth. Cardus would not let the truth get in the way of constructing a good story. On occasion it looks as if he recorded what he wished had happened rather than what really happened. Further, his writing could be designed to give an impression quite different from the truth; in such cases, certainly not the higher truth.

Chapter 15

FINALES

———— ❧ ————

Ada: Neville Cardus's mother

In 1939 Ada was living at Withington Hall, where she was the cook to Beatrice and Paul Schill. They were well-to-do philanthropists, living at what had been one of the most prestigious houses in Manchester, with impressive gardens.[1] However, the family went through difficult times after losing out in the 1930s crash. The Hall was later demolished. Ada was using her mother's maiden name, Rawlinson, as her surname. Perhaps she decided she did not want to be a Cardus, leading to the memory of being the mother of the famous journalist, the mother who left her son to live with the disreputable Eliahoo Joseph. However, at this stage, *Autobiography*, which revealed her role as a prostitute, had not yet been published.

Ada Rawlinson, as she was then known, died on 17 January 1955.[2] Neville was in Australia at the time.

Her place of death was 7 Marriott Street in the Manchester suburb of Withington. This was where her sister Helena had been living for some time, and also her nephew Cecil Cardus (Beatrice's illegitimate son). Helena would die there in 1957. It appears as if Ada was living with Cecil and Helena, although we do not know for how long. Cecil did not marry and died in 1980 in Manchester.

John Frederick Newsham: Neville Cardus's father

After having been a blacksmith, the demand for which was declining, Neville Cardus's father became a shopkeeper and beer retailer. In 1939 he was living with his wife Jane in Stretford.

He died, aged 75, in Stretford in 1941. His wife had died in the previous year.

Edith: Neville Cardus's wife

Edith Cardus passed away on 26 March 1968 in Marylebone. Her death certificate indicated that she died of coronary thrombosis and old age.

Neville Cardus: his death in 1975

On 26 February 1975 Cardus was admitted to hospital after suffering a slight stroke.[3] He died on 28 February in the Fitzroy Nuffield Nursing Home in 10 Bryanston Square, London. He had been living in Bickenhall Mansions. The cause of death was lower lobe pneumonia and arteriosclerosis. His occupation was given on the death certificate as knight, journalist and music critic.

His obituary in the *Guardian* called him "creative critic of international fame" and intriguingly referred to him as "one of the two most internationally renowned journalists the *Guardian* had produced in the century."[4] Death didn't end his contributions to the newspaper; following the death of cricketer Frank Woolley in 1978 the *Guardian* published a tribute that Cardus had prepared.[5]

His memorial service took place at St Paul's, Covent Garden, the actors' church in London, on 4 April 1975. Over 700 people attended, and those taking part included Alan Gibson (Cardus's favourite conversationalist among cricket commentators on radio[6]), Dame Wendy Hiller,

Dame Flora Robson and David Gray; James Loughran conducted the Hallé Orchestra.[7] The soloists were Antony Pay (clarinet) and, on piano, Clifford Curzon, who Cardus thought the best interpreter of Mozart.[8]

He was cremated, and his ashes were scattered on the lawns of remembrance at Golder's Green crematorium, London, with no personal memorial.[9]

The Hallé concert at the Free Trade Hall, Manchester on 6 March was dedicated to Cardus's memory by the Hallé Concerts Society. The programme included Mahler's first symphony, which was "an obviously divinely ordered coincidence."[10]

The Royal Philharmonic Orchestra made its performance of Verdi's *Requiem* at the Royal Albert Hall on 18 April a memorial concert for Cardus. The orchestra was conducted by Carlos Paita and was joined by the London Philharmonic Choir. The soloists were Heather Harper, Josephine Veasey, John Mitchinson and Hans Sotin.[11]

Neville Cardus's estate amounted to £12,559.29 (net £10,792.75).[12] His will, completed on 23 April 1968, shortly after his wife's death, gave his name as Sir John Frederick Neville Cardus. So, was that the truth about his name? After a life in which he had risen high up life's ladder, he had not forgotten his modest roots.

Cardus divided opinion. In Australia his music criticism was denounced by Alphonse Silbermann, but his radio broadcasts on music were widely applauded. In post-war England Larry Montague and A.P. Wadsworth differed about the value of his cricket contributions to the MG. Those readers looking for the literal truth are unlikely to appreciate Cardus; his value was elsewhere. Geoffrey Howard didn't rate Cardus's knowledge of cricket but did regard him as a very gifted writer.[13] One comment was that he used "words which were plain but which could also sing."[14]

Cardus denied that he could properly be described as a writer on cricket or a music critic, and went on to conclude,

"I am, … before else simply a writer, with summer and cricket and the English scene one of my themes; and music and what it means of genius and art, the other."[15]

In his obituary in *The Musical Times*, Michael Kennedy wrote that Cardus had an eye for character; he was "truly a writer, a *writer* [*italics in original*], a prose-poet."[16] The truth was that, for Cardus, his writing wasn't always the truth but that writing came first.

ACKNOWLEDGEMENTS
AND REFERENCES

I would like to thank the following people who have helped me with this book: Marion Bond, Ron Bullock, Robert Curphey, Paul Fenn, Emma Golding, Michael Gray, Bob Hilton, Icki Iqbal, Gary James, Malcolm Lorimer, Ken Maud, Laurence O'Brien, Russell O'Brien, David Paton, Eleanor Roberts, Adam Sharman and Peter Wynne-Thomas. I also wish to thank the staff at several libraries: namely the British Library, University of Cambridge, University of Manchester (John Rylands Library), University of Nottingham and Manchester Central Library. And a big thank you to Amanda Helm for her assistance in the preparation of the book.

I would like to thank Guardian News & Media for permission to reproduce photographs.

And, without doubt, my greatest debt is to Lesley, for her love and support.

References

Agate, J. (1946). *Ego 8*. London: Harrap.

Anderson, R. & Scaife, N. (2001). "Neville Cardus" in Sadie, S. (ed.), *The New Grove Dictionary of Music and Musicians*, vol. 5. London: Macmillan.

Ayerst, D. (1971). *Guardian. Biography of a Newspaper*. London: Collins.

Bateman, A. (2009a). *Cricket, Literature and Culture*. Farnham: Ashgate.

Bateman, A. (2009b). "'Guilty, M'lud, to Fiction': Neville Cardus and the moment of scrutiny", *Sport in History*, vol.

2(1), pp. 259–276.

Bearshaw, B. (1990). *From the Stretford End*. London: Partridge Press.

Berry, S., ed. (1987). *The Observer on Cricket*. London: Unwin Hyman.

Birley, D. (1979). *The Willow Wand*. London: Queen Anne Press.

Brereton, A. (1908). *The Life of Henry Irving*, volume II. London: Longmans, Green & Co.

Brookes, C. (1985). *His Own Man. The Life of Neville Cardus*. London: Methuen.

Busby, R. (1976). *British Music Hall: an illustrated who's who from 1850 to the present day*. London: Paul Elek.

Cardus, J.F.N. (1916). "Bantock in style and art", *Musical Opinion*, no. 471, December, pp. 158–159.

Cardus, N. (1922). *A Cricketer's Book*. London: Grant Richards.

Cardus, N. (1924). *Days in the Sun*. London: Grant Richards.

Cardus, N., ed. (1929). *Samuel Langford*. London: Oxford University Press.

Cardus, N. (1930). *Cricket*. London: Longmans Green.

Cardus, N. (1937). *Australian Summer*. London: Jonathan Cape.

Cardus, N. (1945). *Ten Composers*. London: Jonathan Cape.

Cardus, N. (1947). *Autobiography*. London: Collins.

Cardus, N. (1948). "Music in Australia", *Tempo*, no. 7, pp. 8–11.

Cardus, N. (1949). *The Essential Neville Cardus*. London: Cape.

Cardus, N. (1950). *Second Innings*. London: Collins.

Cardus, N. (1952). *Cricket all the Year*. London: Collins.

Cardus, N. (1954). *Kathleen Ferrier: a memoir*. London: Hamish Hamilton.

Cardus, N. (1956). *Close of Play*. London: Collins.

Cardus, N. (1957). *Talking of Music*. London: Collins.

Cardus, N. (1958). *A Composers Eleven*. London: Jonathan Cape.

Cardus, N. (1960a). "Errol Holmes, perhaps one of the last dandies", *Playfair Cricket Monthly*, vol. 1(6), October, pp. 10–11.

Cardus, N. (1960b). "Review of 'The Hallé tradition: a century of music' by Michael Kennedy", *The Musical Times*, vol. 101, no. 1413, pp. 704–705.

Cardus, N. (1961). *Sir Thomas Beecham, a memoir.* London: Collins.

Cardus, N. (1963). *The Playfair Cardus.* London: Dickens Press.

Cardus, N. (1965). *Gustav Mahler: his Mind and his Music.* Volume 1. London: Gollancz.

Cardus, N. (1966). "Fifty years with the Guardian" in Fay, G. (ed.), *The Bedside 'Guardian' 15.* London: Collins.

Cardus, N. (1970). *Final Score.* London: Cassell.

Cardus, N. (1977). *Cardus on Cricket.* London: Souvenir Press.

Cardus, N. (1979). *Play Resumed with Cardus.* London: Souvenir Press.

Cardus, N. (1985). *A Cardus for All Seasons* (ed. M. Hughes). London: Souvenir Press.

Chalke, S. (2001). *At the Heart of English Cricket.* Bath: Fairfield Books.

Chaney, L. (2006). *Hide-and-seek with Angels: a life of J.M. Barrie.* London: Arrow.

"Cricketer" (1922). *The Club Cricketer.* Manchester: *Manchester Guardian.*

Daniels, R. (1976). *Conversations with Cardus.* London: Victor Gollancz.

Daniels, R. (2008). *Cardus. Celebrant of Beauty.* Lancaster: Palatine.

Engel, M., ed. (1986). *The Guardian Book of Cricket.* London: Pavilion.

Engel, M. (1990). "Introduction" to Kilburn, J.M., *In Search of Cricket.* London: Pavilion.

Fingleton, J. (1981). *Batting from Memory.* London: Collins.

Green, B., ed. (1989). *The Wisden Papers of Neville Cardus.*

London: Stanley Paul.

Griffin, H.M. (1986). "Marjorie Florence Lawrence" in *Australian Dictionary of Biography*, vol. 10.

Hamilton, D., ed. (2008). *Sweet Summers*. Ilkley: Great Northern Books.

Hamilton, D. (2019). *The Great Romantic. Neville Cardus and the Golden Age of Cricket*. London: Hodder & Stoughton.

Hettena, S. (2014). "An extraordinary breach of promise case", http://www.sethhettena.com/2014/01/an-extraordinary-breach-of-promise-case.html,
downloaded 17 September 2017.

Heyworth, P. (1996). *Otto Klemperer, His Life and Times*, volume 1. Cambridge: Cambridge University Press.

Hilton, B. (2007). *My Dear Michael...* Manchester: Lancashire County Cricket Club library.

Hilton, B. (2009). *The Elusive Mr Cardus*. Manchester: Lancashire County Cricket Club library.

Hilton, B. (2012). *Cardus: a Reader's Guide*. Manchester: Lancashire County Cricket Club library.

Hilton, B. (2014). *Neville Cardus Reflects*. Manchester: Lancashire County Cricket Club library.

Hilton, B. (2017). *Cardus Undimmed: the Last Decade*. Manchester: Lancashire CCC Library in association with Max Books.

James, C.L.R. (1963). *Beyond a Boundary*. London: Hutchinson.

Jones, M. (2016). The curious case of Neville Cardus's birth-date. http://www.cricketcountry.com/articles/the-curious-case-of-neville-cardus-birth-date-430632, downloaded 2 August 2017.

Kennedy, M. (1975). "Neville Cardus", *The Musical Times*, vol. 100, no. 1394, pp. 204–205.

Kennedy, M. (1982). *The Hallé 1858–1973. A history of the orchestra*. Manchester: Manchester University Press.

Lamb, A. (1985). "The truth about Cardus", *Wisden Cricket Monthly*, December, pp. 34–35.

Lamb, A. (1988). "Cardus reaches his century", *The Musical*

Times, vol. 172, no. 1742, pp. 177–180.

Major, J. (2007). *More than a Game: the story of cricket's early years*. London: HarperCollins.

Mason, R. (1967). *Sing a Green Willow*. London: Epworth Press.

Mather, G, (2004). "Cricket – the sound of music", http://www.northtrek.plus.com/cardus.htm, downloaded 17 May 2017.

Miller, D. (2014). "The changing character of county cricket", *The Cricket Statistician*, no. 167, autumn, pp. 27–30.

National Liberal Club (1946). *Officers, Committees, List of Members, etc.*

Nichols, H.D. (1946). "The Sports Page" in Haley, W. et al, *C. P. Scott 1846–1932*. London: Frederick Muller.

Phillips, P. (2009). "Out of the ashes", *The Musical Times*, vol. 150, no. 1908, pp. 91–95.

Redmonds, G., King, T. & Hey, D. (2011). *Surnames, DNA, and Family History*. Oxford: University Press.

Robertson-Glasgow, R.C. (1949). *46 Not Out*. London: Hollis and Carter.

Ronayne, M. (2017). *A Guide to the Memorials of Cricketers*. Cardiff: Association of Cricket Statisticians and Historians.

Sale, R. (1951). "Shrewsbury" in Roe, W.N. (ed.), *Public Schools Cricket 1901–1950*. London: Max Parrish.

Sengupta, A. (2014). Myth-busting – Ranji, C.B. Fry, Sussex and the fertile mind of Neville Cardus. http://www.cricketcountry.com/articles/myth-busting-ranji-cb-fry-sussex-and-the-fertile-mind-of-neville-cardus-181550, downloaded 23 August 2017.

Somerville, R. (2002). "Leo Paul Schramm" in *Australian Dictionary of Biography*, vol. 16.

Taylor, G. (1973). *Changing Faces. The History of the Guardian 1956–88*. London: Fourth Estate.

Ward, D. (1963). *King of the Lads. The story of Charles Peace*. London: Elek Books.

Wright, D., ed. (1988). *Cardus on Music*. London: Hamish Hamilton.

Appendix 1

CARDUS'S MUSIC NOTICES IN THE
DAILY CITIZEN

Date	Title	Lines	Byline
1913			
Monday 3 November	The promenade concert Popular appreciation of Mr Balling's work	48	J.F.N.
Friday 7 November	"The Rose Bearer" Strauss succeeds Wagner at the Theatre Royal	46	J.F.N.
Friday 14 November	The Halle concert Mr Joseph Holbrooke's "Queen Mab"	55	J.F.N.
Tuesday 25 November	Brand Lane concert Superb playing by the orchestra [Brand Lane Symphony Orchestra]	50	J.F.N.
Friday 28 November	The Halle concert Manchester's first hearing of Elgar's 'Falstaff'	46	J.F.N.
Monday 1 December	Promenade concert Manchester composer's further success [reference to Mr J.H. Fould's 'Miniature suite']	42	J.F.N.

Friday 5 December	The Halle concert Dr Brodsky's success in Elgar's violin concerto	29	J.F.N.
Friday 12 December	The Halle concert Intellectual piano playing by Mr Frederick Lamond	34	J.F.N.
Monday 15 December	The Promenade concert Mr Frank Mullings's conspicuous success	40	J.F.N.
Friday 19 December	The Halle concert Huge audience for Handel's 'Messiah'	42	J.F.N.
Monday 22 December	Handel's Messiah Exhilarating performance at the Brand Lane concert	33	J.F.N.
1914			
Monday 12 January	Brand Lane concert Mr Mark Hambourg and Miss Ruth Vincent	40	J.F.N.
Friday 16 January	The Halle concert Mr Gustav Holst's Fine Oriental Suite	40	J.F.N.
Monday 19 January	The Promenade concert Miss Kantorovitch and Miss Doris Carte	51	J.F.N.
Friday 23 January	The Halle concert Strauss's extraordinary 'Festal Prelude'	44	J.F.N.
Friday 30 January	The Halle concert Rachmaninoff plays his own compositions	51	J.F.N.

Wednesday 4 February	Harrison concert Popular favourites' appearance in Manchester	43	N.
Friday 6 February	The Halle concert Fine rendering of Bach's Mass in B minor	47	N.
Monday 9 February	Brand Lane concert Mixed programme capitally performed	52	J.F.N.
Friday 13 February	The Halle concert Mr Siloti's triumph as a pianist	39	J.F.N.
Saturday 14 February	Brodsky concert More brilliant playing by Siloti	34	J.F.N.
Monday 16 February	Promenade concert Appreciation of Schubert's 'Unfinished' Symphony	46	J.F.N.
Friday 20 February	The Halle concert Miscellaneous programme by a brilliant quartette	47	J.F.N.
Friday 27 February	The Halle concert Superb performance of Brahms's first symphony	41	J.F.N.
Tuesday 3 March	Chamber concert Mr Max Meyer's splendid effort	39	J.F.N.
Wednesday 4 March	Harrison concert Mr Arthur Nikisch relates things about himself	35	J.F.N.

Friday 13 March	The Halle concert Examples of early Wagnerian opera	47	J.F.N.
Friday 20 March	Pension fund concert Sir Edward Elgar's appearance in Manchester	48	J.F.N.
Tuesday 21 April	Carl Rosa Opera Company Spirited performance of Tales of Hoffman	33	J.F.N.

Note: the concerts took place on the preceding day except that notices on a Monday relate to a concert on the Saturday.

Appendix 2

BACKGROUND TO CHOICE OF MUSIC ON *DESERT ISLAND DISCS*

Schumann: Fantasia

Cardus referred to this work in *Conversations*, praising Horowitz's fluency of technique.[1] Horowitz was one of Cardus's favourites; he "had extraordinary magnetism of touch."[2]

Wagner: *Liebestod*

Kirsten Flagstad had sung in *Tristan and Isolde* at Covent Garden and Cardus's comment about the *Liebestod* was, "Mme Flagstad can indeed be described as a beautiful but not a poignant singer, who lends point and eloquence to her phrases by 'expression'."[3] He later described her as "the finest of all Isoldes".[4] Cardus, when asked who was the greatest conductor, had no hesitation in deciding that, for *Tristan and Isolde*, it had to be Furtwängler.[5] He had heard Furtwängler conduct *Tristan and Isolde* with the Berlin Philharmonic Orchestra at Manchester's Free Trade Hall on 17 February 1933 although, in relation to *Liebestod*, he was somewhat critical of the conductor's frenzied arrangement.[6] The same conductor's performance at Covent Garden on 21 May 1935 was reviewed much more enthusiastically.[7] In *Autobiography* he wrote, "I could bow the head at Furtwängler's intensely tragic 'Tristan and Isolde'."[8]

Mozart: Clarinet Concerto

Mozart's Clarinet Concerto was regarded as an "incredible piece of music", with pathos and romantic undertones, with the descending notes in the adagio touching him deeply.[9]

Beethoven: Symphony No.4

This was the record that Cardus would take if permitted only one. This is not a surprise: in 1939 he wrote about the gramophone record of this work with Toscanini, describing a performance that "comes as close to the ideal as could well be imagined in an imperfect universe."[10] It should be added that although Cardus described Toscanini as "All Highest amongst conductors",[11] his live performance of this work given at the Queen's Hall also in 1939, impressed Cardus rather less.[12]

Mahler: *Das Lied von der Erde*

Mahler was a composer whom Cardus particularly admired: "I can not only *feel* [italics in original] Mahler in nearly every bar he wrote; I can see him."[13] When in Australia he was particularly pleased about the reception of his discussion on the radio about a performance of Bruno Walter conducting *Das Lied von der Erde*,[14] a piece about which he expressed the view: "All the best of Mahler is in this work…"[15] One further element has to be added: he regarded Kathleen Ferrier as "one of the most wonderful and beautiful creatures who has ever been born into this world."[16] He introduced himself to her at the inaugural Edinburgh Festival in 1947 when she was singing *Das Lied von der Erde*, with Bruno Walter conducting. He later wrote, "The whole woman of her sang, sang through the music sounded by the composer through her being."[17] She became a favourite of Cardus, although was to suffer a tragically early death at the age of 41 in 1953. Cardus edited a memoir to her, published in 1954.[18]

Schubert: Symphony No.8

Cardus's enjoyment of Schubert's *Unfinished* Symphony is apparent from his review of the Hallé performing it in 1922.[19] It was also a work he heard at the 1947 Edinburgh Festival, with Bruno Walter conducting, when he wrote that "The blend and eloquence of all the instruments were of voices calling to voices."[20] Cardus described the symphony, with its haunting opening bars, as "like dawn; its sun has been shining all the time"; it was "uniquely beautiful music; a product of the mind and metabolism of rare genius".[21]

Prokofiev: Symphony No.1

The *Classical* Symphony "belongs to fancy and caprice; it is charming in its epigrammatic way and should be heard often at our concerts" was Cardus's verdict when he reviewed a performance by the British Women's Symphony Orchestra conducted by Malcolm Sargent in 1935.[22]

Strauss: *Im Abendrot*

Cardus felt that the recording by Lisa della Casa of Strauss's *Four Last Songs* with the Vienna Philharmonic Orchestra on gramophone was excellent, the artists being flawless,[23] although he was disappointed by her singing at the Royal Festival Hall in 1957.[24] Nevertheless, as Cardus was choosing records, this made its way into the eight for his desert island.

And also...

In 1973 Cardus wrote that, "I'd give up a vast number of established classical piano sonatas for the Schumann Fantasia in C major (preferably played by Horowitz or Muriel Cohen, the Australian pianist). I would not part with my 'Unfinished' Symphony of Schubert, or with my memory of 'Tristan and Isolde' conducted by Furtwängler."[25]

Appendix 3

THE EMERGENCE OF NEVILLE CARDUS'S NAMES

The table reflects the first-known references to names by which Neville Cardus was known.

15/5/1888	John Frederick Cardus	Registration of birth
3/6/1888	John Henry Newsham	Baptism record
5/4/1891	Frederick Newsham	Census
31/3/1901	John Frederick Cardus	Census
2/4/1911	Frederick Cardus	Census
3/11/1913 to 21/4/1914	J.F.N.	*Daily Citizen*
4/2/1914 to 6/2/1914	N.	*Daily Citizen*
20/5/1916	JFN	Letter to George Popper
9/6/1916	J.F.N. Cardus	Concert programme
December 1916	J.F. Neville Cardus	*Musical Opinion*
10/4/1917	N.C.	*Manchester Guardian*
27/1/1919	Neville Cardus	*Manchester Guardian*
27/4/1920	Cricketer	*Manchester Guardian*
23/4/1968	John Frederick Neville Cardus	Will

Appendix 4

NEVILLE CARDUS'S INTER-WAR CRICKET REPORTS IN THE *MANCHESTER GUARDIAN*

	First-class				Non First-class	Total (Lord's)
	Lancs home	Lancs away	Tests	Other		
1919	12	1	0	0	0	13 (0)
1920	12	11	0	4	1	28 (3)
1921	15	5	5	3	0	28 (2)
1922	14	10	0	4	0	28 (3)
1923	17	11	0	6	1	35 (3)
1924	13	9	5	3	0	30 (3)
1925	17	10	0	5	1	33 (4)
1926	14	4	5	6	2	31 (3)
1927	14	8	0	7	1	30 (3)
1928	13	6	3	5	0	27 (3)
1929	14	4	4	5	0	27 (1)
1930	11	6	5	5	0	27 (5)
1931	11	8	3	4	1	27 (4)
1932	10	8	1	9	1	29 (6)
1933	8	7	3	8	0	26 (9)
1934	8	6	5	8	0	27 (5)
1935	9	7	5	9	0	30 (7)
1936	10	3	3	6	0	22 (5)
1937	10	6	3	5	2	26 (6)

	First-class				Non First-class	Total (Lord's)
	Lancs home	Lancs away	Tests	Other		
1938	5	6	5	10	0	26 (8)
1939	11	8	3	4	0	26 (5)
Total	248	144	58	116	10	576 (88)

Notes: covers home English seasons; abandoned Test 1938 included.

Surrey v Lancs 1939 relocated to Old Trafford is treated as "Lancs home"

Counties visited*: Lancs 270 (265), Middx 88 (86), Yorks 51, Surrey 42 (41), Notts 28, Kent 14, Glos 12, Leics 11, Oxon 9, Warwicks 9, Essex 8, Sussex 8, Worcs 8, Cambs 4, Derbys 4, Somerset 3, Northants 2, Berks (Holywell) 1 (0), Denbigh (Colwyn Bay) 1 (0), Glam 1, Hants 1, Staffs (Burton-on-Trent) 1.

Top grounds*: Old Trafford 223 (220), Lord's 88 (86), The Oval 42 (41), Liverpool 30, Trent Bridge 28, Headingley 22, Bramall Lane 14, Bradford 11, Blackpool 11, Leicester 10.

* Figures in brackets are first-class matches only

Appendix 5

FAMILY HISTORY DATA

❧

Abbreviations

B	Birth
B.C.	Birth certificate
Bp	Baptism
BpRec	Baptism record
C-o-M	Chorlton-on-Medlock, Manchester
D	Death
D.C.	Death certificate
E.R.	Electoral register
FS	www.familysearch.org
GRO Index	General Register Office Index of births and deaths
M	Marriage
M.C.	Marriage certificate
M.R.	Marriage record

Note: {} indicates data shown in the source but which is known to be incorrect.

FAMILY TREE

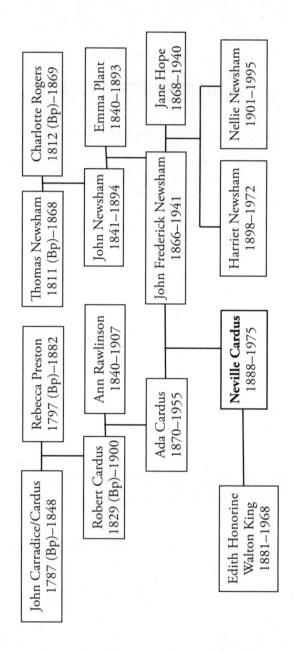

Neville (born John Frederick) Cardus

Father, John Frederick Newsham; Mother, Ada Cardus; Spouse, Edith Honorine Walton King

Date		Residence	Occupation	Birthplace	Age	Source
2/4/1888	B					BpRec*
3/4/1888				4 Summer Place		B.C.
3/6/1888	Bp					BpRec
5/4/1891		4 Summer Place		Manchester	3	Census
31/3/1901		12 Claremont St	scholar	Manchester	12	Census
5/4/1909		129 Rosebery St				Letter to *Manchester Courier*
2/4/1911		129 Rosebery St^R	insurance clerk	Manchester	{21}	Census
13/1/1917		154 Moseley Rd, Fallowfield				Letter to MG♣
17/6/1921	M	154 Moseley Rd, Fallowfield	journalist		{31}	M.C.#

1923, 1924		154 Moseley Rd, Fallowfield	not stated		Slater
1925		2 Barnsfield Ave			Phone book
1929		2 Barnsfield Ave	journalist		Slater
29/9/1939		2 Barnsfield Ave	journalist, editorial staff, M/c Guardian, music critic, lecturer		Register
1939		National Liberal Club			E.R.
1947		National Liberal Club			E.R.
1948		73 Lyall Mews West			E.R.
1949		73 Lyall Mews West			Phone book
1949, 1950		National Liberal Club			E.R.
1951		112 Bickenhall Mansions			E.R.

1952–65		National Liberal Club & 112 Bickenhall Mansions			E.R.
26/3/1968		112 Bickenhall Mansions	knight, writer		Edith's D.C.
28/2/1975	D	112 Bickenhall Mansions, Bickenhall St, London W1	knight, journalist and music critic		D.C.^

* see text for date of birth

R 5 rooms for Neville, uncle Robert and his wife Eliza

♣ *The Elusive Mr Cardus*, p. 14.

married at the register office, Chorlton

^ place of death: 10 Bryanston Square, St Marylebone

Ada Cardus – Neville's mother

Father, Robert Cardus; Mother, Ann Cardus, née Rawlinson; Spouse, John Frederick Newsham

Date		Residence	Occupation	Birthplace	Age	Source
15/10/1870	B			Summer Place		B.C.*
2/4/1871		4 Summer Place	none	Rusholme	0	Census
3/4/1881		4 Summer Place	scholar	Manchester	10	Census
3/4/1888		4 Summer Place	laundress			Neville's B.C.
14/7/1888	M	21 Victoria St[E]	none		17	M.C.#
5/4/1891		4 Summer Place	laundress	Manchester	20	Census
5/1896 to 3/1898		3 Clyde Rd, Withington (with Eliahoo Joseph)				JFN senior in divorce papers
31/3/1901		Park Avenue, Timperley (with Eliahoo Joseph)	none	Manchester	{29}	Census
2/4/1911		10 Old Hall Lane [later renamed Old Moat Lane][R]	laundress	Rusholme	40	Census
29/9/1939		Withington Hall	cook			Register
17/1/1955	D		see note		84	D.C.^

* consistent with 1939 Register

E not verified

married at St Clement's church, Longsight

^ place of death: 7 Marriott St, Withington, residence of C. Cardus, nephew and informant

R 6 rooms for Ada, sister Beatrice and her son Cecil

Notes: occupation given on D.C. as "widow of … Rawlinson (occupation unknown) (deceased)"

Surname shown as Cardus (up to 1888 and 1911), Newsham (1891 and divorce papers), Joseph (married, 1901 census), Rawlinson (1939, 1955)

Robert Cardus – Neville's maternal grandfather						
Father, John Carradice; Mother, Rebecca Carradice, née Preston Δ; Spouse, Ann Rawlinson						
Date		Residence	Occupation	Birthplace	Age	Source
1/11/1829	Bp	Switchers Farm, Hellifield				BpRec†
6/6/1841		Switchers Farm, Hellifield		Yorkshire	11	Census
30/3/1851		Village of Airton, Yorkshire (West Riding)	common carrier	Hellifield, Yorkshire	21	Census
3/6/1854		Skipton [but joining police at Much Woolton]	joined police, was labourer at Skipton Castle	Long Preston	24	Police records
23/7/1859	M	Much Woolton	policeman		28	M.C.#
9/1/1860		Allerton Rd, Much Woolton	poulterer			George's B.C.
3/10/1860		Much Woolton	rejoined police, was greengrocer on own account	Long Preston	30	Police records
7/4/1861		Police station, Silver St, Prestwich	police constable	Airton, Yorkshire	29	Census

Date		Address	Region	Occupation	Source
4/10/1861				police officer	Alice's B.C.
1/2/1865				police officer	Samuel's B.C.
24/6/1866				police officer	Annie's B.C.
28/9/1868				police officer	Arthur's B.C.
15/10/1870				domestic gardener	Ada's B.C.
23/10/1870		Platt Lane, Rusholme (see note)		domestic gardener	Arthur's D.C.
2/4/1871	38	4 Summer Place	Kirkby, Yorkshire	labourer	Census
4/8/1873		4 Summer Place		domestic gardener	Helena's B.C.
25/8/1874				general labourer	Robert (son)'s B.C.
22/11/1876				gardener	Jessie's B.C.
21/5/1879				farmer	Beatrice's B.C.
3/4/1881	49	4 Summer Place	Yorkshire	greengrocer	Census

Date		Address	Occupation	Place	Age	Source
24/12/1882			greengrocer			George's M.C.
9/7/1888			gentleman			Samuel's M.C.
28/1/1889			retired farmer			Annie's M.C.
5/4/1891		4 Summer Place	porter	Yorkshire	55	Census
27/5/1893			retired farmer			Alice's M.C.
11/4/1896			police officer			Helena's M.C.
1899		Church Rd, Northenden				E.R.
9/5/1900			police officer, retired			Jessie's M.C.
16/10/1900	D		formerly a police constable		70	D.C.^

△ Father John: B Yorkshire (1841 census); Bp at Great Mitton, Yorkshire 25/7/1787 (BpRec); M at Long Preston, Yorkshire 14/2/1824 (M.R.); died at Airton 9/7/1848 (D.C.); labourer (D.C.); Mother Rebecca, née Preston: B Slaidburn, Yorkshire (1851, 1861 censuses); Bp Slaidburn 12/3/1797

(BpRec); D Settle 1/5/1882 (D.C., surname Carradice)

† baptised at Long Preston, Yorkshire

married at Childwall parish church

^ place of death: 12 Claremont St

Note: some ages are incorrect

23/10/1870 address presumably Summer Place as this was wife Ann's address on 15/10/1870

Occupations shown on children's M.C.s post-1900: police constable (Robert 1908), laundryman (Beatrice 1912), laundry proprietor (Robert 1921)

Ann Cardus, née Rawlinson – Neville's maternal grandmother

Father, John Rawlinson; Mother, Ann Rawlinson, née Martin Δ; Spouse, Robert Cardus

Date		Residence	Occupation	Birthplace	Age	Source
28/3/1840	B			Allerton		B.C.
9/4/1840	Bp	Allerton				BpRec†
6/6/1841		Allerton	none	Lancs	1	Census
30/3/1851		Rose Lane, Mosley Vale, Wavertree	scholar	Allerton, Lancashire	11	Census
23/7/1859	M	Much Woolton	none		19	M.C.#
7/4/1861		Police station, Silver St, Prestwich	none	Allerton, Lancashire	21	Census
4/10/1861		Woolton St, Much Woolton				Alice's B.C.
1/2/1865		Union St, Rusholme				Samuel's B.C.
24/6/1866		Union St, Rusholme				Annie's B.C.

28/9/1868		Union St, Rusholme				Arthur's B.C.
15/10/1870		Summer Place				Ada's B.C.
2/4/1871		4 Summer Place	none	Childwall, Lancashire	31	Census
25/8/1874		Summer Place				Robert's B.C.
22/11/1876		4 Summer Place				Jessie's B.C.
21/5/1879		4 Summer Place				Beatrice's B.C.
3/4/1881		4 Summer Place	laundress	Liverpool	41	Census
5/4/1891		4 Summer Place	none	Liverpool	51	Census
7/1893		4 Summer Place				JFN senior in divorce papers
Pre-25/3/1898		Rose Cottage, Northenden				JFN senior in divorce papers

					Robert's D.C.
16/10/1900		12 Claremont St			
31/3/1901		12 Claremont St	retired laundress	Allerton, Lancashire	61	Census
17/12/1907	D		widow		{68}	D.C.^

Δ parents married 11/12/1826 at Childwall (source: FS)
† baptised at St Anne's church, Aigburth
# married at Childwall parish church
^ place of death: 12 Claremont St
Note: father's occupation: labourer on Ann's B.C. and BpRec, agricultural labourer in 1841 census, parter
(?) in 1851 census, gardener on Ann's M.C.

Children of Robert and Ann – Neville's aunts and uncles		Source
George	9/1/1860, born at Allerton Rd, Much Woolton	B.C.
	7/4/1861, living at police station, Silver St, Prestwich	Census
	2/4/1871, living at 4 Summer Place, scholar	Census
	3/4/1881, living at 4 Summer Place, tin man	Census
	24/12/1882, married Sarah Ann Gaul, age 21, no occupation (father's occupation tinplate worker) at St Mary Magdalene church, Liverpool; George's occupation, tinplate worker	M.C.
	5/4/1891, living at 61 Loom St, Manchester, trunk maker (employer) with wife (here called Selina) and 4 children (ages 0–7) and servant	Census
	31/3/1901, living at 9 Syndall St, C-o-M, trunk maker (employer), with wife Sarah A. and 8 children aged 0–18	Census
	2/4/1911, living at 2 Greenhill St, C-o-M, tin trunk worker (on own account) with wife Sarah Ann (head of household) and 7 children aged 8–16; had had 12 children, of whom 9 alive	Census
	23/10/1937, died at 110 Moss Lane West, Moss Side; occupation, nightwatchman	D.C.

Name	Details	Source
Alice	4/10/1861, born at Woolton St, Much Woolton	B.C.
	3/11/1861, baptised at Woolton, Liverpool	BpRec
	2/4/1871, living at 4 Summer Place, scholar	Census
	27/1/1878, gave birth to Harry at 4 Summer Place (Alice's residence); occupation, laundress	B.C.
	14/8/1878, Harry died at 4 Summer Place	D.C.
	3/4/1881, living at 4 Summer Place, laundress (no father named)	Census
	5/4/1891, living at 4 Summer Place, dress maker	Census
	27/5/1893, married John Fallows, age 29, coach builder, at Chorlton register office; Alice, no occupation, living at 36 Rosamund St West, Manchester	M.C.
	5/7/1897, died at 36 Rosamund St West	D.C.
Samuel	1/2/1865, born at Union St, Rusholme	B.C.
	2/4/1871, living at 4 Summer Place, scholar	Census
	3/4/1881, living at 4 Summer Place, blacksmith's apprentice	Census
	9/7/1888, married Maria Agnes Mines, age 21, no occupation (father's occupation, labourer) at Holy Trinity church, Hulme; Samuel's occupation, farrier, living at 12 Foy Grove	M.C.
	31/3/1896, died of exhaustion at 10 Oak St, New York (his residence), occupation horseshoer, had been in US for 7 years	D.C.
	Note: widow Maria was a servant in Manchester at 31/3/1901	Census

Name	Details	Sources
Annie	21/6/1866, born at Union St, Rusholme 2/4/1871, living at 4 Summer Place, scholar 3/4/1881, living at 4 Summer Place, scholar 28/1/1889, married Arthur Albert Smith, age 22, commercial traveller, at St Matthew's church, Toxteth Park; Annie had no occupation, living at 12 Clive St	B.C. Census Census M.C.
Arthur	28/9/1868, born at Union St, Rusholme 23/10/1870, died of scarlet fever at Platt Lane, Rusholme [presumably meant to be nearby 4 Summer Place]	B.C. D.C.
Ada	See above	

Helena		
	4/8/1873, born at 4 Summer Place	B.C.
	3/4/1881, living at 4 Summer Place, scholar	Census
	5/4/1891, living at 4 Summer Place, laundress	Census
	11/4/1896, married George Wilkinson, age 26, warehouse man, at Chorlton register office; Helena, no occupation, living at 4 Summer Place	M.C.
	31/3/1901, living at 31 Watts St, Levenshulme, no occupation; with husband George, brickseller's labourer	Census
	2/4/1911, living at 4 Chapel Cottages, Withington, no occupation; with husband George, bricklayer	Census
	29/9/1939, living at 7 Marriott St, Manchester, with husband George, bricklayer	Register
	11/3/1957, died at 7 Marriott St, Withington (widow of George, oven builder); informant, C. Cardus, nephew, 7 Marriott St	D.C.

Robert		
	25/8/1874, born at 4 Summer Place	B.C.
	3/4/1881, living at 4 Summer Place, scholar	Census
	5/4/1891, living at 4 Summer Place, estate agent's clerk	Census
	22/2/1893, departed for New York on *Teutonic*, clerk	Passenger list
	31/3/1901, living at 12 Claremont St, stone mason	Census
	4/7/1908, married Eliza Idle, sewing machinist, age 32, at Chorlton register office; Robert's occupation was foreman, stonemasons, living at 3 Kippax St, Moss Side	M.C.
	1910, 1911, living at 129 Rosebery St, Moss Side, storekeeper	Slater
	2/4/1911, living at 129 Rosebery St, Moss Side, stone mason (steel work) for Manchester corporation; living with wife Eliza and Neville (called Frederick) Cardus	Census
	1920, Eliza died	GRO Index
	12/2/1921, married Alice Phillips, age 38, no occupation, at Chorlton register office; Robert's occupation, municipal clerk, living at 154 Moseley Rd, Fallowfield; Neville and wife-to-be Edith were witnesses	M.C.
	29/9/1921, died at Manchester Infirmary; was living at 154 Moseley Rd, Fallowfield; occupation, municipal clerk (highways)	D.C.
	Note: Alice died in Wythenshawe, 9/3/1974	D.C.

Jessie	22/11/1876, born at 4 Summer Place	B.C.
	3/4/1881, living at 4 Summer Place, scholar	Census
	5/4/1891, living at 4 Summer Place, scholar	Census
	9/5/1900, married Harry Davies, age 22, store keeper, at Chorlton register office; Jessie, no occupation, living at 122 Raby St, Moss Side	M.C.
	31/3/1901, living at 12 Claremont St, usher (Comedy Theatre) with husband, mother, brother Robert, sister Beatrice and Neville (shown as John Frederick) Cardus	Census

Beatrice	21/5/1879, born at 4 Summer Place	B.C.
	3/4/1881, living at 4 Summer Place	Census
	5/4/1891, living at 4 Summer Place, scholar	Census
	31/3/1901, two entries in census: at 12 Claremont St with mother and others (working at home); and at Park Ave, Timperley with Ada and Eliahoo Joseph (no occupation in either entry)	Census
	15/10/1903, son Cecil born at 65 Roebuck Lane, Sale; Beatrice living at 14 South Grove, C-o-M; name given as Cardross	Cecil's B.C.
	2/4/1911, living at 10 Old Hall Lane, Withington, laundress; with son Cecil and sister Ada	Census
	1911, 1912, living at 10 Old Hall Lane, Withington, householder, shown as Mrs Beatrice Cardus	Slater
	26/8/1912, married Edward Mann, age 61, widower and day gardener, at Chorlton register office; Beatrice, no occupation; both shown living at 10 Old Hall Lane, Withington	M.C.
	2/10/1912, daughter Irene born at 10 Old Hall Lane (Beatrice's address); father's occupation, domestic gardener	B.C.
	14/1/1916, son Edward James born at 10 Old Hall Lane; father's occupation, gardener	B.C.
	14/6/1918, died aged 39, at Baguley sanatorium; address 10 Old Hall Lane; husband Edward was a cotton warehouseman	D.C.
	Note: Cecil, retired labourer, died 4/3/1980 in Manchester	D.C.
	Irene, widow of postman Frank Dyos, died 3/9/2003 in Manchester	D.C.

John Frederick Newsham – Neville's father

Father, John Newsham; Mother, Emma Newsham, née Plant; Spouses, Ada Cardus (divorced), Jane Hope; for pronunciation see chapter 3 (help from Marion Bond acknowledged)

Date		Residence	Occupation	Birthplace	Age	Source
27/11/1866	B			5b York St, C-o-M		B.C.*
3/3/1867	Bp					BpRec†
2/4/1871		3 Gray St, C-o-M		Manchester	4	Census
3/4/1881		42 Duke St, Rusholme	apprentice to smith	Manchester	14	Census
14/7/1888	M	21 Victoria St^E	smith		21	M.C.#
6/4/1898		17 Water St	smith			JFN senior in divorce papers
2/2/1899	M	28 Moston Lane, Harpurhey	smith		32	M.C.##
21/6/1901			journeyman blacksmith			Nellie's B.C.

2/4/1911		28 Moston Lane, Harpurhey^R	engineer's smith	Manchester	44	Census
18/8/1917			smith			Harriet's M.C.
20/8/1919			smith			Nellie's M.C.
21/2/1931			engineer			Nellie's M.C.
29/9/1939		43 Ryecroft Rd, Stretford	engineer tool maker, retired			Register
19/12/1941	D		grocer		75	D.C.^

* date confirmed by school admission record (Ducie Street school) and 1939 Register

† baptised at All Saints, C-on-M

married Ada Cardus at St Clement's church, Longsight

See text for passenger journeys to and from USA

married Jane Hope by licence at the Holy Innocence church, Fallowfield; Jane was born 19/3/1868 (BpRec) and died 9/11/1940 (D.C.); occupation patent lint maker (1891 census), assistant shopkeeper, provisions (1901 census), none on M.C. or in 1911 census

E not verified

R 4 rooms for JFN senior, wife, 2 children, father-in-law, visitor

Directory entries: 1921, beer retailer, 39 Alexandra Rd, Moss Side; 1926, 155 Cowesby St, Moss Side; 1931 and 1936, beer retailer, 17 Dudley St, Brooks's Bar [Slater]

^ place of death: 43 Ryecroft Rd, Stretford, buried in Southern Cemetery, Manchester

1901 census entry not confirmed: could be Fred Newsham, blacksmith, lodging at 61 Cottenham St, C-o-M, shown as age 30 and unmarried; wife Jane was living with her parents and daughter Harriet at 28 Moston Lane

John Newsham – Neville's paternal grandfather

Father, Thomas Newsham; Mother, Charlotte Newsham, née Rogers Δ; Spouse, Emma Plant

Date		Residence	Occupation	Birthplace	Age	Source
6/4/1841	B			Durham Place, C-o-M (father's residence)		B.C.
30/3/1851		25 Chester St, Hulme, C-o-M	scholar	Lancashire	9	Census
7/4/1861		20 Brindle St, Hulme, C-o-M	blacksmith	Manchester	20	Census
20/8/1864	M		blacksmith		>21	M.C.#

Date		Address	Occupation	Place	Age	Source
27/11/1866		5b York St, C-o-M	farrier's smith			JFN senior's B.C.
18/12/1868			blacksmith			William Henry's B.C.
2/4/1871		3 Gray St, C-o-M	whitesmith	Manchester	29	Census
15/5/1871			blacksmith			Thomas's B.C.
3/4/1881		42 Duke St, Rusholme	blacksmith	Manchester	39	Census
14/7/1888			master smith			JFN senior's M.C.
5/4/1891		27 Duke St, Rusholme	blacksmith	Manchester	49	Census
23/1/1893		27 Duke St, Rusholme	blacksmith (master)			Emma's D.C.
22/1/1894	D		blacksmith (master)		52	D.C.^

△ Father Thomas: B Lytham (1851, 1861 census), Bp Lytham 21/8/1811 (BpRec); M Lytham 17/5/1831 (M.R.); shoemaker (John Frederick's B.C.), foreman of vulcanised rubber factory (1851 census), foreman

247

(1861 census), manager of India rubber works (John Frederick's M.C.); D Manchester 23/6/1868 (D.C.)

Mother Charlotte, née Rogers, B Chichester (1851 census), Bp Chichester 11/9/1812 (BpRec); no occupation in censuses; D Manchester 8/2/1869 (D.C.)

married at St John the Baptist church, Hulme

^ place of death: 68 Upper Duke St, Hulme (where son Henry was residing)

Not traced in 1841 census

Children in addition to John Frederick (Neville's uncles): William Henry, B Manchester 18/12/1868 (B.C.); Thomas, B Manchester 15/5/1871 (B.C.)

Servant in household at 1851, 1861, 1871 and 1891 censuses

Emma Newsham, née Plant – Neville's paternal grandmother						
Father, John Plant Δ; Mother, Catharine Plant, née Kay; Spouse, John Newsham						
Date		Residence	Occupation	Birthplace	Age	Source
27/10/1840	B			Hunt Green, Blackley		B.C.
6/6/1841		Barnes Green, Manchester		Lancs	0	Census

7/4/1861		19 Ruby St, Hulme	cotton weaver	Blackley	20	Census
20/8/1864	M		crinoline maker		>21	M.C.#
18/12/1868		66 York St, C-o-M				William Henry's B.C.
2/4/1871		3 Gray St, C-o-M		Blackley	30	Census
15/5/1871		3 Gray St, C-o-M				Thomas's B.C.
3/4/1881		42 Duke St, Rusholme		Blackley	40	Census
5/4/1891		27 Duke St, Rusholme		Blackley	50	Census
23/1/1893	D				52	D.C.^

Δ Father's occupation: grinder in factory (Emma's B.C.), cotton carder (1861 census), carder (Emma's M.C.)

Not traced in 1851 census

married at St John the Baptist church, Hulme

^ place of death: 27 Duke St, Rusholme

Children of John Frederick Newsham and Jane Hope – Neville's half-sisters

			Source
Harriet		7/10/1898, born at 38 Furness Rd, Fallowfield, named Harriet Newsham Hope	B.C.
		16/2/1899, baptised Harriet Newsham	BpRec
		31/3/1901, living at 28 Moston Lane, Harpurhey	Census
		2/4/1911, scholar, 28 Moston Lane, Harpurhey	Census
		18/8/1917, married 20-year-old Alfred Alexander Scowen, musician on *HMS Lion*, at Harpurhey; Harriet living at 28 Moston Lane; occupation, seamstress	M.C.
		1919, son Alfred Neville Scowen born; he died at sea in 1944	FS; www.traffordwardead.co.uk
		1935, Alfred Alexander Scowen died	GRO Index
		29/9/1939, known as Hetty, shop assistant; living with parents at 43 Ryecroft Rd, Stretford	Register
		10/2/1945, married Alfred George Grist, a 45-year-old engineer, at Stretford; Harriet living at 21 Newstead Rd, Davyhulme, no occupation	M.C.
		Later emigrated to South Africa, occupation English teacher	Passenger lists
		21/11/1972, died in Durban (had been living at Umhlanga Rocks, Kwa-Zulu Natal)	Death record

Nellie	21/6/1901, born at 28 Moston Lane, Harpurhey	B.C.
	2/4/1911, scholar, 28 Moston Lane, Harpurhey	Census
	20/8/1919, married Harry Hides, 25-year-old band corporal; Nellie living at 34 Kemp St, Middleton, Lancashire, no occupation	M.C.
	Divorced Harry Hides	M.C. (Meyers)
	21/2/1931, married Rudolph Edward Meyers, 29-year-old export merchant; Nellie living at 134 Hulton St, Moss Side, no occupation	M.C.
	Note: Meyers was Dutch citizen living in S Africa	Passenger lists
	28/8/1995, died in Johannesburg	Correspondence with Ken Maud

Edith Honorine Walton Cardus, née King – Neville's wife

Father, John Thomas Sissons King Δ; Mother, Fanny Jane King, née Walton; Spouse, Neville Cardus

Date		Residence	Occupation	Birthplace	Age	Source
19/6/1881	B			Carr Hill, Mossley, Saddleworth		B.C.*
5/4/1891		18 Livingstone St, C-o-M	scholar	Mossley, Yorkshire	9	Census
31/3/1901		Stockwell Training College	future professional teacher	Mossley, Yorkshire	19	Census
2/4/1911		18 Livingstone St, C-o-M	assistant schoolmistress	Mossley, Yorkshire	29	Census
17/6/1921	M	Sindow, Albany Rd, Victoria Park	schoolmistress		{33}	M.C.#

29/9/1939		2 Barnsfield Ave	art mistress, Ducie Ave school, Manchester	{54}	Register
1951-1965		112 Bickenhall Mansions, Westminster			E.R.
26/3/1968	D	112 Bickenhall Mansions, Westminster	wife of Neville Cardus, knight, writer	{82}	D.C.^

Δ father's occupation: certificated schoolmaster (1881 census), schoolmaster (Edith's B.C., 1891, 1901 censuses), headmaster (1911 census); all of 1881–1911 censuses indicate he was born in Bottesford, Leicestershire

* 1881 census shows parents living at Carr Hill Road

\# married at the register office, Chorlton

^ place of death: 22 St Edmund's Terrace, St Marylebone.

ENDNOTES

Chapter 1: It's a matter of style

1 *Manchester Guardian*, 2 May 1927.
2 *Manchester Guardian*, 31 August 1921.
3 *Full Score*, p. 100.
4 *Manchester Guardian*, 9 October 1953.
5 *Manchester Guardian*, 10 October 1951.
6 *Manchester Guardian*, 7 July 1945.
7 *Wisden*, 1951.
8 *Cricket all the Year*, p. 17.
9 *Manchester Guardian*, 5 June 1957.
10 *Play Resumed with Cardus*, p. 13.
11 *Manchester Guardian*, 25 July 1899.
12 This was pointed out by Brookes, *His Own Man*, p. 21.
13 *Autobiography*, p. 15.
14 *Autobiography*, p. 15.
15 Bateman (2009a), p. 115.
16 Green (1989), introduction.

Chapter 2: Family background

1 *Autobiography*, p. 13.
2 Redmonds, King & Hey (2011), p. 118.
3 This and following paragraphs in this section are drawn from census returns and the GRO Index.
4 *Liverpool Mercury*, 5 April 1859.
5 Lancashire police archives; and *Liverpool Mercury*, 17 November 1859.
6 This paragraph draws on the Lancashire police archives.
7 *Manchester Guardian*, 8 July and 6 August 1867.
8 *Manchester Courier*, 6 August 1867.
9 *Manchester Guardian*, 6 August 1867.

10 p. 13.
11 Ward (1963).
12 This paragraph draws on the Lancashire police archives.
13 *Autobiography*, p. 14.
14 *Autobiography*, pp. 25–26.
15 The Manchester rate books show Robert Cardus in Union Street from 1866, at house no.1.
16 According to a sample of 10 houses.
17 Using the information in Manchester rate books for Union Street in 1866 and Summer Place in 1870.
18 The earliest date where houses in Summer Place have been traced in Manchester rate books is 1838.
19 p. 14.

Chapter 3: A secretive early life

 1 The examples quoted are from p. 58 and p. 269; there are similar examples on pp. 50, 93, 127, 182 and 254. A reference on p. 62 implies birth in 1891.
 2 p. 11.
 3 *Celebrant of Beauty*, p. 3.
 4 p. 17.
 5 Brookes (1985), p. 18, acknowledged this.
 6 Lamb (1985), p. 34.
 7 Peter Calver: https://www.lostcousins.com/ newsletters2/midnov17news.htm#Birthdate, downloaded 21 November 2017.
 8 From the list of "Baptisms solemnized in the Cathedral and parish church of Manchester".
 9 Jones (2016).
10 *His Own Man*, p. 18.
11 Further, implying that he was born in 1890 went beyond what was required to avoid a charge of illegitimacy; although using 1890 may have reflected faulty arithmetic, referred to below.
12 *Autobiography*, p. 254.
13 An inconsistency is that he disclosed his birthdate as 2 April 1890 in *Who's Who in Australia* (1947 and later),

perhaps because he had just completed *Autobiography*, with the implication that he was born in 1890.

14 In March 1937 he travelled on *Orontes* from Australia to England, age shown as 41: this is so far out that it is unreliable and may reflect a transcription error.

15 In *Ten Composers*, p. 19, he wrote, "In May, 1933, when I had passed my forty-third birthday…".

16 He wrote that he was 15 when Henry Irving died (in October 1905) and 19 at the time of the Old Trafford Test in 1909 (pp. 194, 121).

17 *Second Innings*, p. 58.

18 He wrote that he had been 50 in 1939 (p. 163) and was then in his 82nd year (p. 199). One suggestion (Lamb, 1988), p. 177, was that the change from 1890 to 1889 may have dated from when he was eligible for his state pension. That doesn't fit with his using 1889 as his birthdate in the 1930s.

19 In the list of illustrations.

20 p. 13.

21 Ada's husband referred to this in papers for their divorce (see later).

22 *Autobiography*, p. 7; also used for the remainder of this paragraph. Cardus also referred to it as a slum on p. 280.

23 *His Own Man*, ch. 1; Lamb (1988), p. 177; in *Neville Cardus Reflects* Hilton refers to it as "not quite the slum of legend" (p. 3).

24 *Second Innings*, p. 84; *Full Score*, p. 202.

25 *Full Score*, p. 120; Mather (2004).

26 *Conversations*, pp. 28, 268.

27 Rooms from 1911 census (except no.10, from 1891 census) and include kitchen but exclude scullery and bathroom.

28 *Autobiography*, p. 18.

29 pp. 15, 16.

30 *Celebrant of Beauty*, p. 4.

31 Jones (2016) used this information to deduce that JFN senior was the father.

32 His 1956 and later *Who's Who* entries omit any mention of his parents; this followed his mother's death in 1955.

33 Available from www.ancestry.co.uk.

34 *The Times*, 25 June 1898.

35 *Manchester Courier*, 25 June 1898.

36 *Autobiography*, pp. 15–16.

37 Manchester schools admission registers.

38 This section draws on the court papers, *Manchester Courier*, 25 June 1898, *Lloyd's Weekly Newspaper*, 26 June 1898 and the newspapers from which quotations are taken.

39 *The Times*, 25 June 1898.

40 Samuel's death certificate. However, Samuel was not on the passenger list to America that included JFN senior.

41 *The Times*, 25 June 1898.

42 *Lichfield Mercury*, 25 June 1898.

43 *Lichfield Mercury*, 25 June 1898.

44 *Autobiography*, pp. 14, 15.

45 *Autobiography*, p. 16.

46 *Autobiography*, pp. 28, 35.

47 Memorandum from Larry Montague, *Manchester Guardian* sports editor, 1952, University of Manchester Library Special Collections, ref GB 133 GDN/A/M87.

48 p. 204.

49 The 1901 census referred to him as 45 years old, i.e. born about 1856; the prison record of 1903 has him as age 42, i.e. born about 1861.

50 *Manchester Courier*, 11 July 1903.

51 The details of the case are from *Manchester Guardian*, 5 and 6 December 1892; *Manchester Times*, 9 December 1892, other newspapers as referenced; and Hettena (2014).

52 *Freeman's Journal and Commercial Advertiser*, 6 December 1892.

53 *Manchester Times*, 9 December 1892.

54 *Bristol Mercury and Daily Post*, 8 February 1893.

55 Hettena (2014).

56 *Autobiography*, p. 28.

57 *Manchester Courier*, 21 November 1903.

58 Hettena (2014).

59 *Manchester Guardian*, 11 December 1903.

60 *Manchester Courier*, 21 November 1903.

61 *Derby Daily Telegraph*, 23 November 1903.

62 *Autobiography*, pp. 7–8.

63 *Who's Who in Australia*, 1947.

64 *Second Innings*, p. 82.

65 *Full Score*, p. 203. The 1901 census shows him to be at school, then aged 12.

66 *Second Innings*, p. 82.

67 p. 203.

68 *Second Innings*, p. 99.

69 *Autobiography*, p. 280.

70 *Autobiography*, p. 80.

71 *Second Innings*, p. 57.

72 *Manchester Guardian*, 3 December 1861.

73 *Autobiography*, pp. 16, 18.

74 *Second Innings*, pp. 24, 38.

75 *Second Innings*, p. 100; *Conversations*, p. 35.

76 *Autobiography*, p. 16.

77 *Conversations*, p. 255.

78 *Autobiography*, p. 55.

79 *Autobiography*, pp. 22, 40; *Guardian*, 7 September 1973.

80 *Autobiography*, p. 22.

81 *Autobiography*, p. 49; *Second Innings*, p. 105.

82 *Second Innings*, p. 110; *Manchester Guardian*, 22 October 1906.

Chapter 4:
More difficulties with family and friends

1 *His Own Man*, p. 22.

2 *Autobiography*, p. 26.

3 *Second Innings*, p. 39; *Autobiography*, p. 22.

4 The electoral register for 1899 confirms this.

5 *Manchester Courier*, 22 April 1902.

6 pp. 42–43. The reference to the grandmother suggests it may be after Robert's death in 1900.

7 *Manchester Guardian*, 21 May 1936.

8 *Autobiography*, p. 28.

9 *Autobiography*, p. 30.

10 pp. 36–37.

11 Published on 6 April 1909. The name underneath the letter is "J.T. Cardus". However, it is possible that he signed the letter as J.F. Cardus and that this was mis-read.

12 Slater's entry for the house shows Robert Cardus as the householder in 1910; it is blank for 1909 but given an annual publication cycle Robert may have been there some time in 1909.

13 Her death certificate indicates that she had suffered from dilatation of the heart for 6 months, and also suffered from syncope.

14 p. 170.

15 *Autobiography*, p. 15.

16 The court case is described in *Manchester Guardian*, 14 May 1903.

17 The court case is described in several newspapers, including *Manchester Courier*, 6, 7 and 8 August 1903, 19, 20, 21 and 23 November 1903; *The Times*, 23 November 1903.

18 Prison register.

19 *Manchester Guardian*, 11 December 1908.

20 Details of the court case are from *Manchester Guardian*, 11 December 1908 and *The Times*, 3 March 1909.

21 *Manchester Guardian*, 11 December 1908.

22 *Autobiography*, p. 27.

23 *Autobiography*, p. 26.

24 *Autobiography*, p. 28.

25 Details of the court case from the *Manchester Courier*, 22 April 1902.

26 *Manchester Guardian*, 1 October 1881.

27 *Manchester Guardian*, 17 May 1898.

28 General Register Office Index.

29 The 1901 census shows seven children living with their parents. The court case referred to eight: perhaps the other was Gladys (present in the 1891 census) or Zullfie (a child mentioned in some family trees on www.ancestry.co.uk but not verified independently). Hence, the couple may have had nine children: the seven in 1901 and both Gladys and Zullfie.

30 *Manchester Guardian*, 25 August 1902. It is not clear when he originally became Consul.

31 The court hearing established that Karsa had given Beatrice about £50 in cash and £30 in clothes.

32 *Autobiography*, p. 29. Cardus indicated that she bet at the Manchester races on the day following the court verdict; however, there was no racing at Manchester that week.

33 On 19 August: *Manchester Guardian*, 20 August 1907.

34 Details of this case from *Manchester Guardian*, 27 September 1909.

35 *Autobiography*, p. 30.

36 *Second Innings*, pp. 145 et seq.

37 *Second Innings*, pp. 148–149.

38 *Second Innings*, pp. 146–147.

39 I am grateful to Dr Gary James for his assistance on this point.

40 *Manchester Guardian*, 27 March 1953.

41 *Spectator,* 3 September 1953.

42 *Close of Play*, p. 177.

43 *Second Innings*, p. 150.

44 *Full Score*, p. 203.

45 The information in this paragraph is from *Second Innings*, pp. 150–155.

46 Downloaded 5 December 2016.

47 *Autobiography*, p. 249. There is no mention of the Ceylon match in *Australian Summer*.

48 In minor matches on www.cricketarchive.com his highest score was 82 not out.

49 *Autobiography*, pp. 34, 74.

50 *Autobiography*, pp. 9, 22, 60, 249; Cardus's notebook,

late 1949, *Neville Cardus Reflects*, p. 11.

51 *Autobiography*, p. 9; *Second Innings*, p. 24.

52 *Autobiography*, p. 251.

53 *Autobiography*, p. 22.

54 The information about this group is from *Second Innings*, pp. 133–136.

55 *The Elusive Mr Cardus*, pp. 7–11; *Neville Cardus Reflects*, pp. 17–23.

56 The name Spengler on the marriage certificate is not clear.

57 Probate record.

58 Jane's marriage certificate.

59 Correspondence with Ken Maud.

Chapter 5: Young Neville takes to cricket

1 *Manchester Guardian*, 27 March 1953; *Close of Play*, p. 88; it was a three-day match.

2 p. 33.

3 31 May 1934.

4 *Australian Summer*, p. 10.

5 *Chronicle,* Adelaide, 17 October 1940.

6 *Manchester Guardian*, 27 March 1953.

7 *Days in the Sun*, p. 22.

8 *Cricket*, p. 117; in *Cricket all the Year*, p. 109 and *Manchester Guardian*, 5 June 1957, he wrote that he was present when England lost. In *Second Innings*, p. 87, he mentioned Trumper's century but did not indicate that he witnessed it.

9 27 December 1927.

10 *A Cardus for all Seasons*, p. 183 (originally in *World Sports*, May 1960); *Cricket all the Year*, p. 24.

11 p. 55.

12 p. 121.

13 *Manchester Guardian*, 7 July 1945; *Wisden*, 1951; *Cricket all the Year*, p. 17; *Manchester Guardian*, 5 June 1957.

14 *Wisden*, 1975. The error was that Kent were 401–6 rather than 420 all out at close of play.

15 *Guardian*, 6 May 1964. The error was that the batsman

who scored 56 was Perkins rather than Patterson.

16 *Cricket all the Year*, p. 21.

17 In *Wisden*, 1951 and *Cricket all the Year*, pp. 17–19, he wrote that he had previously seen the matches against Gloucestershire in 1899 and Worcestershire in 1900. Also see *Manchester Guardian*, 28 May 1931.

18 *Manchester Guardian*, 6 August 1931.

19 p. 32. Cardus wrote that he had just passed his 12th birthday but in view of the difficulties with Cardus's age, this is discounted.

20 pp. 59–60. Cardus wrote that he was aged 15 or 16, but that can be discounted.

21 This paragraph draws on *Manchester Guardian*, 25–29 July 1901.

22 *Autobiography*, p. 31.

23 *Playfair Cardus*, p. 74.

24 *Guardian*, 28 May 1971.

25 *Autobiography*, p. 72.

26 *Full Score*, p. 105; *Guardian*, 28 May 1971.

27 *Cricket*, p. 33.

28 *Manchester Guardian*, 26 May 1904.

29 p. 33.

30 *Cricket all the Year*, p. 22.

31 *Manchester Guardian*, 8 June 1927.

32 p. 76.

33 *Manchester Guardian*, 31 December 1921.

34 *Manchester Guardian*, 21 May 1936; *Autobiography*, p. 35; *Wisden*, 1951.

35 *Manchester Guardian*, 6 August 1931.

36 *Cricket*, p. 78; *Cricket all the Year*, p. 28.

37 *Manchester Guardian*, 22 June 1933.

38 *Manchester Guardian*, 6 June 1929.

39 *Second Innings*, p. 89.

40 *Manchester Guardian*, 6 June 1929.

41 *Manchester Guardian*, 12 April 1923. The Cardus family lived in Union Street before Summer Place.

42 *A Cricketer's Book*, p. 57.

43 *Autobiography*, p. 31; *Second Innings*, p. 82.

44 See the 1977 edition of *Cardus on Cricket*.

45 p. 89 et seq.

46 *Manchester Guardian*, 20 June 1910.

47 *Second Innings*, p. 93.

48 *Second Innings*, p. 151.

49 *Second Innings*, p. 94.

50 *Second Innings*, p. 90.

51 *Autobiography*, p. 65.

52 *Guardian*, 2 April 1969.

53 The archives at Shrewsbury School confirm that the senior coach was Walter Attewell: see *The Elusive Mr Cardus*, back cover.

54 See *Autobiography*, p. 63 et seq.

55 *Cricket all the Year*, p. 50. The Attewells were cousins not brothers.

56 *Autobiography*, p. 72; *Birmingham Daily Gazette*, 2 March 1914; Sale (1951), p. 171.

57 *Close of Play*, p. 29.

58 *Manchester Guardian*, 13 May 1929.

59 *Autobiography*, p. 66.

60 Sale (1951), p. 163.

61 *Manchester Guardian*, 19 May 1919.

62 *Manchester Guardian*, 29 October 1919. The obituary gives Wainwright's age as 53 whereas he was actually 54.

63 *Manchester Guardian*, 28 April and 3 May 1922. See also "Cricketer" (1922).

64 This paragraph draws on *Autobiography*, pp. 79–86.

65 p. 62.

66 *Manchester Guardian*, 28 June 1974 (the book was over 400 pages long).

Chapter 6: Introduction to music, the arts and work

1 *Second Innings*, p. 23.

2 *Manchester Guardian*, 23 December 1895.

3 *Second Innings*, p. 25; *Manchester Guardian*, 24 December

1900.

4 *Second Innings*, pp. 33–35; *Manchester Guardian*, 3 March 1903.

5 *Second Innings*, pp. 30–31; *Manchester Guardian*, 26 December 1904.

6 *Autobiography*, p. 28.

7 *Autobiography*, pp. 17, 32; Brereton (1908), p. 315.

8 *Second Innings*, p. 58.

9 *Autobiography*, p. 25.

10 *Second Innings*, p. 102.

11 *Manchester Guardian*, 8 September 1908.

12 *Conversations*, pp. 35–36.

13 *Conversations*, p. 27.

14 *Conversations*, p. 35.

15 Busby (1976), p. 139.

16 *Manchester Guardian*, 22 January 1907.

17 *Autobiography*, p. 52. The first performance had been on 30 March: *Manchester Guardian*, 6 March 1907.

18 *Manchester Guardian*, 1 and 9 April 1907.

19 *Autobiography*, p. 53.

20 *Manchester Guardian*, 2 July 1930.

21 *Talking of Music*, p. 34.

22 *Second Innings*, p. 121.

23 *Manchester Guardian*, 24 January 1908.

24 *Autobiography*, p. 52; *Second Innings*, p. 127; *Ten Composers*, p. 126; *Conversations*, p. 37.

25 *Conversations*, p. 39.

26 *Manchester Guardian*, 1 November 1910.

27 *Second Innings*, pp. 118–120. In *Conversations*, pp. 37–38, Cardus mentions some singing engagements before the lieder training.

28 *Second Innings*, pp. 122–123.

29 *Second Innings*, p. 121.

30 *Second Innings*, pp. 9–11; the information on Max Mayer is from his naturalisation papers and probate record.

31 Heyworth (1996), pp. 12–13.

32 Cardus reviewed a concert by Mayer on 2 March 1914 in

the *Daily Citizen*.

33 For this paragraph, see *Autobiography*, pp. 8, 23–24, 36–37; he said (p. 8) that his parents conducted a home laundry, but this should instead refer to his grandparents, assisted by his mother and her sisters.

34 *Full Score*, p. 15.

35 *Conversations*, p. 38.

36 *Conversations*, p. 254.

37 Probate record using his real name of George Galvin.

38 The information in this paragraph is from census returns and *Autobiography*, pp. 37–42.

39 Slater, 1904; consistent with Cardus's recollection in Mather (2004).

40 *Autobiography*, p. 39; *Full Score*, p. 199.

41 *Autobiography*, pp. 49–50.

42 This paragraph draws on *Conversations*, p. 259.

43 This paragraph draws on *Autobiography*, pp. 86–89. Note that his *Who's Who* entry gave the correct year of 1913.

44 *The Elusive Mr Cardus*, p. 8.

45 *Second Innings*, pp. 8, 124.

46 *Autobiography*, p. 45.

47 Also as stated in *Celebrant of Beauty*, p. 21.

48 *Full Score*, pp. 199, 216.

49 The works mentioned in the article were Ambroise Thomas's *Mignon* overture; Percy Grainger's *Mock Morris*; an excerpt from Wagner's *Die Walküre*; Sullivan's "Woo thou the snowflake"; and Saint-Saëns' *Phaeton*.

50 *Guardian*, 2 April 1989.

51 *Neville Cardus Reflects*, p. 19.

52 Cardus (1916).

53 *Autobiography*, p. 50; *Conversations*, p. 40; Lamb (1988), p. 177; *Neville Cardus Reflects*, p. 19.

54 Cardus (1916), p. 159.

55 *Autobiography*, p. 55.

56 *Autobiography*, p. 86, puts his work for the *Daily Citizen* in this period, whereas it was in 1913–14.

57 *Autobiography*, p. 86.

58 *Autobiography*, p. 89.
59 *Autobiography*, p. 90. In his notebook Cardus wrote that he read the first edition of Agate's *Responsibility* while delivering insurance policies in Manchester (*Neville Cardus Reflects*, p. 38). This could have referred to his work for the Fleming brothers (1904–12) or his work with burial policies (1916), but the book was not published until 1919, so there is a memory problem here.
60 Ayerst (1971), p. 441.
61 This and the following paragraph draw on *Autobiography*, pp. 90–93.
62 *Autobiography*, p. 94.
63 Ayerst (1971), p. 417.
64 *The Elusive Mr Cardus*, pp. 14, 16. Cardus's letter shows his address as 154 Moseley Road, Fallowfield.
65 https://artuk.org/discover/artworks/search/actor: dodd-francis-18741949/page/2#artwork-edward-taylor-scott-18831932-134597; downloaded 30 May 2017. Laurence Scott died in 1908 (probate records).
66 In *His Own Man* Brookes (1985), p. 80, indicated that Cardus wrote a further letter to Scott in early March, stressing his reduced circumstances.
67 *Autobiography*, p. 93.

Chapter 7: The *Manchester Guardian* and a cricket writer

1 *Autobiography*, pp. 96, 99.
2 *Autobiography*, pp. 99–100; *Manchester Guardian*, 27 March 1917.
3 *Conversations*, p. 163. There are similar comments in *Autobiography*, p. 10 and *Full Score*, p. 6.
4 *Conversations*, p. 33.
5 p. 3.
6 *Autobiography*, p. 103.
7 John Arlott, *Guardian*, 2 April 1989.
8 *Autobiography*, p. 104; *Conversations*, pp. 33–34.
9 *Autobiography*, p. 110.

10 p. 114.
11 *Autobiography*, p. 111; *Full Score*, p. 7. It is unclear how long this lasted.
12 *Autobiography*, p. 118, where the book is referred to as *Reminiscences*.
13 *Manchester Guardian*, 25 November 1919.
14 Ayerst (1971), p. 481.
15 Bearshaw (1990), p. 204.
16 pp. 127–128.
17 *West Australian*, 16 October 1936. He refers to a breakdown in 1918 not 1919. Parkin took 6 wickets in the first innings, 8 in the second.
18 p. 61. In *Second Innings*, p. 172, Cardus incorrectly refers to 1921 as the start of his cricket-writing.
19 p. 13.
20 p. 89.
21 Nichols (1946), p. 153.
22 *Celebrant of Beauty*, p. 47.
23 *Conversations*, p. 61.
24 *Conversations*, p. 61. The title "cricket correspondent" was not, however, used in his match reports.
25 *A Cricketer's Book*, p. 55.
26 *Manchester Guardian* archive, University of Manchester Library Special Collections, ref A/C/13/2.
27 pp. 174–185.
28 pp. 61–62.
29 *Second Innings*, p. 175.
30 *Conversations*, p. 159.
31 *Conversations*, p. 62.
32 This paragraph is based on the *Guardian*, 18 June 1975. Miss Linford was born in Scotland on 16 January 1895 (birth certificate) and died in Grange-over-Sands on 16 June 1975 (probate record).
33 *Manchester Guardian*, 25 September 1922.
34 *Manchester Guardian*, 3 June 1924.
35 *Autobiography*, p. 130.
36 *Manchester Guardian*, 17 May 1920.

37 *Manchester Guardian*, 21 June 1920.

38 *Manchester Guardian*, 7 July 1920.

39 *Manchester Guardian*, 8 July 1920.

40 *Manchester Guardian*, 15 July 1920.

41 *Manchester Guardian*, 19 July 1920.

42 *Manchester Guardian*, 23 August 1920.

43 *Manchester Guardian*, 25 August 1920.

44 *Manchester Guardian*, 20 September 1920.

45 *Second Innings*, pp. 169–172.

46 *Second Innings*, p. 173.

47 *Manchester Guardian*, 21 June 1921. "Murmurous" was a much more commonly used word in the 1920s and 1930s than since.

48 *Manchester Guardian*, 23 July 1921.

49 *Manchester Guardian*, 25 July 1921.

50 *Manchester Guardian*, 23 July 1921.

51 *Manchester Guardian*, 17 August 1921.

Chapter 8: Cricket develops

1 pp. 176–178.

2 *Autobiography*, p. 177.

3 Brookes pointed out that the alternative match was not Surrey v Yorkshire at The Oval but Middlesex v Surrey at Lord's to decide the championship: *His Own Man*, p. 100.

4 31 August 1921.

5 *Guardian*, 3 June 1970; *Spectator*, 23 August 1974.

6 *Manchester Guardian*, 11 June 1919.

7 An article on Woolley is an example: *Guardian*, 27 May 1967.

8 *Manchester Guardian*, 1 May 1936.

9 *Full Score*, pp. 100–101.

10 *Manchester Guardian*, 29 May 1930.

11 *Close of Play*, p. 39.

12 *Manchester Guardian*, 22 June 1933.

13 *Full Score*, p. 15.

14 *Conversations*, p. 62.

15 *A Cricketer's Book,* pp. 109–111.

16 *Autobiography*, p. 143.

17 *Autobiography*, p. 152.

18 *Autobiography*, p. 153.

19 Calculations regarding the Roses matches made by the author using Cricket Archive. Eight-ball overs used in 1939 were converted to an equivalent number of six-ball overs.

20 Miller (2014), p. 28, found an average rate of 2.74 in 1920–29 and 2.73 in 1930–39.

21 *Manchester Guardian*, 6 June 1922.

22 *Spectator*, 4 June 1964.

23 18 May 1939.

24 Kinneir and Quaife were caught by Worsley in the second innings, not the first, when his victim was Byrne.

25 pp. 144–147.

26 This paragraph draws on *His Own Man*, p. 130; Ayerst (1971), pp. 489–490; *Sporting Globe*, Melbourne, 29 November and 6 December 1941; *Daily Telegraph*, Sydney, 13 May 1932; *The Great Romantic*, pp. 184–187.

27 *Manchester Guardian*, 3 December 1932.

28 Berry (1987), pp. 144–145.

29 *Manchester Guardian*, 24 June 1937.

30 *Sun,* Sydney, 3 January 1937.

31 This paragraph draws on *Autobiography*, pp. 187–191.

32 Chaney (2006), p. 358.

33 *Manchester Guardian*, 7 June 1926.

34 Chaney (2006), p. 127.

35 *His Own Man*, p. 134.

36 Nichols (1946), p. 153.

37 The articles appeared from 24 April to 12 May 1922. Also see *Manchester Guardian*, 17 and 22 May 1922 and an item by Martin Chandler, http://www.cricketweb.net/cardus-on-how-to-play-cricket/ downloaded 1 December 2019.

38 *Manchester Guardian*, 28 June 1922; *The Times*, 11 July 1922.

39 *The Times*, 16 September 1932.
40 *Manchester Guardian* archive, University of Manchester Library Special Collections, ref A/C/13/2.
41 *Radio Times*, 3 June 1927.
42 *Radio Times*, 29 July 1927.
43 *Manchester Guardian*, 17 August 1931.
44 *Sydney Morning Herald*, 8 June 1934.
45 *Register News-Pictorial*, Adelaide, 27 April 1929.
46 This section draws on the reports in *The Times* and the *Manchester Guardian* on 16 and 17 July 1929.
47 *Manchester Guardian*, 16 July 1929.
48 *The Times*, 16 July 1929.
49 *The Times*, 17 July 1929.
50 The incident is described in *Full Score*, pp. 129–134.
51 *Full Score*, p. 130.
52 *Sun,* Sydney, 7 October 1936.
53 *Autobiography*, p. 62.
54 *Who's Who*, 1936.
55 National Liberal Club (1946); also *His Own Man*, p. 76.
56 *Autobiography*, p. 192; I am grateful to Michael Gray of the Savage Club for the joining date.
57 *Full Score*, p. 134.
58 *Cricket*, p. 4.
59 p. 223.
60 *Second Innings*, p. 198.
61 Information about the match from *The Argus,* Melbourne, 3 March 1938 (from which the quotation is taken) and *Manchester Guardian*, 26 March 1938.
62 *The Times*, 15 June 1950.
63 *Second Innings*, pp. 94–98.
64 *Manchester Guardian*, 24 May 1934 and *Second Innings*, pp. 86–87; Duckworth's first stumping in a county match at Old Trafford was against Surrey on 12 June 1923.
65 *Autobiography*, p. 179. This appears to be the match referred to in *Manchester Guardian*, 5 June 1957.
66 *Second Innings*, p. 90.
67 *Autobiography*, pp. 193–195.

68 *Advertiser,* Adelaide, 28 October 1936.
69 p. 66.
70 *The Elusive Mr Cardus*, p. 19.
71 *Close of Play*, pp. 31–32.
72 28 June 1974.

Chapter 9: Not only cricket

1 A letter from Edith in 1916, possibly 31 July, mentioning "Fred", is included in *The Elusive Mr Cardus*, p. 11.
2 John Arlott, *Guardian*, 2 April 1988.
3 In *His Own Man* (p. 76) and *The Great Romantic* (p. 61) it is referred to as Watten.
4 *Autobiography*, p. 143.
5 p. 101. Lamb (1985), p. 34, pointed out some errors in the account in *His Own Man*.
6 Brookes (1985), p. 76, indicated that it was 1929 when Neville and his wife moved to the property, Edith being the purchaser; the above information indicates that the move was in 1924 or 1925. According to Daniels (2009), p. 354, Neville Cardus never owned a property.
7 *West Australian*, 21 October 1936.
8 *Full Score*, p. 179.
9 p. 143.
10 *Full Score*, pp. 178, 207–208.
11 *Guardian*, 16 May 1963. He also paid tribute to Langford in *Conversations*, pp. 42–46.
12 pp. 131–134, used for this paragraph.
13 *Manchester Guardian*, 9 and 16 April, 10 and 26 November 1919 (concerts on 8 and 15 April, 8 and 25 November).
14 *Manchester Guardian*, 9 April 1919.
15 *Manchester Guardian*, 12, 13 and 14 January 1920.
16 *Manchester Guardian*, 14 January 1920.
17 *Manchester Guardian*, 12 and 13 January 1920.
18 p. 134.
19 *Manchester Guardian*, 6 October 1920.
20 *Full Score*, pp. 4–6.

21 The concert took place on 17 April 1920.

22 *Manchester Guardian*, 6 December 1922.

23 Obituary in *Wisden*, 1944.

24 *Autobiography*, p. 142.

25 *Autobiography*, p. 134.

26 *Samuel Langford*, p. x.

27 *Manchester Guardian*, 21 October 1927. Wright (1988) referred to Cardus's first notice as senior music critic on 28 October, when he praised Harty's performance of Brahms' third symphony, but omitted reference to the earlier concert.

28 pp. 37–39.

29 *Manchester Guardian*, 1 and 22 October 1928.

30 *Manchester Guardian*, 19 October 1931.

31 *Full Score*, p. 37; *Manchester Guardian*, 19 October 1931.

32 *Autobiography*, pp. 223–224.

33 *Manchester Guardian*, 12 November 1928.

34 I am grateful to Ron Bullock for the information in this paragraph.

35 *Manchester Guardian*, 31 August 1931. This is also the source for the following sentence.

36 *Manchester Guardian*, 2 September 1931.

37 *Autobiography*, p. 237; *Sir Thomas Beecham*, p. 17.

38 *Manchester Guardian*, 22 and 23 October 1931. The problems between Gray and Cardus are documented in the *Manchester Guardian* archives, University of Manchester Library Special Collections, A/G 38.

39 *Manchester Guardian*, 14, 17 and 25 November 1931.

40 *Manchester Guardian*, 19 November 1931.

41 *Autobiography*, p. 265

42 *Manchester Guardian*, 8 May 1933.

43 *Autobiography*, pp. 265–266.

44 *Conversations*, p. 214; *Autobiography*, pp. 221–222, also referred to problems involving Harty.

45 Kennedy (1982), pp. 26–27; *Sir Thomas Beecham*, p. 64.

46 Cardus (1960b), p. 705.

47 Letter dated 25 September 1937, *The Elusive Mr Cardus*,

p. 29.

48 *Sir Thomas Beecham*, pp. 35, 38.

49 *Manchester Guardian*, 21 October 1938.

50 *Conversations*, pp. 40–41.

51 *Ten Composers*, p. 6.

52 Lamb (1988), p. 177.

53 Anderson & Scaife (2001), p. 125.

54 *Autobiography*, p. 88; Manchester Guardian, 9 October 1933.

55 *Manchester Guardian,* 29 June 1926; Engel (1986), p. 311. Cardus refers to other misprints in a letter dated 26 August 1960 (*My Dear Michael...*, p. 10).

56 *Cardus: a Reader's Guide.*

57 *Manchester Guardian*, 21 February 1919, referred to Neville Cardus by name as a contributor to *Voices*.

58 Cardus (1965).

59 *Autobiography*, pp. 269–270.

60 British Library catalogue.

61 *Autobiography*, p. 270.

62 *Manchester Guardian,* 25 February 1969; Guardian News & Media Archive, NCA/1/1, letters 25 and 26 February 1969.

63 p. 123.

64 *His Own Man*, p. 123, indicated that the couple met in autumn 1928.

65 Undated fragment in notebook, *Neville Cardus Reflects*, p. 27.

66 *Neville Cardus Reflects*, p. 31. Although the comment is that it was 29 years since he met Milady, this is thought to be an error for 19 years. Hilton suggests that the section of the notebook was probably September.

67 The Canterbury festival is in August; but, in 1929, the Roses match in August was in Yorkshire.

68 *Full Score*, p. 72.

69 *Manchester Guardian*, 4 August 1930.

70 p. 73.

71 *Manchester Guardian*, 10 October 1933.

72 p. 73.

73 *Neville Cardus Reflects*, p. 28.

74 *Manchester Guardian*, 25 February 1969; *Full Score,* p. 73.

75 *His Own Man*, p. 125 (also relates to following sentence).

76 *Kent Messenger,* 4 July 1931.

77 *Manchester Guardian*, 30 August 1934; *Kent Messenger,* 1 September 1934.

78 *Kent Messenge*r, 25 September 1937.

79 Death certificate.

80 The text of the letter is in *His Own Man*, p. 125.

81 The remainder of this section draws on birth, marriage and death certificates, together with census returns and other sources mentioned in the text.

82 See Hamilton's (2019) helpful research on Barbe and Elton Ede; in particular, *The Great Romantic*, p. 165.

83 *The Sunday Times*, 25 August 1935.

84 *The Sunday Times,* 18 April 1937.

85 Marriage certificate and probate record.

Chapter 10: Extending horizons in the late 1930s

1 *Manchester Guardian*, 12 August 1936.

2 The match reports in the *Manchester Guardian*, 13–15 August 1936, were by a special correspondent.

3 *Manchester Guardian*, 19 August 1936.

4 *Manchester Guardian*, 17 October 1936.

5 *Manchester Guardian*, 14 September 1936.

6 *Australian Summer*, p. 22.

7 18 September 1936.

8 22 October 1936.

9 *Sporting Globe,* Melbourne, 13 March 1937.

10 *News,* Adelaide, 1 March 1937.

11 *Advertiser,* Adelaide, 28 October 1936.

12 *West Australian*, 21 October 1936.

13 *Mirror,* Perth, 24 October 1936.

14 *Sun,* Sydney, 13 November 1936.

15 *Advertiser,* Adelaide, 29 January 1937.

16 *Sun,* Sydney, 6 March 1937.

17 p. 202.

18 Letter dated 28 February 1937, *The Elusive Mr Cardus*, p. 27.

19 *Manchester Guardian*, 3 May 1937.

20 *Manchester Guardian*, 27 August 1937 (also the source of the next quotation).

21 *Manchester Guardian*, 13 September 1937.

22 *Sydney Morning Herald*, 19 January 1938; *West Australian*, 19 January 1938.

23 *Manchester Guardian*, 26 February 1938.

24 p. 271.

25 Letter included in *The Elusive Mr Cardus*, pp. 29–30.

26 *Second Innings*, pp. 169–170.

27 Letter to W.P. Crozier dated 5 January 1937, *The Elusive Mr Cardus*, p. 26.

28 Letter to W.P. Crozier dated 28 February 1937, *The Elusive Mr Cardus*, p. 27.

29 *Sun,* Sydney, 30 January 1938.

30 *Camperdown Chronicle*, 1 March 1938.

31 *Age,* Melbourne, 24 February 1938.

32 *Advertiser,* Adelaide, 19 January 1938.

33 *Sydney Morning Herald,* 27 January 1938.

34 *Newcastle Morning Herald and Miners' Advocate,* 5 February 1938.

35 *Argus,* Melbourne, 9 March 1938.

36 *Manchester Guardian*, 2 May 1938.

37 *Manchester Guardian*, 11 July 1938.

38 *Manchester Guardian*, 17 August 1929.

39 *Manchester Guardian*, 13 August 1931.

40 *Manchester Guardia*n, 22 May 1939.

41 James (1963), p. 123.

42 *The Great Romantic*, p. 221.

43 pp. 166–167.

44 Letter to W.P. Crozier, *The Elusive Mr Cardus*, p. 33. *Full Score*, p. 163, confirms that Edith accompanied evacuated children.

45 *Sydney Morning Herald*, 18 January 1941.
46 p. 164.
47 *Manchester Guardian*, 30 August 1939.
48 *Manchester Guardian*, 22 August 1941. Another error is that Cardus referred to the Middlesex v Surrey match as one which was to be the last day's play at Lord's for a long time; however, it was followed by the game against Warwickshire mentioned above.
49 *Manchester Guardian*, 28 August 1939.
50 *Manchester Guardian*, 22 August 1941.
51 *Manchester Guardian*, 26 August 1939.

Chapter 11: A celebrity in Australia 1940–47

1 p. 163.
2 *Full Score*, p. 164.
3 *Manchester Guardian*, 17 November 1939.
4 *Manchester Guardian*, 27 December 1939.
5 *Manchester Guardian*, 27 December 1939.
6 Kennedy (1982), p. 30.
7 *Sydney Morning Herald*, 18 January 1941.
8 This paragraph from *Manchester Guardian*, 15 March 1940; *Full Score*, p. 164.
9 Cardus's comment in *Second Innings*, p. 223, errs in saying that he landed in Australia in September 1939.
10 *Newcastle Morning Herald and Miners' Advocate*, 12 February 1940.
11 p. 165.
12 p. 48.
13 *Argus,* Melbourne, 11 June 1940; *Sir Thomas Beecham*, pp. 49–50.
14 *Sir Thomas Beecham*, p. 52.
15 *Manchester Guardian*, 29 November 1940.
16 *Manchester Guardian*, 9 October 1943.
17 *Truth,* Sydney, 13 October 1940.
18 *Conversations,* p. 54; *West Australian*, 13 June 1944.
19 *News,* Adelaide, 12 August 1943.
20 *Advertiser,* Adelaide, 4 April 1940.

21 *Conversations*, p. 115.
22 *Full Score*, p. 166.
23 Letter from E.I.M. Henchman, 5 April 1941.
24 *News,* Adelaide, 13 August 1941.
25 *Full Score*, p. 173.
26 *Sydney Morning Herald*, 12 September 1941.
27 *Full Score*, p. 172.
28 https://www.parliament.nsw.gov.au/members/Pages/ profiles/concannon_james-matthew.aspx, downloaded 31 August 2017.
29 *Sydney Morning Herald*, 10 February 1944.
30 p. 172.
31 *Sydney Morning Herald*, 14 September 1944.
32 p. 168.
33 12 June 1944.
34 *Full Score*, p. 170.
35 Griffin (1986).
36 p. 170.
37 *Sydney Morning Herald*, 9 October 1944.
38 *Full Score*, p. 172.
39 *Sydney Morning Herald*, 31 October 1940.
40 *Daily Telegraph*, 7 February 2005.
41 p. 172.
42 *Sydney Morning Herald*, 23 August 1946; also used in the remainder of this paragraph.
43 *Full Score*, p. 173.
44 *Sydney Morning Herald*, 27 September 1946.
45 p. 173.
46 *Sydney Morning Herald*, 6 November 1946.
47 Somerville (2002).
48 *Full Score*, pp. 173–176.
49 *Sydney Morning Herald*, 10 and 21 May 1945.
50 *Full Score*, pp. 167–168.
51 *Sun,* Sydney, 10 June 1951.
52 22 August 1941.
53 *The Courier-Mail*, Brisbane, 9 March 1940.
54 *Sydney Morning Herald*, 3 January 1947.

55 Edith's photo album is in the Guardian News & Media
    Archive. She exhibited paintings at exhibitions (*Sun,*
    Sydney, 4 February 1944; *Sydney Morning Herald,* 25
    April 1945); produced *Asmodée* by the French playwright
    François Mauriac (*Sun,* Sydney, 1 August 1945); and
    gave a speech on England and rationing (*Cumberland
    Argus,* 18 August 1943).

56 Letter to A.P. Wadsworth (*Manchester Guardian* editor,
    1944–1956), dated 4 June 1944, *The Elusive Mr Cardus,*
    p. 37.

57 *Full Score,* p. 179.

58 *Smith's Weekly,* 31 January 1948.

59 *Smith's Weekly,* 28 December 1940.

60 *Full Score,* p. 178.

61 *The Elusive Mr Cardus,* p. 36.

62 *Sydney Morning Herald,* 31 May 1947.

63 p. 238.

64 p. 193.

65 *Full Score,* p. 193; *Mail,* Adelaide, 29 May 1947.

66 Agate (1946), p. 221. The letter was dated 1 September
    1945.

67 *Sun,* Sydney, 25 May 1947.

68 *Weekly Times,* Melbourne, 4 June 1947.

69 pp. 47, 58.

Chapter 12: The metronome years and settling back in England

1 *Sun,* Sydney, 24 February 1949.

2 Letter dated 16 December 1945 to A.P. Wadsworth, *The
   Elusive Mr Cardus,* p. 40.

3 *Manchester Guardian,* 23 June 1947.

4 *Manchester Guardian,* 7 July 1947.

5 *Manchester Guardian,* 21 August 1947.

6 *Manchester Guardian,* 6 September 1947.

7 *Manchester Guardian,* 2 September 1947.

8 *Manchester Guardian,* 13 September 1947.

9 *Sydney Morning Herald,* 1 December 1947.

10 *Sydney Morning Herald*, 20 December 1947.

11 Cardus (1948), p. 9.

12 *Sydney Morning Herald*, 4 March 1948.

13 *Northern Standard*, 12 December 1947.

14 *Age,* Melbourne, 24 January 1948.

15 *West Australian*, 1 December 1947.

16 *Advertiser,* Adelaide, 9 February 1948.

17 *National Advocate*, 10 March 1948.

18 *Manchester Guardian*, 2 May 1938.

19 *West Australian*, 20 March 1948.

20 *Sun,* Sydney, 29 January 1948.

21 *National Advocate*, 10 March 1948.

22 *Full Score*, p. 198.

23 *Full Score*, pp. 198–9.

24 *Observer*, 5 September 1948.

25 *Sydney Morning Herald*, 24 August 1948.

26 *West Australian*, 19 February 1949.

27 Letter dated 3 December 1948, *The Elusive Mr Cardus*, p. 41.

28 *West Australian*, 7 January 1949.

29 *Sunday Herald*, 23 January 1949.

30 *News,* Adelaide, 7 January 1949; *Brisbane Telegraph*, 11 January 1949.

31 *Sunday Times,* Perth, 27 March 1949.

32 *Sunday Herald*, 27 February 1949.

33 *Sun,* Sydney, 8 April 1949.

34 *A Cardus for all Seasons*, p. 114 (originally in *World Sports*, August 1949).

35 *The Essential Neville Cardus*, p. 15. Cardus would take a greater interest in financial matters in later years (*His Own Man*, p. 234).

36 *Sun,* Sydney, 24 February 1949; *Scone Advocate,* 15 March 1949.

37 *Second Innings*, p. 242.

38 *Daily News,* Perth, 26 April 1949.

39 *Brisbane Telegraph*, 16 April 1949.

40 The phone book for 1949 shows him at 73 Lyall Mews

West, but this may have been out of date.

41 *Sun,* Sydney, 26 January 1950.

42 *West Australian*, 10 October 1950.

43 *The Times*, 15 September 1950; *West Australian*, 10 October 1950.

44 *Advertiser,* Adelaide, 20 December 1950.

45 *Barrier Miner,* Broken Hill, 20 December 1950.

46 10 February 1951.

47 *West Australian*, 14 March 1951.

48 *Daily Commercial News*, 12 April 1951.

49 *West Australian*, 14 March 1951.

50 *The Elusive Mr Cardus*, p. 43.

51 Writer's notebook, 12 October 1951, *Neville Cardus Reflects*, p. 50.

52 Letter dated 16 July 1951 to A.P. Wadsworth, *Neville Cardus Reflects*, p. 40.

53 *Manchester Guardian*, 10 October 1951; see also *Neville Cardus Reflects*, p. 40.

54 Kennedy (1975), p. 205.

55 *Manchester Guardian*, 19 November 1951.

56 *Manchester Guardian*, 5 November 1955.

57 *Guardian*, 7 April 1960.

58 This is documented in the *Manchester Guardian* archive, University of Manchester Library Special Collections, ref A/M 87 (the source of the quotation).

59 This paragraph draws on letters in *The Elusive Mr Cardus*, pp. 48–49; and *Brisbane Telegraph*, 11 November 1954.

60 *A Cardus for all Seasons*, p. 144 (originally in *World Sports*, September 1954).

61 *Sun-Herald,* Sydney, 28 November 1954.

62 Manchester Guardian, 5 March 1955; *Picture Post*, 9 April 1955.

63 Chalke (2001), p. 158.

64 *Manchester Guardian*, 5 March 1955.

65 For example, *Sydney Morning Herald*, 27 November 1954; *Age,* Melbourne, 16 December 1954 for radio.

66 *Manchester Guardian*, 8 January 1955.

67 *Manchester Guardian*, 25 November 1954.

68 Phillips (2009), p. 95.

69 Letter dated 7 August 1958 to Else Mayer-Lismann, Guardian News & Media Archive, NCA/2/1.

70 *Conversations*, p. 253.

71 *Guardian*, 5 February 1971.

72 *Guardian*, 4 April 1966.

73 *His Own Man*, p. 245; *Private Eye*, 29 April 1975.

74 *Guardian*, 15 April 1966.

75 *Guardian*, 15 April 1966. Brookes (1985), p. 245, is also correct in referring to a celebration of his 50th year with the *Guardian*.

76 *Guardian*, 16 April 1966.

77 Letter dated 15 March 1957 to Else Mayer-Lismann, Guardian News & Media Archive, NCA/2/1; it refers to starting work on 16 March 1916.

78 Cardus (1966), pp. 5–13.

79 p. 244.

80 http://www.bbc.co.uk/programmes/p009y2vy/segments, downloaded 25 May 2017. Also see *Cardus Undimmed,* p. 37.

81 Writer's notebook, 25 October 1949, *Neville Cardus Reflects*, p. 27.

82 For example, *Talking of Music*, pp. 18, 19, 65, 215.

83 For example, *Cricket*, p. 96; *Manchester Guardian*, 29 December 1922.

84 *Conversations*, p. 259.

85 *Ten Composers*, p. 46.

86 *Full Score*, p. 149.

87 This paragraph draws on *Conversations*, p. 81.

88 This paragraph draws on *Conversations*, p. 133.

89 He was registered there as an elector in 1948 and this was his address shown in the 1949 phone book (which may have been out of date).

90 Ernest Bradbury, *Yorkshire Post*, 2 April 1959.

91 Stanley Parker, *John O'London's,* 5 November 1959.

92 Rupert Hart-Davis, *The Essential Neville Cardus,* p. 15.

93 Guardian News & Media Archive, NCA 2/2/1(2), 22 August 1964.

94 Elizabeth Grice, *Cardus Undimmed*, p. 6.

95 *The Times*, 6 May 1953, 7 June 1954, 5 January 1960, 22 July 1961, 12 October 1965, 14 January 1967; *The Elusive Mr Cardus* has letters to the *Manchester Guardian* from his club.

96 Letter dated 27 July 1958, Guardian News & Media Archive, NCA/2/1.

97 Rob Steen, obituary of Margaret Hughes, 9 February 2005, https://www.theguardian.com/news/2005/feb/09/guardianobituaries.cricket, downloaded 12 January 2017.

98 *Cardus Undimmed*, p. 7.

99 *Rochdale Observer*, 23 January 1954; Fingleton (1981), pp. 134, 137; *His Own Man*, p. 220; John Woodcock, *The Times*, 30 July 2016.

100 Letter dated 1 September 1970 to Michael Kennedy, *My Dear Michael...*, p. 34.

101 Letter dated 9 January 1973 to Michael Kennedy, *My Dear Michael...*, p. 12.

102 Letter dated 1 August 1958 to Else Mayer-Lismann, Guardian News & Media Archive NCA/2/1.

103 Letter dated 7 May 1965 to Michael Kennedy, *My Dear Michael...*, p. 17.

104 Undated letter, Guardian News & Media Archive, NCA.

105 Guardian News & Media Archive, NCA 2/1/1(2), 28 July 1958.

106 *His Own Man*, pp. 257–258; letters from Cardus in *The Elusive Mr Cardus*, pp. 51–52, 55–56, 58; *My Dear Michael...*, pp. 12, 14.

107 Taylor (1993), pp. 58, 135; also see *Full Score*, pp. 200–201.

108 *The Sunday Times,* 30 May 1971.

109 *Guardian*, 10 September 1971.

110 *Guardian*, 20 April 1968 (also covers following 3 sentences).

111 *Full Score*, p. 97; *Guardian*, 28 June 1974.

112 *Full Score*, p. 99; *Guardian*, 8 August 1973; *Spectator*, 23 August 1974.

113 *Guardian*, 24 January 1975.

114 Letter to Michael Kennedy, 8 July 1974 (*My Dear Michael...*, p. 38); *The Sunday Times*, 7 July and 29 December 1974.

115 *Guardian*, 12 December 1974.

116 *Guardian*, 9 and 14 August 1974.

117 *Celebrant of Beauty*, p. 351.

118 *Guardian*, 29 March and 7 September 1973.

Chapter 13: To be personal ...

1 *Manchester Guardian*, 17 June 1926.

2 *Manchester Guardian*, 18 May 1925.

3 *Manchester Guardian*, 21 June 1926.

4 *Manchester Guardian*, 25 May 1933.

5 *Manchester Guardian*, 13 July 1937.

6 *Manchester Guardian*, 27 June 1921.

7 *Manchester Guardian*, 16 January 1933.

8 *Manchester Guardian*, 7 July 1920.

9 *Manchester Guardian*, 27 May 1937.

10 *Manchester Guardian*, 9 July 1932.

11 *Manchester Guardian*, 21 June 1926.

12 *World Sports*, June 1948.

13 *Manchester Guardian*, 24 July 1920 and *Daily Mail*, 24 July 1920.

14 *Manchester Guardian*, 5 August 1919.

15 *Manchester Guardian*, 4 July 1932.

16 *Manchester Guardian*, 16 August 1934.

17 *World Sports,* June 1948.

18 *Manchester Guardian*, 2 August 1934.

19 *Manchester Guardian*, 6 June 1922.

20 *Manchester Guardian*, 15 August 1938.

21 *Manchester Guardian*, 8 June 1920.

22 *Manchester Guardian*, 31 May 1932.

23 *Manchester Guardian*, 25 May 1939.

24 *Manchester Guardian*, 6 June 1938.
25 *Manchester Guardian*, 15 July 1970.
26 *Manchester Guardian*, 16 May 1927.
27 *Manchester Guardian*, 2 May 1921.
28 *Manchester Guardian*, 3 June 1970 and 22 August 1941.
29 *Manchester Guardian*, 25 June 1934.
30 *Manchester Guardian*, 5 June 1939.
31 *Manchester Guardian*, 3 July 1924.
32 *Manchester Guardian*, 9 July 1932.
33 *Manchester Guardian*, 4 August 1937.
34 *Manchester Guardian*, 1 and 2 July 1926.
35 *Manchester Guardian*, 20 August 1925.
36 *Manchester Guardian*, 20 August 1920.
37 *Manchester Guardian*, 11 August 1932 (also applies to next sentence).
38 *Manchester Guardian*, 16 June 1925.
39 *Manchester Guardian*, 16 September 1931.
40 *Manchester Guardian*, 23 July 1929.
41 *Manchester Guardian*, 24 July 1925.
42 *Manchester Guardian*, 14 August 1970.
43 *Manchester Guardian*, 8 August 1973.
44 This paragraph draws on *Manchester Guardian*, 14 August 1970.
45 *Manchester Guardian*, 30 July 1969.
46 *Manchester Guardian*, 15 July 1970.
47 *Manchester Guardian*, 30 April 1970.
48 *Manchester Guardian*, 17 July 1924.
49 *Manchester Guardian*, 1 July 1926 (and 3 July for next quotation).
50 *Daily Express*, 22 October 1965.
51 *Manchester Guardian*, 27 May 1967.
52 *The Times*, 25 May 1937.
53 Robertson-Glasgow (1949), p. 182.
54 *Manchester Guardian*, 25 June 1934.
55 *Manchester Guardian*, 12 August 1929
56 *Manchester Guardian*, 14 August 1970.

57 *Manchester Guardian*, 18 June 1931.
58 *Manchester Guardian*, 5 June 1939.
59 Bateman (2009a), p. 98.
60 *Manchester Guardian*, 5 May 1938.
61 *Manchester Guardian*, 16 June 1921.
62 *Manchester Guardian*, 28 April 1921.
63 *Manchester Guardian*, 25 July 1930.
64 *Australian Summer,* p. 232.
65 *Manchester Guardian*, 2 July 1936.
66 *Manchester Guardian*, 9 July 1931.
67 *Manchester Guardian*, 15 June 1933.
68 *Manchester Guardian*, 15 July 1970.
69 *Manchester Guardian*, 1 June 1973.
70 *Manchester Guardian*, 8 August 1935.
71 *Manchester Guardian*, 12 July 1939.
72 *Manchester Guardian*, 5 June 1933.
73 *Manchester Guardian*, 22 June 1922.
74 *Manchester Guardian*, 18 May 1931.
75 *The Essential Neville Cardus*, pp. 14, 15.
76 *Manchester Guardian*, 11 July 1938.
77 *Manchester Guardian*, 12 June 1922, 26 August 1930; *The Sunday Times*, 15 August 1948.
78 For example, *Manchester Guardian*, 19 April 1920: "haec olim meminisse juvabit!"
79 *Manchester Guardian*, 15 August 1927.
80 *Manchester Guardian*, 3 July 1930.
81 *Manchester Guardian*, 22 August 1937.
82 For example, *Manchester Guardian*, 6 July 1927.
83 *Manchester Guardian*, 29 June 1922.
84 *Manchester Guardian*, 11 July 1922.
85 *Manchester Guardian*, 12 May 1921.
86 *Manchester Guardian*, 28 May 1931.
87 *Manchester Guardian*, 5 June 1933.
88 *Manchester Guardian*, 28 June 1974, also applies to the rest of this paragraph.
89 10 August 1958, Guardian News & Media Archive,

NCAS2/1/1(2).

90 *Daily Telegraph*, Sydney, 5 February 1947.

91 *Manchester Guardian*, 25 February 1969.

92 *Manchester Guardian*, 5 August 1926.

93 In Hamilton (2008), p. 330.

94 Birley (1979), pp. 231, 232.

95 *Manchester Guardian*, 20 June 1924, 24 July 1929 and 5 August 1926.

96 *Manchester Guardian*, 26 April 1922.

97 James (1963), p. 179.

98 *The Cricketer,* January 1971, p. 17.

99 *Wisden*, 1965.

100 Major (2007), p. 292.

101 Taylor (1993), p. 58; Ayerst (1971), p. 417.

102 Michael Kennedy, *The Elusive Mr Cardus*, p. 3.

Chapter 14: The truth but not always the truth

1 *Manchester Guardian*, 14 June 1934.

2 *Manchester Guardian*, 6 July 1927.

3 *Days in the Sun*, pp. 117–124.

4 *Manchester Guardian*, 25 April 1928.

5 Bateman (2009a), p. 103.

6 *Manchester Guardian*, 7 January 1922.

7 *Days in the Sun*, p. 16.

8 Bateman (2009b), pp. 263–264.

9 *Manchester Guardian*, 17 August 1921.

10 *Manchester Guardian*, 24 May 1921.

11 *Manchester Guardian*, 22 May 1925.

12 *A Cricketer's Book*, p. 1.

13 Bateman (2009b), p. 275.

14 Engel (1990), p. i.

15 Lamb (1988), p. 177.

16 *Cricket all the Year*, p. 34.

17 *Neville Cardus Reflects*, p. 31.

18 *Autobiography*, p. 197.

19 *Guardian*, 9 August 1967.

20 *Manchester Guardian*, 8 August 1927.

21 *Autobiography*, p. 159.

22 *A Cardus for all Seasons*, p. 171 (originally in *World Sports*, September 1958).

23 *Spectator*, 4 April 1952.

24 *Conversations*, p. 223.

25 *Full Score*, p. 105.

26 *Cricket all the Year*, p. 21.

27 *Manchester Guardian*, 21 May 1936.

28 p. 34.

29 *Autobiography*, p. 172.

30 Cardus (1960a), pp. 10–11.

31 Mason (1967), p. 14.

32 20 October 1967.

33 *Manchester Guardian*, 5 June 1922. The words from Henry VI are actually spoken by a soldier.

34 This paragraph draws on *Manchester Guardian*, 15 June 1933.

35 *Guardian*, 20 October 1967.

36 Mason (1967), p. 15.

37 *Manchester Guardian*, 2 May 1927. I am grateful to Bob Hilton for his assistance on this incident.

38 *Guardian*, 20 October 1967.

39 *Spectator*, 23 August 1974.

40 *Conversations*, p. 219.

41 *Spectator*, 23 August 1974.

42 *Manchester Guardian*, 30 May 1928.

43 Sengupta (2014).

44 *Spectator*, 13 July 1929.

45 Bateman (2009a), pp. 118–119.

46 *Spectator*, 25 July 1935.

47 *Manchester Guardian*, 18 April 1936. I am grateful to Bob Hilton for his assistance in researching this incident.

48 *Wisden*, 1970.

49 *Manchester Guardian*, 22 May 1934.

50 *Guardian*, 31 October 1972.

51 *Guardian*, 9 August 1967.

52 *Manchester Guardian*, 5 June 1933.

53 *Spectator*, 3 September 1953.

54 Michael Henderson, *Spectator*, 19 February 2005.

55 This paragraph draws on the *Spectator*, 2 December 1972.

56 Green (1989), p. 131.

57 Green (1989), p. 22.

58 Green (1981), p. 23.

59 Green (1989), p. 132.

60 *The Times*, 23 July 1945.

61 This paragraph draws on *The Times*, 30 July 1945. To tarradiddle = to tell petty lies (*Oxford English Dictionary*).

62 *The Elusive Mr Cardus*, p. 36.

63 *Manchester Guardian*, 2 March 1957.

64 *Second Innings*, pp. 162–163. Cardus also wrote in the *Mercury*, Hobart, 23 September 1940 that he saw Rathnally fall 20–30 years before.

65 *Second Innings*, pp. 162, 164.

66 p. 31.

67 *Manchester Guardian*, 5 May 1921.

68 p. 186.

Chapter 15: Finales

1 The information about the Schill family is from the obituary of Eleanor Beatrice Schill in the *British Medical Journal* 2006:332:918 and data supplement.

2 Brookes (1985), p. 19, indicates that Ada died in December 1954, but this is not the case.

3 *Guardian*, 27 February 1975.

4 *Guardian*, 1 March 1975.

5 19 October 1978.

6 *Guardian*, 29 July 1970.

7 *Guardian*, 5 April 1975 and *Celebrant of Beauty*, p. 366.

8 Guardian News Media Archive, service programme and NCA/3/2.

9 Ronayne (2017).

10 Source for this paragraph: *Guardian*, 7 March 1975.

11 *Guardian*, 19 April 1975.

12 Probate record.
13 Chalke (2001), p. 158.
14 *Guardian*, 1 March 1975.
15 *Autobiography*, p. 131.
16 Kennedy (1975), p. 205.

Appendix 2

1   p. 150.
2   *Conversations*, p. 119.
3   *Manchester Guardian*, 20 May 1936.
4   *Conversations*, p. 103.
5   *Conversations*, pp. 131–132.
6   *Manchester Guardian*, 18 February 1933.
7   *Manchester Guardian*, 22 May 1935.
8   p. 267.
9   *Conversations*, pp. 71, 94, 97.
10 *Manchester Guardian*, 11 December 1939.
11 *Autobiography*, p. 263.
12 *Manchester Guardian*, 10 May 1939.
13 *Ten Composers*, p. 68.
14 *Conversations*, p. 48.
15 *Ten Composers*, p. 76.
16 *Conversations*, p. 106.
17 This paragraph draws on *Guardian*, 20 January 1972.
18 *Kathleen Ferrier: a memoir.*
19 *Manchester Guardian*, 6 December 1922.
20 *Manchester Guardian*, 13 September 1947.
21 *Conversations*, pp. 193, 235.
22 *Manchester Guardian*, 14 February 1935.
23 *Manchester Guardian*, 2 January 1954.
24 *Manchester Guardian*, 22 March 1957.
25 *Guardian*, 10 July 1973.

INDEX

Rhys, Hubert 68
Richards, Grant 102
Richardson, Tom 60,
199–200
Richter, Hans 71
Ringwood 108
Roberts, F.G. 56
Robertson-Glasgow, R.C.
181
Robey, George 69, 82
Robinson, Emmott 60–1,
98, 196–8
Robinson, Stanford 171
Robson, Dame Flora 206
Rochdale 90, 116–17
Rodin, Auguste 190
Romiley 107–8
Root, Fred 101
Rose, Captain 62–3, 110
Roses matches 57–9, 84,
87–8, 98–9, 103, 123–4,
135, 158, 170, 174–5,
177–8, 185, 192, 196–8
Rosing, Vladimir 115–17
Rossall School 62–3, 67
Rowbotham, Denys 162
Royal Air Force 68
Royal Albert Hall 206
Royal Festival Hall 160,
164, 219
Royal Philharmonic
Orchestra 167, 206
Rusholme 17–18, 20, 28,
35–6, 49, 57, 68
Rusholme cricket club 62,
90, 109

Saffrons: see Eastbourne
St Bede's College 107–8
St Helens 14
St Paul's Church, Covent
Garden 205
Sale 44, 47
Sale, R. 67
Salzburg Festival 120, 124,
127–8, 131–3, 136
Salzman, Pnina 149
Santley, Sir Charles 71
Sargent, Malcolm 141, 219
Saunders, Helen: see Karsa,
Helen
Savage Club 105
Scarborough 97
Schalk, Franz 166
Schill, Beatrice & Paul 204
Schönberg, Arnold 120
Schramm, Paul 147–9
Schubert, Franz 128, 142,
145–6, 167, 219
Schumann, Robert 71, 119,
167, 217, 219
Schwartzkopf, Elisabeth 166
Scott, C.P. 77–81, 83, 87,
89, 102, 116–17, 133,
202
Scott, Malcolm 69
Scott, Percy 83
Scowen, A.A. & A.N. 51–2
Sell, W.H. 63
Sengupta, Arunabha 197
Settle 12–13
Seymour, J. 185
Shakespeare, William 70,
189, 193
Sharp, Jack 9

Wayland, Muriel 144
Weber, Carl Maria von 142
Weingartner, Felix 166
Wellington 103
Werneth 136
West Australian 130
West Indies 180
Western Australia 135
Westhoughton 195–6
Whalley Range, Manchester 62–4
Whincup, Frank 67
White City, Manchester 8
Who's Who 19, 21, 26, 74–5, 105, 118, 202
Who's Who in Australia 36
Whysall, W.W. 194
Wild, Isaac 15
Wilkinson, George 47
Wilkinson, Helena: see Cardus, Helena
William Collins 152, 154
Wills, Justice 44
Wilson, George 60
Winser, W.L. 63
Wisden 57, 67, 76, 85–6, 102–3, 192
Withington, Manchester 30,

47, 50, 108, 114, 204
Wolf, Hugo 160, 165–6
Wollstonecraft, Mary 89
Women's cricket 100–1, 125
Women's International League 81
Woodcock, John 169
Woolley, Frank 98, 122, 181, 205
Worcester 135, 183–4
Worcestershire 55, 60, 93, 109, 184
Worsley, Bill 99–100
Worthington, Stan 177
Wrathall, H. 9
Wythenshawe, Manchester 47

Yorkshire cricket 57–62, 66, 84, 87–8, 91, 93, 96, 98–9, 103, 123–4, 132, 135, 170, 172, 177–8, 196–8
Yorkshire (general) 12, 112, 119, 176
Yorkshire Post 187

Zinovieff letter 152